SOUTH A...
THE SANCTIONS REPORT

PREPARED FOR
THE COMMONWEALTH COMMITTEE
OF FOREIGN MINISTERS ON
SOUTHERN AFRICA

FOREWORD BY
SHRIDATH RAMPHAL
COMMONWEALTH SECRETARY-GENERAL

PENGUIN BOOKS
IN ASSOCIATION WITH
JAMES CURREY

PENGUIN BOOKS

Published by the Penguin Group
27 Wrights Lane, London w8 5tz, England
Viking Penguin Inc., 40 West 23rd Street, New York, New York 10010, USA
Penguin Books Australia Ltd, Ringwood, Victoria, Australia
Penguin Books Canada Ltd, 2801 John Street, Markham, Ontario, Canada l3r 1b4
Penguin Books (NZ) Ltd, 182–190 Wairau Road, Auckland 10, New Zealand

Penguin Books Ltd, Registered Offices: Harmondsworth, Middlesex, England

First published 1989
1 3 5 7 9 10 8 6 4 2

Made and printed in Great Britain by
Richard Clay Ltd, Bungay, Suffolk
Filmset in Monophoto Sabon

CONTENTS

TABLES

FOREWORD

SHRIDATH RAMPHAL
COMMONWEALTH SECRETARY-GENERAL

*We believe that sanctions
remain the most effective peaceful
path to the ending of apartheid.*

That is the specific conclusion of the Commonwealth Committee of Foreign Ministers on Southern Africa, which requested the independent study now being published as this book. It is, as well, the quintessential message of the book.

The formation of the Committee of Foreign Ministers – an unusual step for the Commonwealth – took place two years ago at Vancouver, under the Okanagan Statement and Programme of Action on Southern Africa; its purpose was to provide high-level impetus and guidance in the furtherance of the objectives of the statement. Among those objectives was that the 'wider, tighter and more intensified application of economic and other sanctions must remain an essential part of the international community's response to apartheid', that Commonwealth leaders would continue their efforts to 'secure a more concerted application of a global sanctions programme' and would 'evaluate on a continuous basis the application of sanctions in order to assess their impact'. Britain did not share these particular objectives, nor did it agree with the establishment of the Committee, which was chaired by the Secretary of State for External Affairs of Canada and included the Foreign Ministers of Australia, Guyana, India, Nigeria, Tanzania, Zambia and Zimbabwe.

One of the very first decisions of the Committee, taken at its meeting in Lusaka in February 1988, was to invite me to commission an independent evaluation of the application and impact of sanctions. This report is that study, carried out by a group of distinguished experts and researchers headed by Dr Joseph Hanlon, responsible as individuals for its conclusions and recommendations. The report confirms the legitimacy and effectiveness of sanctions as an instrument

of policy to induce the dismantling of apartheid. While acknow-
ledging that as an independent study the report does not necessarily
represent the views of governments, the Committee of Foreign Ministers agreed that the study and its recommendations deserve detailed
consideration by all countries, most of which already apply sanctions
of one kind or another against South Africa. They therefore requested
that it be made available not only to Commonwealth governments
but also to the wider international community.

The issue of sanctions against South Africa is not one that can be
divorced from the brutal realities of the South African tragedy. These
realities have been of acute concern to the Commonwealth ever since
1961, when South Africa was forced to leave the Commonwealth
following the Sharpeville massacre – which made clear to the whole
world the inherent violence of the apartheid state. Apartheid itself
has been recognized by Commonwealth leaders over the years to be
the root cause of the problems of Southern Africa; particular issues
in Southern Africa that have become Commonwealth preoccupations
– such as UDI in Rhodesia and the eventual independence of Zimbabwe, or economic and security issues in Mozambique, or freedom
in Namibia, or the destabilization of the Front-line States or, of
course, oppression and suffering within South Africa itself – all had
roots in the apartheid system of South Africa. It is a system I have
elsewhere described as 'the modern face of slavery'; it is certainly one
whose eradication presents to the world the same formidable moral
and political challenges as slavery did.

One of the Commonwealth's best-known initiatives was the dispatch to South Africa in 1986 of the Eminent Persons Group – or
EPG for short. The Group had been established in 1985 to advance
the process of change in South Africa by all practicable means, and it
sought to do so by facilitating a process of dialogue among South
African leaders for the dismantling of apartheid and the establishment
of a non-racial representative government. The Group's report, *Mission to South Africa*, remains the most authoritative description of
the South African political landscape and of the reality behind the
façade of reform. As I wrote in the foreword to the EPG report, the
central message of the EPG was clear: 'Apartheid must end. It will
end – if necessary, through a bloody struggle whose cost in lives may
be counted in millions and whose agonies will reverberate in every
corner of our multiracial world. But it could end by peaceful means –
by a genuine process of negotiation – once white South Africa

accepts that the evil system by which it has sustained its dominance must end, and is ready by deeds to bring it about.'

Sanctions were not the primary concern of the members of the EPG, but, in the context of their findings, they inevitably turned to them. As they said in their report, 'against the background in which ever-increasing violence will be a certainty, the question of further measures immediately springs to mind.' The 'further measures' to which they were referring were sanctions: effective economic pressure applied particularly by those major economic powers that are South Africa's principal trading partners and to which it looks for major financial flows; pressure that demands change while there is still time to bring it about by peaceful means. If the Government of South Africa, said the EPG, 'comes to the conclusion that it would always remain protected' from effective economic measures against it, 'the process of change in South Africa is unlikely to increase in momentum and the descent into violence would be accelerated' – with the cost of lives counted possibly in millions. Sanctions against South Africa and peaceful change within South Africa had become synonymous.

At the special Heads of Government Review Meeting in London in mid-1986 called to consider the EPG report, and later at Vancouver in 1987, the Commonwealth (with Britain dissenting) came out strongly for a strategy of sanctions to persuade South Africa to end apartheid – sanctions supplementary to those already agreed at Nassau in 1985. It was in this context that *The Sanctions Report* was commissioned by the Commonwealth Committee of Foreign Ministers on Southern Africa, established in 1987 to spearhead Commonwealth efforts to end apartheid. The group's brief was to take a hard, expert look, independently of governments, at the actual and potential impact of sanctions in the current political situation. It is being published at the Committee's request. The report speaks for itself.

Yet this hard look, resulting in the advocacy of stronger sanctions, comes at a time of an apparently 'softer' approach by Pretoria. Hiding the realities of apartheid behind an iron curtain of censorship, Pretoria has been trying to present to the world the face of reasonableness and reform. Inevitably, those who are opposed to applying economic sanctions, as well as some who may be genuinely uncertain about their scale and timing, wonder whether new sanctions, or even an emphasis on existing sanctions now, would send the wrong signals at a time when Pretoria appears to be behaving more moderately, when the Namibian independence process is under way, and

when a change in leadership may pave the way for faster change in
South Africa. Such hesitations ignore the fact that South Africa
procrastinated for more than a decade over independence in Namibia
and withdrawal from Angola and agreed only when it was under
pressure. Peace in Angola and Namibia comes not because of a
sudden outbreak of good will in Pretoria. Rather, heavier trade and
financial sanctions, an increasingly effective arms embargo and conse-
quential military reverses, especially at Cuito Cuanavale in Angola,
all helped to convince Pretoria that its illegal occupations of Namibia
and Angola were unsustainable. It was only the wave of sanctions in
1985 and 1986, led by the Commonwealth, helped by US Con-
gressional action and combined with other internal and international
pressure, that jolted Pretoria into a sense that change was becoming
unavoidable. Will the international community send to F. W. de
Klerk the same signal that it sent to P. W. Botha a decade ago – that
he will have several years without further real international pressure,
that all he need face is international exhortation? Or will it send a
new message – that the international community will not allow time
for apartheid simply to be facelifted, that pressure will be increased
until Pretoria abandons apartheid – until fundamental change in
South Africa becomes irreversible?

As if in answer to such questions, *The Sanctions Report* stresses
that sanctions are an essential part of the negotiating process, not an
alternative to it; that their object is not to punish, but to facilitate;
that they are not an end in themselves, the end being genuine
negotiations in the context of the dismantling of apartheid. The
report identifies concrete ways in which the Commonwealth and the
wider international community can escalate the pressure for peaceful
change. Sanctions have already had an impact, but it has been
limited because sanctions themselves have been limited. In order to
achieve the desired impact, the study concludes, a significant increase
in pressure will be necessary. This increase is within the reach of the
governments of the industrialized world, given the political will to
contribute to the ending of apartheid in this way.

The study also stresses that South Africa's debt crisis in 1990–91
opens a special window of opportunity to exert maximum pressure
because the debt crisis will multiply the effects of other economic
measures. Moreover, financial sanctions are cost-free to governments
and in tune with the instincts of financial markets. The study warns,
however, that if governments merely tinker with existing sanctions

and defer stronger action until a later date, South Africa's white minority will justifiably feel that it is being protected from sanctions and will conclude that fundamental political change can be deferred. Pressure on the financial front is a role for sanctions already highlighted by the Commonwealth Committee of Foreign Ministers, who have made clear recommendations on the strength of an Australian initiative designed to demonstrate 'why financial sanctions are needed to compel change in South Africa and how they can work'.

These and other aspects of the sanctions issue are subjected in the report to clear-headed analysis. Altogether it makes some thirty recommendations. They cover some of the measures already adopted by the Commonwealth (minus Britain), the USA and the Nordic States. The vast majority of Commonwealth countries have long ago embargoed all trade with South Africa and have no relations with Pretoria. But these actions were weakened by the non-adoption of equivalent measures by some of the major trading partners of South Africa. The Committee of Foreign Ministers expressed concern at the unwillingness of these countries with the most leverage to apply pressure on South Africa through more concerted action on sanctions.

All the recommendations deserve careful consideration by all countries. As the Foreign Ministers recognized, important questions of timing arise in the application of additional sanctions, as does the need to place them in the framework of overall strategy. These are some of the decisions that lie ahead for governments. It is to that decision-making process that the report makes some of its most significant contributions.

The Foreign Ministers Committee had the benefit, over an eighteen-month period, of testimony from a wide cross-section of black South Africans of their own view of sanctions, including the impact of sanctions on them – an impact that is sometimes advanced as a reason for not applying sanctions. In its own report to the Kuala Lumpur Meeting, the Committee had this to say on the matter:

> Our deliberations and consultations with several black South African leaders have confirmed our view that most black South Africans continue to look principally to sanctions as the international community's most necessary form of pressure on Pretoria for peaceful change. Pretoria's campaign, supported by massive financial resources, to convince Western countries that black South Africans are opposed to sanctions demonstrates its fear of them, and is tantamount to an

admission that sanctions have been effective. They must remain an essential part of the response to apartheid. If Pretoria does, indeed, turn towards the dismantling of apartheid, sanctions will have contributed to forcing that change. They will need to be sustained until progress in that direction becomes irreversible.

That, too, is the key conclusion of this important report.

This is a professional evaluation of the application of sanctions and their impact, but it is written for a wide reading public and makes its case clearly and convincingly. I am delighted that its publication by Penguin Books will enable it to reach that public.

Yet it remains immensely important, in any reflection on sanctions and South Africa, that the core humanitarian issues at stake in Southern Africa and the great moral challenge that apartheid presents should remain in the forefront of our minds. We cannot judge sanctions as if they were to do only with money or exports or even strategic considerations. In the end, they are to do with people. In the South African situation it is all too easy to miss the true scale of the horror of the whole because of the immediate outrage generated by particular parts. It is one of the least pardonable crimes against contemporary humanity that, under the label of 'apartheid', false doctrines of racial superiority continue to be employed against the black people of South Africa through the most entrenched state apparatus of racism in the entire community of nations: the most blatant and systematic denial of freedom of the many by the few anywhere in the world. It is a cruel irony that while the family of man arose in Africa – indeed, very probably in Southern Africa itself – it is there today, in that cradle of mankind, that the rights of man must fight and win their final victory against the denial of human oneness.

It is that denial of human oneness that has been at the heart of the apartheid system. So long as it persists, apartheid will persist under whatever name – unless forced to change by pressures from within South Africa and beyond it. The sad truth is that in South Africa so little has changed at this most basic level of the supremacy of otherness over common humanity.

In 1897 the British statesman Lord Bryce described how a white farmer in South Africa had flogged his African servant to death, was tried and acquitted by a white jury and was triumphantly escorted home by his neighbours 'with a band of music'. Nearly a hundred years later, the London *Times* of 23 March 1989 carried a commentary on the recent case of a white South African who beat a black farm worker to death and was fined some £700, with £1,800 to pay to the man's family over a five-year period. Is it any wonder that apartheid stirs fierce passions? Its evil roots run deep. Its iniquity is unique, its horrors too numerous to recount. The whole world agrees – more than that, insists – that apartheid must end. That is not in question; the only question is how. This book provides some of the answers.

Its message is addressed not only to governments but to all who are committed to the ending of apartheid in South Africa and are engaged in the now universal effort to secure it. A justifiable sense of outrage has stirred people throughout the world and stiffened the resolve of their governments. It is important to acknowledge the moral fibre of those governments and peoples in Western countries who, despite racist elements within their own societies, have made the most militant stand against apartheid. For them it is a stand that can rest on no kinship save that of the human family. The Scandinavian countries have virtually imposed a trade boycott against South Africa; people in the United States and in Europe have kept high the anti-apartheid banner within their own societies. The United States Congress carried the day in its fight against the Reagan Administration for the comprehensive Anti-Apartheid Act. Millions of people throughout the West continue to make their quiet – or not so quiet – protests in their everyday lives, whether by refusing to do business with banks linked with the South African economy, or by telling their shopkeepers not only that they will not buy South African fruit but that they will cease to shop where the fruit is stocked, or by any other way they can.

This 'people' pressure, human solidarity, is the ultimate sanction against apartheid. Human solidarity with the victims and opponents of apartheid in South Africa is what will ensure one day a free, non-racial, democratic society in South Africa, one in which all its people, black and white, will dwell in freedom and in peace. If this report helps to sustain and strengthen that solidarity, it will have served South Africa, and all South Africans, well.

AUGUST 1989   MARLBOROUGH HOUSE
                                  LONDON SW1

PART I

SANCTIONS ARE ESSENTIAL FOR NEGOTIATIONS

I

INTRODUCTION

Exhortation will never end apartheid. Even diplomatic pressure will not be enough. Economic pressure will be needed before the white minority yields its monopoly of power. Sanctions add to that pressure and thus are an essential part of the process leading to genuine negotiations in South Africa.

Pretoria's agreement to withdraw from Angola and to grant independence to Namibia raises hopes of a negotiated settlement inside South Africa itself, but the 1988 Namibia talks, and the background against which they were held, provide important lessons for any future negotiations. South Africa 'agreed' to Resolution 435 and independence in Namibia more than a decade ago but then refused to implement that Resolution. 'Negotiation' included endless talks with the Contact Group and became a way of maintaining control over Namibia rather than relinquishing it. South Africa agreed to withdraw from Angola in 1984, then invaded again.

It was the success of sanctions, combined with the growing strength of the Angolan military, with Cuban support, and the weakness of the South African economy that finally forced South Africa into genuine negotiations in 1988. The arms embargo played a critical role. Prevented from obtaining modern weapons, Pretoria lost military superiority and could not maintain its occupation of southern Angola without a death rate that was unacceptable to the South African white minority. Economic and financial sanctions made it increasingly difficult to pay the rising cost of the occupation of Namibia and southern Angola.

After a decade of talking, negotiations became serious when Pretoria was under pressure. Thus sanctions were an essential part of the negotiating process, not an alternative to it. Yet even these negotiations were aimed at sustaining apartheid, not at replacing it. South Africa was retreating from expensive involvement in neighbouring states so that it could concentrate on the goal of maintaining apartheid in South Africa itself.

In 1986 the Commonwealth Eminent Persons Group (EPG) warned that 'while the Government claims to be ready to negotiate, it is in truth not yet prepared to negotiate fundamental change, nor to countenance the creation of genuine democratic structures, nor to face the prospect of the end of white domination and white power in the foreseeable future. Its programme of reform does not end apartheid, but seeks to give it a less inhuman face. Its quest is power sharing, but without surrendering overall white control.'[1]

That remains true today. Pretoria is negotiating to defend apartheid, not to end it. Action by the international community in the next two years will play a decisive role in determining the nature of negotiations in South Africa.

The political climate in southern Africa *is* changing. Negotiations over Angola and Namibia could be a prelude to talks about South Africa itself. White politics are showing a new fluidity as more South Africans are realizing that apartheid cannot continue in the present form. Such an opportunity should not be lost.

Neither, however, should we be prepared to accept anything like the decade of prevarication that passed for negotiation over Namibia. The Pretoria Government always says that it is prepared to talk, but the EPG warned that 'the Government is not yet ready to negotiate in any genuine way the establishment of a non-racial and representative government in South Africa'.[2] The acting State President, F. W. de Klerk, stressed soon after his election as leader of the National Party that this remains true.

The economic climate in southern Africa is also changing, however. South Africa will be particularly vulnerable to pressure in the next two years because it will face in 1990 and 1991 debt problems potentially as damaging as those of 1985, when banks refused to roll over (renew) loans and Pretoria was forced to halt repayments on nearly US$14 billion in short-term debt. The agreement with international banks on the frozen short-term debt expires in June 1990 and must be renegotiated; this could involve substantial additional payments. Furthermore, in 1990–91 nearly US$3 billion* in long-term debts outside the 1985 freeze are due to be repaid. The prospect of

* Throughout this book the term 'billion' signifies 1,000 million.

much larger payments looms at a time when the South African economy is already seriously constrained by the effects of decades of apartheid, sanctions imposed in 1985–6 and a gold price well below its 1987 peak. Thus any new measures introduced during this period will have additional impact because they will compound the problems that the apartheid state already faces.

In the coming two years the international community will make a choice. It could help Pretoria to weather the debt crisis and maintain apartheid, or it could take this opportunity to exert maximum pressure and provide some of the conditions essential for an end to apartheid.

Two windows of opportunity, one economic and the other political, are opening at the same time. Taken together, they provide a special opportunity for genuine negotiation, but *sanctions are essential if any such negotiations are to take place*. As the EPG stressed, 'the South African Government is concerned about the adoption of effective economic measures against it. If it comes to the conclusion that it would always remain protected from such measures, the process of change in South Africa is unlikely to increase in momentum and the descent into violence would be accelerated. In these circumstances, the cost in lives may have to be counted in millions.'[3]

The white minority is extremely worried about sanctions. In 1988 a small economic upturn had to be curbed because of the constraints of sanctions. Some businessmen talked openly of the need for political concessions to prevent further sanctions. Foreign Minister Pik Botha and other South African leaders have been touring the world desperately trying to fend off sanctions. They argue that negotiations for Namibian independence should be taken as evidence of commitment to peace and reform rather than of retreat in the face of sanctions and internal pressure. They are also anxious to claim that South Africa is regaining international credibility. 'The thrust of foreign interference recently showed signs of subsiding,' wrote Gerrit Olivier, a chief director in the Department of Foreign Affairs, in late 1988.[4] In part this is because detentions and bannings, combined with ever stricter controls on the foreign press, have succeeded in pushing South Africa off the world's TV screens and out of the public consciousness. The apartheid Government takes comfort from the fact that no major new sanctions have been imposed in more than two years. In South Africa wide publicity has been given to the failure of the United States, Europe and the Commonwealth to take significant new economic actions. Statements against sanctions by leaders in the United States, Britain and West Germany are also given prominence as evidence of support for the apartheid regime.

Pretoria hopes to spin out negotiations, as it did over Namibia. It will use the prospect of negotiation to defer new sanctions, to secure easy repayment terms on outstanding debt and even, perhaps, to gain new loans, thus weathering the debt crisis. National Party leaders want to use this breathing space to restructure apartheid based on a mix of economic 'reform' with continued repression and censorship. The goal is a new form of white hegemony that will be tolerated both internationally and internally.

Failure to tighten and widen sanctions, as urged by Commonwealth leaders (except Britain's) at their meeting in Vancouver in October 1987, will be seen as the international stamp of approval for maintaining white rule and will doom any talks to failure. *Delaying new sanctions until after 1991 will give Pretoria the breathing space it needs, while more effective sanctions now would have their impact multiplied and could ensure the success of negotiations.* Thus the international community must make a choice now to support the majority or the minority.

The Expert Study Group has assessed the impact of sanctions so far and has come to a two-edged conclusion: past sanctions have had some impact but not enough. The Nordic countries, the United States, the Commonwealth (except Britain) and other nations have already imposed significant sanctions. These sanctions have curbed Pretoria's military power and limited its regional terrorism; they have pushed Pretoria towards the conference table; they have restrained some internal excesses; they have imposed considerable economic constraints; and they have prompted more and more whites to question the desirability of continued apartheid.

Nevertheless, South Africa has tried to accommodate itself to existing sanctions through greater self-sufficiency, import restraints, sanctions busting, sharply increased repression and, more recently, partial withdrawals from Namibia and Angola. There has been a cost, but white living standards remain high. Thus the sanctions imposed so far can be counted as only a partial success.

We have looked particularly closely at this matter and conclude that further sanctions could have a more significant political effect only if they were strong enough, and were imposed rapidly enough, to have a noticeable impact on white living standards. This means that it will be necessary substantially to widen and tighten existing measures, to impose some new sanctions and to act quickly if sufficient pressure is to be put on the apartheid regime.

If only limited new measures were imposed, or if new measures were imposed slowly, the South African economy would have time to adapt. White living standards might continue to decline but not rapidly enough to have a decisive political impact. In particular, it would not be sufficient simply to plug a few loopholes in existing measures.

We specifically considered the question of whether an additional limited sanctions package might be effective. It is obvious that the smaller the sanctions package, the more the lifelines available for the apartheid regime. Nevertheless, the Expert Study Group concludes that there is a practical and targeted package of measures, short of comprehensive sanctions, that could take advantage of the economic window of opportunity caused by the anticipated 1990–91 debt crisis. *If widely and rapidly applied*, this package should provide a catalyst for genuine negotiations. The package stresses wider, tighter and more extensive bans on bulk imports from South Africa. It is practical for immediate implementation because it excludes all the commodities normally considered problematic, including ferro-alloys and gold.

In the remainder of Part I of this report we outline the way in which sanctions will encourage negotiations (Chapter 2) and look at the impact of sanctions so far (Chapter 3). In Part II we outline current sanctions as imposed by Governments, organizations and individuals. We detail their successes and assess their weaknesses (Chapters 5–10). In Part III we show how some Governments and agencies are frustrating attempts to impose sanctions. We stress that the most important problem is that countries like West Germany, Spain, Taiwan and others are openly increasing their trade with the apartheid state. They are taking advantage of sanctions by purchasing more of commodities such as coal and steel, the prices of which are depressed because of sanctions imposed by the United States, the Commonwealth and the Nordic states (Chapter 11). We also look at ways to prevent sanctions busting (Chapters 12–14). South Africa is extremely vulnerable to sanctions, and this issue is evaluated in Part IV. We quantify vulnerability to trade sanctions (Chapter 15) and to restrictions on technology transfer (Chapter 16). Then we estimate how much pressure will be needed to lead the Pretoria regime to genuine negotiations (Chapter 17). This leads, in Part V, to a strategy of increasing sanctions to apply further pressure (Chapter 18), which would involve expanded economic measures (Chapter 19) and various ways of tightening existing measures (Chapters 20, 22 and 23). We take note of the concern in some quarters that sanctions will cost black people their jobs, and we propose a pair of sanctions that will weaken the morale of white people while increasing the number of jobs for black people (Chapter 21).

As part of our study we conducted detailed investigations into a number of specific topics related to sanctions. These papers are published in a companion volume to this report, which also contains more detailed trade data.*

In the first instance our report is directed at Commonwealth Governments, which we encourage to take the lead in imposing wider, tighter and extended sanctions. But we recognize the dearth of serious research on sanctions and on the importance of the Commonwealth lead. Therefore we have made several recommendations that are directed at non-Commonwealth states.

It is not sufficient simply to condemn apartheid and tinker with existing sanctions. New and effective measures are essential to force the Pretoria regime to negotiate an end to apartheid and not to use negotiations to sustain institutionalized racism.

We have assessed what action would be effective against the apartheid regime. We conclude that it will require a significant increase in pressure but one that is within the reach of the Governments of the industrialized world if they act quickly.

This means that individual states and international groups must act now, on their own; they cannot afford to wait for consensus. Indeed, the Experts note that the sanctions imposed in 1985 and 1986 were not coordinated. Rather, each new set of sanctions further strengthened an international climate of opinion that generated still more sanctions. Single actions by individual countries to ban fruit or coal imports played a part, and the 1985 and 1986 Commonwealth packages were important spurs to other countries, some of which imposed much more extensive sanctions than the Commonwealth. Similarly in 1989 and 1990, with a debt crisis facing South Africa, initiatives by the Commonwealth and individual states will change

* *South Africa: The Sanctions Report – Documents* (James Currey, London, 1989).

the international mood. Commonwealth countries can show the way by intensifying and widening their own sanctions to include the entire package. This is a time for leadership, not for delay.

2

HOW SANCTIONS WORK

The Commonwealth has always stood for a peaceful settlement in South Africa, rooted in the ending of apartheid. It has always seen the apartheid system as the essential source of violence in South Africa and recognized that only the ending of apartheid will lead to peace and political freedom.

Commonwealth Heads of Government who met in Nassau in October 1985 adopted the Commonwealth Accord on Southern Africa, which called on the authorities in Pretoria to take five steps 'in a genuine manner and as a matter of urgency:

(a) Declare that the system of apartheid will be dismantled and specific and meaningful action taken in fulfilment of that intent.
(b) Terminate the state of emergency.
(c) Release immediately and unconditionally Nelson Mandela and all others imprisoned and detained for their opposition to apartheid.
(d) Establish political freedom and specifically lift the existing ban on the African National Congress and other political parties.
(e) Initiate, in the context of a suspension of violence on all sides, a process of dialogue across lines of colour, politics and religion, with a view to establishing a non-racial and representative government.'

Sadly, little progress has been made on these five steps despite the talks over Angola and Namibia and the supposed new mood in southern Africa. This underlines our fear that the apartheid regime is negotiating to sustain white hegemony, not to end it.

The Commonwealth (other than Britain) has always recognized that it will be necessary to intensify the pressure on Pretoria if these steps are to be taken and fundamental change is to be achieved. After all, Governments normally act only when the cost of doing nothing becomes higher than the cost of change. Sanctions have already been partly successful because they have raised the cost to South Africa of doing nothing. But the white minority is divided on what to do now: should it abandon apartheid, or can it reconstruct apartheid in a form that will be internationally tolerated and internally sustainable? The next goal of sanctions must be to make the second route impossible and to show that the only way out is negotiation with true representatives of the majority black population. The ultimate goal of sanctions must be to 'bring Pretoria to the negotiating table', in the words of the Okanagan Statement adopted by Commonwealth Heads of Government in Vancouver in October 1987.[1]

Sanctions are a practical diplomatic tool, intended to apply pressure. They are not a sop to a guilty conscience.

Opponents of sanctions often describe them as 'punitive' – as punishment for South Africa because it maintains apartheid. This is wholly erroneous and a wilful misunderstanding. Sanctions should be seen as 'persuasive' – as a means of bringing pressure to bear and so persuading the white minority of the necessity of entering into genuine negotiations. As the EPG made clear, sanctions are designed to prevent a further 'descent into violence' and to promote negotiations instead. This is why sanctions are an essential component of negotiations and not an alternative to them.

It is sometimes argued that sanctions will push whites 'into the *laager*'. In fact, whites are already in the *laager*. As the EPG observed, they are unprepared 'to face the prospect of the end of white domination and white power in the foreseeable future'. The question, then, is what sanctions will do to whites who are already in the *laager*.

Far from coming together, the white power bloc is fragmenting in the face of economic pressure and political insecurity. The divisions are increasingly economic rather than ethnic. Under P. W. Botha the National Party became less a party of Afrikaner nationalism as it largely abandoned the white working class to the Conservatives and other far-right parties while gaining the support of English speakers and especially of English-speaking capital.

White politics remain fluid, and under the pressure of sanctions this new alliance seems likely to fragment as well. Increasing numbers of whites, and especially business leaders, will see that government schemes to pacify the black majority while regaining international acceptability are pure fantasy. Some are already thinking the formerly unthinkable and talking of negotiations and majority rule, but a much larger white group must abandon traditional attitudes and create a powerful lobby for negotiation before the regime will be prepared to admit that the only route out of the deepening crisis is by way of the conference table. Leaders of transnational companies who see a viable future under majority rule and who, in growing numbers, are in contact with the African National Congress (ANC), the United Democratic Front (UDF) and the Congress of South African Trade Unions (Cosatu) will be a vital element in this lobby. Sanctions will play an essential role in crystallizing that lobby for negotiation.

Sanctions will help to convince white South Africans that it is in their own interests to dismantle apartheid and enter negotiations to establish a non-racial and representative government. As part of that process sanctions should reduce the ability of the minority regime to suppress the black majority. The minority must see that apartheid is no longer a viable option because the economic and political cost is too high, while continued repression of the black majority is not sustainable.

BUILDING A LOBBY FOR NEGOTIATION

It is important to distinguish three levels of objectives for sanctions. Their ultimate goal is a political one – negotiation. The intermediate goal is to create a growing group of people who will press for genuine talks – to build a lobby for negotiations. And the immediate tactical objective is to raise the political and financial cost of alternatives to negotiation.

There are four aspects of this tactical objective.

1 The denial of essential goods, such as arms and oil.
2 The acceleration of the general economic strain.
3 The battering of white morale.
4 The encouragement of those who are struggling to end apartheid.

All four aspects are intimately related. The economic strain imposed by many sanctions will make it impossible simultaneously to satisfy white consumption demands, to build up the military and to finance showpiece development projects designed to create a false impression of change for urban black people. Thus white living standards will be harder to maintain, and this will strike at morale. Further, the arms and oil embargoes will impose an additional economic strain because Pretoria will have to pay ever higher prices for essential goods. The arms embargo and the economic strain will make it harder for the Government to maintain an effective military presence in the townships and neighbouring states; as the minority realizes that it will be harder to suppress the majority, morale will sink even lower. Meanwhile sanctions will encourage black morale in two ways. First, they are an important show of international solidarity that reminds people inside that they have not been forgotten and that their struggle is receiving practical help. Second, the steady weakening of the apartheid regime will give increasing space for the black struggle. This, of course, will weaken white morale and increase the economic strain. Thus the four different impacts of sanctions will feed each other in an accelerating spiral.

The business community plays a central role. The level of business confidence is determined by white morale, the intensity of economic strain and an assessment of the Government's ability to maintain control. Rising business confidence means support for the Government and its sanctions-busting efforts. Collapsing business confidence means less investment (and thus further economic strain) and increasing pressure on the Government to enter into serious negotiations. Disinvestment and sanctions such as the sports boycott and cutting air links hit white morale and increase the sense of international isolation and unacceptability.

The speed with which sanctions are imposed is a critical factor, for both practical and political reasons. Given enough time, South African industry will be able to find some alternative markets and suppliers and develop ways to produce local versions of some sanctioned goods. This in turn will relate to morale; a slow decline in living standards will be less noticeable and more acceptable than the sudden disappearance of goods from supermarket shelves. Thus if limited measures are imposed slowly, the minority will have time to adapt to them. In that case sanctions are unlikely to have the intended political effect.

Even rapidly applied sanctions will not bring instant results; this is unlikely to be a quick or easy process. But strong sanctions quickly imposed will work more effectively than weak sanctions imposed over a long period of time. Indeed, sanctions can be compared with antibiotics; taken in the right dose, they cure the disease; administered too weakly, they allow the development of resistance that makes it harder to cure the disease later.

It is important to reiterate that sanctions – and especially partial sanctions – will not work on their own. The agent for change is South Africans themselves, especially the black majority. But the international community can tip the balance. By reducing the power and will of the apartheid state and its beneficiaries to resist change, sanctions will support and shorten the struggle. Indeed, it is unlikely that a large group of white moderates favouring negotiation will emerge without the pressure of sanctions.[2]

3

PARTIAL SANCTIONS: A PARTIAL SUCCESS

Sanctions against South Africa have a long history. India imposed a comprehensive trade ban in 1946. South Africa was forced to leave the Commonwealth in 1961. In 1977 the United Nations mandatory arms embargo and the Gleneagles Commonwealth sports boycott were both agreed. An international wave of new financial and economic sanctions hit South Africa in 1985 and 1986.

The sanctions imposed so far are partial, not total. Nevertheless, it is reasonable to ask how successful these measures have been, judged against the three different levels of goals set out in the previous chapter.

At the immediate tactical level sanctions have had a perceptible impact, even though that impact has not been sufficient. Although South Africa's economic crisis is due mainly to apartheid, sanctions have added to the economic problems. 'Our economy is hamstrung by a host of politically motivated and internationally orchestrated restrictions,' commented the South African Finance Minister, Barend du Plessis, in his Budget speech in March 1988. 'Sanctions and boycotts are a fact of our economic and financial life.'

We show in Chapter 5 that the trade sanctions imposed since 1985 alone have cut South Africa's export earnings by 7 per cent. Sanctions busting has proved an enormous economic drain. Ex-President P. W. Botha himself estimated the cost of breaking the oil embargo between 1973 and 1984 at US$25 billion. South Africa is proud of its arms industry, but this has been built at enormous cost.

South Africa's Trust Bank estimates that in the 1985–90 period sanctions and disinvestment will have cost South Africa R40 billion (about US$20 billion). The bank estimates that in 1990 the average South African will be 10 per cent poorer than he or she would have been without sanctions and disinvestment and that by 1990 real disposable incomes will be below 1970 levels because the 'strangle-hold of international trade and financial sanctions' will combine with the lower gold price to hit the economy.[1]

SANCTIONS DO FORCE CONCESSIONS

We present more detailed discussions of the economic impact of sanctions in Chapters 5 and 19. In the rest of this chapter we look at the political questions. It is apparent that partial sanctions have succeeded in helping to convince Pretoria that it cannot continue with apartheid in its present form; thus sanctions are having some success in building the lobby for negotiation. And sanctions have been crucial in putting Pretoria on the defensive, but they have not been strong enough to convince the apartheid regime to open a genuine dialogue with the majority; thus they have not yet succeeded in reaching the ultimate political goal. Our verdict is that partial sanctions have been a partial success.

A *New York Times* article pointed out that while 'most business leaders argue that increased pressure retards reform . . . recent history may contradict this. The twelve months following the banks' 1985 refusal to roll over South Africa's loans was a period of negative economic growth for the country. Yet it was a time when the most fundamental political reforms were made. These included the scrapping of the hated pass laws . . . and the granting of property rights to blacks.'[2] Indeed, it is widely reported that the 'reforms' of early 1986 were a condition of the acceptance of debt rescheduling by international banks.

Most important, partial sanctions (and the threat of their being increased) helped to promote the first, tentative, negotiations. It was not a coincidence that when businessmen met the ANC in 1985 it was just after the United States imposed its first sanctions and soon after Western banks had imposed financial sanctions.

Similarly, ex-President P. W. Botha linked the talks with Angola in May 1988 directly with the United States sanctions debate.[3] 'One of the clearest results of sanctions that have been put in place is what we see now in the peace process in Angola,' said Dr Allan Boesak, President of the World Alliance of Reformed Churches, in January

1989. 'The pressure of sanctions ... forced them to the negotiating table.'[4]

Sanctions alone did not bring about the withdrawal from Angola and the Namibian independence process: key roles were played by the people of Namibia and Angola and by Cuba. But it was sanctions that, in the end, propelled the South African Government to the conference table and kept it there. Without sanctions Namibian independence would not be in prospect now.

CURBING THE WORST EXCESSES

The threat of further sanctions has also stopped the South African Government from perpetrating a few of its worst excesses. For example, it was widely reported that fear of a new United States sanctions law prevented the execution of the Sharpeville Six. And threats of sanctions have forced some reduction in raids into neighbouring states.[5] The problem, however, is that the threat of sanctions halts only the most blatant actions; other acts of destabilization and other executions persist. The Sharpeville Six were not executed, but they remain in jail. Censorship and bannings continue. And the 'reforms' made under pressure in 1986 are purely economic and social – they do not touch the fundamental question of black political rights.

Pretoria has often withdrawn concessions once the pressure is off. Thus in 1988 trade-union rights granted three years before were severely restricted by new legislation and by banning orders. The threats by West Germany to cancel landing rights for South African Airways and of Switzerland to restrict gold sales were behind the South African decision to shelve legislation to restrict foreign funding of anti-apartheid organizations.[6] But funding regulations were then reintroduced in early 1989 when Pretoria was under less pressure because it was negotiating on Namibia. (This also underlines the fact that Pretoria is still negotiating to sustain white rule, not to end it.)

The apartheid regime has become skilled at making grand promises under pressure, then failing to fulfil those promises when the pressure is relaxed. Nelson Mandela's release was promised countless times. The Emergency was lifted during negotiations with international banks in early 1986, only to be reimposed a few months later. The much touted ending of the pass laws turned out not to apply to residents of the Bantustans.

WHITE SOUTH AFRICA IS WORRIED

The minority regime is extremely worried about sanctions precisely because it knows that sanctions do work. As the EPG pointed out, 'South Africa not only believes in the principle of sanctions but has consistently applied them to its neighbours.'[7]

The example of sanctions against Southern Rhodesia is relevant. Erratically applied sanctions there took a decade to be effective, but in a memo to the Rhodesian Cabinet in June 1979 the security head, Ken Flower, was forced to admit that 'with every month that goes by, sanctions become more debilitating'.[8] Thus sanctions were an essential factor in bringing Ian Smith to Lancaster House later that year, ending the bloodshed sooner than would have been the case without sanctions.

A key actor in sanctions against Rhodesia was South Africa itself. At first it served as Rhodesia's 'big brother' and became the main sanctions-busting channel. But in the late 1970s Pretoria concluded that the war in Rhodesia was putting South Africa itself at risk and withdrew its support. The South African Government and the business community know, from direct experience, that if no one is prepared to be their 'big brother' and help them to bust sanctions, then sanctions will have a major impact.

Various studies have confirmed this. For example, a study by the Federated Chamber of Industries (FCI) concluded that 'sanctions can damage the South African economy rather more seriously than appears to be generally perceived'. 'Don't kid yourself. Effective sanctions do work,' commented the *Financial Mail*. 'If, as expected, sanctions intensify, a short-term boom followed by long-term decline into Third World status seems the most likely scenario.'[9]

CAN 'TOTAL FRANCHISE' BE AVOIDED?

Although those in business are potentially members of the lobby for negotiation, this would not necessarily be an automatic development. Sir Michael Edwardes, former chairman of British Leyland and now head of Minorco, spelled out what are probably the goals of much of the business community. He said that South Africa could regain international acceptability 'by sensible representation but without the trauma of one-man-one-vote'. He concluded: 'Before the issue becomes one of a choice between isolation and total franchise, and nothing less, for God's sake get discrimination of all sorts and varieties out of the system totally, for all to see.'[10]

The judgement that business people – and all white South Africans – must make is whether apartheid can be maintained at a reasonable cost. Will the international community, and the black majority, be bought off simply by an end to 'discrimination', an end to petty apartheid, without ending the white monopoly on political power? Or will that not be enough, and will the cost of sanctions and the increasing military budget promote a search for alternatives?

On this the business community is sharply divided, and its opinions shift rapidly. 'I don't think it's a coincidence that the business community became most vocal when the economy was in the worst recession for fifteen years, profits were declining and South African businessmen were shunned in the capitals of the world,' commented Tony Bloom, former chairman of Premier Milling and one of the delegation that met the ANC in 1985. 'At the time of the Lusaka trip there was more of a feeling of urgency,' he explained. Three years later 'there's a lull because we're back into an economic upswing and a lot of people have gone back to just running a business . . . It took a crisis to evoke their conscience.'[11]

But the upswing did not last long. In mid-1988 a sanctions-induced balance-of-payments crisis caused a serious economic squeeze. As the South African magazine *Finance Week* commented, 'The sanctions chickens are coming home to roost.'[12] The result was a series of statements by business leaders calling for political change.

In May 1988 the *Financial Mail*, South Africa's most important business magazine,[13] warned that 'as long as sanctions deprive us of these [export earnings] and political uncertainty remains a part of daily life, we will see more of bust than boom. Without a dramatic change in political policies, economic policies can do little more than provide life support.' In July 1988 Henri de Villers, chairman of Standard Bank of South Africa, at a meeting of the Executive Association of Southern Africa, warned of the need for political change to avoid further sanctions.[14] In August 1988 a number of business leaders formed a new Consultative Business Movement to work for non-racial democracy, in explicit opposition to the government policy of 'reform'. *Finance Week* commented: 'The price of apartheid is growing ever more horrendous.'[15] At about the same time the president of South Africa's Computer Society, Keith Mattison, told a conference that South Africa faced technological stagnation

due to sanctions. The solution, he said, was to get rid of apartheid.[16]
In December 1988 the Afrikaanse Handelsinstituut, an organization
of Afrikaner business people not noted for radicalism, warned that
drastic political change was needed to avoid new European
sanctions.[17]

Other business leaders have not been pushed into looking for an
end to apartheid. The EPG stressed the importance of the belief that
the Government 'can contain the situation indefinitely by force'.[18] A
central issue in business confidence seems to be whether it thinks that
the Government can control black dissent without inviting international retaliation in the form of further sanctions. Gavin Relly,
chairman of Anglo American Corporation of South Africa, said in his
annual statement in 1987: 'The imposition of the State of Emergency
last year and its recent renewal, though regrettable, were necessary.'[19]

In its otherwise gloomy view of the economy Trust Bank in
October 1988 said: 'The 60 per cent increase in South Africa's
security expenditure over the past two years was clearly essential in
the circumstances. In fact, the damper put on socio-political insta-
bility by the security forces has definitely played a role in the recently
improved performance of the economy.'

In March 1988 the *Financial Mail* commented: 'Business confidence, that fragile reed, will probably be bolstered by government's
latest crackdown on black dissent.' A survey in mid-1988 showed
that 86 per cent of whites believed that security forces could keep the
lid on internal unrest for as long as the Government wanted.

The lack of new measures in 1987 and 1988 corresponded to a
period of increased repression, which was supported by business. It
is not weak sanctions that have caused increased repression: rather,
the lack of strong sanctions has permitted it.

REPRESSION AND 'REFORM' AS A STRATEGY

Central to the efforts to maintain a reformulated apartheid is the
minority Government's 'reform' policy, under which economic concessions are seen as an alternative to political change. The late Fred
du Plessis, who was an adviser to President P. W. Botha and
chairman of Sanlam, one of South Africa's largest corporations,
talked in 1988 about 'a situation where people ten years from now
feel things are going so much better for them that they do not feel
anxious about political power'.[20]

The plan is to deliver enough economic benefits to key groups of black citizens to reduce the pressure for political change. This includes *economic concessions* to urban blacks – trade-union rights, changes to job reservation and the Group Areas Act, home ownership, etc. It also involves considerable expenditure in the townships on education, housing and so on. *But there will be no concessions on political rights.* 'I am not considering even to discuss the possibility of black majority government in South Africa,' President P. W. Botha said in 1988.[21] And F. W. de Klerk said after his election as National Party leader that one-person-one-vote would be 'catastrophic for South Africa'.[22] Thus whatever economic changes are made, political apartheid will remain.

This has been widely recognized. The British Government, in its policy paper on South Africa, reports: 'The South African Government have yet to address the fundamental issue of black political rights in central government and to abandon the concepts of separate development and population registration by racial origin.'[23]

President Ronald Reagan was forced to admit in October 1988: 'I am again unable to report significant progress to the end of apartheid and the establishment of of non-racial democracy ... Repression of government opponents has intensified in the past year ... The South African Government has given no sign that it is ready to negotiate with credible black leaders except within narrowly defined contexts established by the Government itself.'[24]

Britain's Prime Minister, Margaret Thatcher, spelled out the impossibility of economic growth before political change when she said: 'Experience teaches us that you can only achieve higher growth, only release enterprise, only spur people to greater effort, only obtain their full-hearted commitment to reform, when people have the dignity and enjoyment of personal and political liberty.'[25]

Because the South African Government has no intention to grant political liberty, economic reform must be linked with repression. Security officials expect censorship, stepped-up military patrols, expanded networks of informers, vigilantes, assassinations and mass detentions to break rent boycotts and popular organizations and to silence any representative black political voices. At the same time the security services hope to establish counter-organizations such as cultural, sport and political groups that support the Government.[26]

Undecided people will be wooed by township-upgrading schemes with new houses, water and electricity. The goal is to create a small property-owning group in key townships with a stake in the apartheid system. It is a strategy that attempts to co-opt the relatively small but vocal black urban middle and working classes while ignoring the destitute majority in the Bantustans. The Government hopes that this key minority will accept economic improvement as a substitute for political rights, but the whole process will be backed up with ruthless repression to eliminate opposition in the townships.

Upgrading is starting in thirty-four of the most turbulent townships, such as Mamelodi and Alexandra. Security officials say that the priority is to regain 'effective control over the population'. These thirty-four townships are called 'oilspots' by the security services, and it is intended that effective control will expand, like a blot of oil, into neighbouring areas.[27]

In espousing this strategy the apartheid state has realized that it must spend hundreds of millions of dollars to try to buy off a relatively small group of urban black people while spending vast amounts on Bantustan armies and apartheid-enforcing bureaucracies to keep the majority quiet. Finance Minister Barend du Plessis argues that whites will have to accept a drop in their standard of living so that money can be spent on projects in black townships;[28] however, the only attempt so far to shift some money from white to black failed. The Civil Service wage freeze in 1988 was intended to free some money for reform in a state budget already stretched by sharply rising military costs. The freeze caused such discontent that large salary rises had to be granted in advance of the 1988 white local elections.

The strategists of the new apartheid hope that some of the money will come from the private sector. Much will be raised by a major programme of privatization of state companies. The Government hopes that private-sector firms that have been unwilling to invest in new plant will at least buy parastatals and that it will be able to use this money in the 'oilspots'.

This would not be enough, however, and more money would have to come from outside. Ex-President Botha and others have even called for an international 'Marshall Plan' to fund the project. The Government and its supporters increasingly argue that sanctions are depriving urban black people of township improvements.

In practice, the whole scheme is needed only because of low wages. Few black wage earners can afford to buy houses built on a commercial basis by the private sector. Thus there must be subsidy, which is where corporate social responsibility programmes come in. Murray Hofmeyr, chairman of Johannesburg Consolidated Investments, admits: 'If proper wages are paid, people will be more able to look after themselves, which will be better.'[29]

THE MONEY MUST BE SPENT

These contradictions mean that money must be spent in any case in a desperate attempt to assuage black discontent over low wages, poor living conditions, a lack of political rights and the general repression. As sanctions bite, this money must come from the white minority, whether they like it or not. Sanctions will make it impossible to pay for white consumption, repression and buying off the black urban class at the same time. White consumption must suffer. This should lead to some rethinking in white homes.

Those who argue that increased investment and trade will lead to economic growth and sweep away apartheid are talking only of economic, not political, apartheid. Increased investment is intended precisely to maintain political apartheid.

The new strategy of 'repressive reform' must inspire even greater moral and political repugnance. Countries that have economic dealings with South Africa can express their odium in a tangible way because 'repressive reform' depends on outside financial and trade links. So economic sanctions are both a moral and a practical response – a cogent way of saying that apartheid cannot be reformed.

'PROTECTION' AGAINST SANCTIONS?

The EPG made the crucial point that if the South African Government believed 'it would always remain protected' from 'effective economic measures', political change would not take place. Indeed, 'it is not whether such measures will compel change; it is already the case that their absence, and Pretoria's belief that they need not be feared, defers change'.[30]

This statement has proved sadly prophetic. When international banks renegotiated South Africa's short-term debt on unexpectedly favourable terms in March 1987, effectively reducing their financial sanctions, the then Governor of the South African Reserve Bank, Gerhard de Kock, called it a 'sign of confidence' in South Africa. In his Budget speech in March 1988 Finance Minister Barend du Plessis said that the slowdown in capital outflow 'reflects a more positive over-seas perception of South Africa's economy and prospects'. In other words, any easing of international pressure is seen as support for the Government. Former Anglo American Corporation head Harry Oppenheimer used the EPG's term when he talked in March 1988 of 'the protection we are currently receiving from the major Western powers' – protection against sanctions.

PRESSURE FOR CHANGE

Business leaders cannot, on their own, force the Pretoria Government to the negotiating table. But it would be impossible for the Government to maintain apartheid in the face of business hostility. Business leaders will be the most sensitive to economic sanctions, and their decision-making will be influenced by potential profits as well as by racism and a desire to maintain apartheid.

The growing debate, then, will be between those on one side who expect sanctions to become very much worse, and therefore press for political change, and those on the other side who believe that foreign pressure is subsiding and that South Africa will remain protected from sanctions. A return to economic prosperity would probably help to reconstruct the consensus within the white community and increase support for 'repressive reform'. In contrast, economic sanctions will deepen the economic crisis and encourage the fragmentation of the white community, enlarging the group who see negotiations as the only sensible way out.

Tighter and much stronger sanctions are essential to back those who are pressing for change. JCI's Hofmeyr is an opponent of sanctions, but even he privately admits, 'If the pressure were removed, I think the Government will continue to do nothing.'

Speaking in London in May 1988, the Roman Catholic Archbishop of Durban, Denis Hurley, said, 'Much stronger pressure is required – pressure that will cause real discomfort to the white community to make it realize that it cannot continue [with apartheid].'

4

WHY IS SOUTH AFRICA THE EXCEPTION?

Many arguments are proffered against sanctions. It is said that more investment and more trade, rather than sanctions, are the way to end apartheid. Yet in the more than three decades since sanctions were first proposed there have been ample investment and major increases in trade, while the position of most black people has become much worse. Increased trade and investment have accompanied increased repression, greater poverty and extensive forced relocation.

Similarly, critics argue that sanctions harm those whom they are supposed to help. We deal with this point in more detail later. But we note here that opponents of sanctions against South Africa were willing to impose sanctions against Argentina, Libya, Poland, Iran, Cuba and Nicaragua. In those cases there was no suggestion that we should wait three decades and hope that increased trade and investment would encourage political change and negotiation. Nor was any concern expressed about hurting the people we meant to help. Thus opposition to sanctions in South Africa runs counter to the tactics applied elsewhere.

Nearly fifty years ago many countries of the world joined together to end fascism in Europe. The war imposed much hardship on the people of occupied Europe as well as on those who helped. But who, then or now, would argue that it would have been better to spend three decades increasing trade with Nazi Germany and talking to Hitler in the hope of internal political reform that would alleviate hardship among the oppressed peoples of Europe?

The opponents of sanctions against South Africa argue that South Africa should be an exception and that the tactics used with a wide range of other countries should not be applied in its case. They suggest as an alternative a tactic that has been a manifest failure for more than three decades. We find no convincing reason why this unusual and unsuccessful policy should be pursued or why South Africa should continue to be treated as a special case. 'In our view, the white regime of South Africa has been tolerated because it is perpetuated by white people. If it had been by any black government, that government would have been thrown out a long time ago, not by the nationals of that country alone, but by a combination of force of the European Governments,' argues Didymus Mutasa, Speaker of the Zimbabwe parliament.[1] Howard Wolpe, chairman of the Africa Sub-Committee of the United States House Foreign Affairs Committee, argues: 'Unconscious racial attitudes and reflexive anti-communism make it possible for there to be expressions of deep concern that sanctions against Pretoria will "hurt the black majority we seek to help" (disregarding the pro-sanctions sentiments of popular black political organizations and unions) when there are no similar cries of conscience about the fate of Polish or Libyan workers.'[2]

HOW MUCH HARDSHIP WOULD SANCTIONS CAUSE?

The willingness to harm Polish or Libyan workers cannot be used as a justification to harm South African workers. There are two relevant questions. First, will sanctions actually cause massive black unemployment inside South Africa? And second, if so, are sanctions worth the price?

Clearly some sanctions will cause some job losses. If mineral exports are curbed, fewer miners will be needed. If fruit exports are ended, some pickers will be redundant. But support for sanctions within the South African trade-union movement reflects a broader view. In the past two decades there have been massive redundancies, very much larger than any job losses likely to be caused by sanctions, that have been the result, in large part, of mechanization – often with imported machinery, some funded by foreign investment. In the decade 1974–84 manufacturing output rose by 2.9 per cent per year, while manufacturing employment rose by only 0.8 per cent per year as companies used new investment to increase productivity rather than to create jobs.[3]

In 1988 the workforce in the gold mines – not subject to sanctions – declined by 40,000, while the workforce in the coal mines fell by

6,000.[4] The reason was the need to reduce production costs and maintain profits. In agriculture state policy encouraged rapid mechanization, largely with imported equipment; 1.1 million jobs were lost in the 1970s and another 120,000 in the first half of the 1980s, before any sanctions were imposed.[5] Many redundant workers and their families were forcibly removed from the white farms and dumped in the Bantustans. Because so many of the permanent agricultural tasks have been mechanized, much of the remaining work, especially in export crops like fruit, is badly paid and seasonal. Farm workers are excluded from the Labour Relations Act (1982), which permitted collective bargaining, although some unionization has taken place.

Trade-union support for the withdrawal of foreign firms is based partly on the view that foreign investment does not increase the total number of jobs; social investment due to the Sullivan and other codes improves the life of the remaining workers, but better wages would be more effective. Furthermore, foreign and South African firms that declare themselves concerned about the sanctions-induced job losses seem quite happy to sack workers by the thousands if they strike.

Finally, some economists within South Africa argue that as the country faces tighter sanctions it must become more self-sufficient and less dependent on modern, computerized imports. This means more labour-intensive industry and perhaps more jobs. Furthermore, now that job reservation has been formally ended, the squeeze on company profits may lead firms to replace expensive white workers with cheaper black ones.

Thus the dominant view within the trade-union movement is that although sanctions will cost some jobs, there are two countervailing factors. First, workers are at risk in any case from mechanization and lock-outs, which are much more serious worries than sanctions, while sanctions should create and protect jobs in other sectors. Second, there is consensus within the black trade-union movement that sanctions will work and will bring the Government to the negotiating table. They are convinced that sanctions will end much worse suffering. Frank Chikane, General Secretary of the South African Council of Churches, put it bluntly:

> I think the victims of apartheid are put in a situation where ... you
> keep your jobs and continue dying [or you] say, well, I may as well

give up my job so that I stop the dying . . . It is the insecurity that goes with the victims of apartheid. If your children are shot in the townships and you are working in a factory, the likelihood is that you leave the factory and go and take care of the dead children because that issue becomes a priority, much more than the salary you get, because it doesn't help you to work for children who aren't there.

WHO SPEAKS FOR BLACK WORKERS?

Does Chikane accurately reflect the views of black workers? There has been much discussion about black views of sanctions, and opinion polls seem to show a wide and contradictory range of views.

At its July 1987 Congress Cosatu reiterated its call for 'comprehensive and mandatory sanctions'. Since then the South African Government has gone out of its way to prevent the discussion of sanctions, through both bannings and legislation. Business is also anxious to prevent debate on sanctions. For example, Gencor chairman Derek Keys, in his 1988 annual report, noted, 'We are, however, concerned about union actions such as support for sanctions.' The new restrictions on trade-union political activity are in part intended to bar just such support.

In such circumstances many people will be afraid to be honest with an unknown poll taker, which partly explains the variation in results. And the trade unions can no longer express an opinion or discuss the issue. Therefore we must trust Church leaders and others whose international reputation gives them some degree of protection and who are thus freer to speak out. They remain firm and consistent advocates of sanctions.

At its meeting in Toronto in August 1988 the Commonwealth Committee of Foreign Ministers on Southern Africa (CFMSA)

recognized that Pretoria's fear of sanctions was leading to a concerted campaign supported by massive financial resources to convince Western countries that black South Africans were opposed to sanctions. The Committee recognized that this was itself an admission by Pretoria of the effectiveness of sanctions. Its deliberations also confirmed throughout the Committee's view that black South Africans continue to look principally to sanctions as the international community's most necessary form of pressure on Pretoria for peaceful change.

'DELIBERATE POLICY IN IMPOVERISHING PEOPLE'

The results of the recent Carnegie inquiry into poverty in southern Africa frame the issue well. One prominent critic of sanctions said that sanctions would 'harm the very people we wish to help' by throwing black South Africans out of work. 'The recent Carnegie report on poverty in South Africa paints a shocking picture. It is very much to the discredit of the South African Government. But are we to make the problem worse? The answer is no.'[6]

The Carnegie report itself argues:

> in South Africa there is no painless way to change: no easy road to freedom. Seen in this light the question about sanctions becomes not so much a matter of debating whether or not it will cause unemployment (although this is certainly an important consideration), but rather a question as to whether or not it will be effective.[7]

It concludes:

> policies of separate development, anti-urbanization, forced removals, Bantu education, the crushing of organization, and, in more recent years, destabilization have been directly responsible for increasing poverty amongst millions of people. Indeed it is precisely this dimension of premeditation or deliberate policy in impoverishing people that makes poverty in South Africa different from that in so many other parts of the world.[8]

Surely when such 'shocking' poverty is the result of 'deliberate policy' of the apartheid state, this is an argument *for* sanctions, not *against* them?

WILL SANCTIONS BENEFIT SADCC?

Opponents of sanctions also stress their belief that sanctions against South Africa will rebound on the neighbouring states: 'Nor would sanctions hit only South Africa. The Front-line States, linked as they are to the South African economy, would suffer severely.'[9]

'Anyone who stands up and says sanctions should not be imposed because they will hurt us is simply being hypocritical,' declared Dr Simba Makoni, Executive Secretary of the Southern African Development Coordination Conference (SADCC). 'We are already suffering. How much more can we suffer?' asks President Robert Mugabe. 'We support sanctions because it will shorten the time we must suffer.'

Like the victims of apartheid inside South Africa, the SADCC states respond that the price of apartheid is so high that any cost of sanctions must be seen as an investment in ending apartheid. The United Nations Children's Fund (Unicef) estimates that 1.3 million people have died in the SADCC states since 1980 because of South African destabilization. The material cost has been more than US$60 billion.[10] In part because they saw sanctions work in helping to end the suffering in Rhodesia, SADCC leaders strongly support sanctions against South Africa. And they see it as a small price to pay.

In any case, those who warn that sanctions will harm SADCC exaggerate the damage that will be done because they base their warning on the false premise that the nine states in SADCC are so dependent on South Africa that any action against South Africa will have knock-on effects that will harm SADCC.

Seven of the nine SADCC states are dependent, to some extent, on South Africa. The central goal of SADCC is to reduce that dependence precisely because it is artificial and is a legacy of colonialism. Substantial progress has been made in reducing links with the apartheid state, although this process has been slowed by South African destabilization. For example, Zimbabwe and Malawi ship goods through South African ports only because South Africa continues to blow up the railways in Mozambique that would normally serve those countries.[11] Similarly, migrant workers are in South African mines because identical minerals in the SADCC states have never been exploited.[12]

Only one of the nine SADCC states, Lesotho, is totally dependent on South Africa. It is surrounded by the apartheid state, and migrant miners in South Africa are its main source of income. Clearly Lesotho is the hostage state. Even so, King Moshoeshoe II of Lesotho is a strong backer of international sanctions: 'In considering the impact of sanctions against South Africa, we have to ask those who oppose such measures in the name of hurting black populations in and near South Africa, "Where were you while South Africa was imposing a blockade around Lesotho?"[13] Having heard little protest from these people over threats to our survival, we do not find their new concern for our interests persuasive.'[14]

WHOSE SANCTIONS?

In discussing the implications of sanctions for the neighbouring states it is important to identify who is imposing sanctions – the major industrialized countries, South Africa or SADCC itself? This issue is treated in detail in the companion volume to this report,[15] and we note only the key conclusions here.

First let us consider the main range of sanctions that have been imposed, or are being discussed, by the industrialized world. The arms embargo clearly helps South Africa's neighbours by reducing South Africa's ability to destabilize them. Some firms that have withdrawn from the apartheid state have moved to SADCC, especially Swaziland. Western sanctions against South African minerals and agricultural products cannot harm SADCC states, except for the problem of migrant labour. But most migrants from the SADCC states (including Lesotho) work in the gold mines, and gold is not proposed as a target for any immediate sanctions. The idea of the air-links ban was to stop direct flights to South Africa from the rest of the world, forcing people to transit through the majority-ruled SADCC states, which would benefit those states. Thus sanctions by the industrialized states will entail some costs but, on balance, will be directly beneficial to the majority-ruled states of southern Africa.

This leaves the two remaining cases – South African sanctions against SADCC and SADCC sanctions against South Africa. These are really two sides of the same coin because they involve cutting the same links and perhaps closing the same border. The differences would lie in order and timing – each side would take the actions that most harmed the other and most benefited itself.

South Africa has imposed sanctions against all of its neighbours, most notably Lesotho in 1986. However, South Africa has an average balance-of-payments surplus of more than US$1,250 million per year from its trade with the SADCC states – after taking into account customs-union and migrant-labour payments. This figure will decline somewhat in the coming two years as SADCC re-opens transport links cut by South African destabilization. Nevertheless, South Africa could expect to retain a significant profit from its regional trade.

Therefore it seems unlikely that South Africa would impose wide-ranging sanctions against SADCC: this would be tantamount to Pretoria's imposing sanctions on itself. Instead South Africa is more likely to respond to more extensive Western sanctions with greater destabilization – particularly by attacking transport links in an attempt to increase SADCC dependence on South Africa. It is hardly rational, however, to argue that sanctions should not be imposed because Pretoria would respond by attacking its neighbours.

It would be much better to impose sanctions strong enough to make such raids impossible.

This leads to the third case, SADCC-imposed sanctions. The Organization of African Unity (OAU) specifically exempts 'some independent states in southern Africa from imposing sanctions'. In practice, only the opponents of sanctions demand that SADCC join in immediately. SADCC has been trying for nearly a decade to reduce its links with South Africa, and its efforts need more international support. But links forged during eighty years of colonialism and reinforced by a decade of destabilization will need time to break. For SADCC to impose wide-ranging sanctions quickly would be highly disruptive and hardly cost-effective because total SADCC trade with South Africa is less than that of any one of the five big trading partners. Hence SADCC sanctions would have a relatively small effect. Furthermore, as international sanctions tighten, South Africa will be increasingly anxious to keep the route to the north open. Continued trade between South Africa and its neighbours may serve as limited protection against destabilization and counter-sanctions.

We come to three conclusions:

1 Existing sanctions imposed by the industrialized countries benefit, not harm, the SADCC states.
2 There will be a cost related to greater destabilization.
3 Extensive sanctions imposed by the SADCC states would be much less useful than sanctions imposed by the industrialized states and much more expensive.

The SADCC summit in 1986 reiterated the position of the SADCC states with respect to sanctions:

> Although individual SADCC member states may not themselves be in a position to impose sanctions, SADCC member states' vulnerability should not be used as an excuse by others for not imposing sanctions;

> SADCC member states will do nothing to undermine the effectiveness of sanctions imposed on South Africa by the international community;

> SADCC member states will cooperate closely with each other to lessen the adverse impact of sanctions on their own economies, and in this respect will expect the international community to render them maximum assistance.

We fully support the SADCC position.

ACCELERATING SUFFERING

Critics of sanctions say they would 'harm the very people we wish to help'. This assertion is based on a circular argument. The Carnegie report shows increasing poverty as a 'deliberate policy' of the apartheid state, and the critics of sanctions declare that action should not be taken against apartheid because it will accelerate that impoverishment. Destabilization causes massive suffering, and opponents of sanctions claim that action should not be taken against apartheid because the white regime will respond by increasing destabilization. In other words, the very horrors of apartheid are cited in support of the argument that the apartheid regime should be protected from sanctions.

Sanctions are not intended to ease the suffering under apartheid but, rather, to speed the end of apartheid. It is a question of extra pain now to prevent even greater suffering later. If sanctions had been imposed in 1960, after the Sharpeville massacre and the first calls for economic sanctions by Chief Albert Luthuli, apartheid would have been overthrown by now and the Carnegie report need never have been written. If sanctions had been imposed in 1976 after the Soweto massacre, destabilization would be over. The total suffering would have been much less, even if some people had been hurt by the sanctions.

As we noted at the beginning of this chapter, South Africa is an exception to the common policy of using sanctions as part of an international effort to change policies in a wide range of countries. We find that none of the excuses put forward can justify this anomalous attitude towards the apartheid state.

PART II

CURRENT SANCTIONS: IMPACT
AND SHORTCOMINGS

5

THE SANCTIONS JUGGERNAUT

Most countries in the world have taken some action against South Africa during the past four decades. In this part of our report we look more closely at the measures that have been taken and attempt to evaluate their success. We also look at shortcomings, loopholes and more overt violations.

India was the first country to impose comprehensive sanctions against South Africa with a set of increasingly tight measures between 1946 and 1964. It banned trade with South Africa in 1946. This involved significant cost, as India lost 5.5 per cent of its exports at that time. Many other countries cut links as they became independent. Indeed, it was the poor countries that made the greatest sacrifices.

Various countries began imposing selected sanctions. Japan banned direct investment in 1964 (although licensing and technology transfer is still permitted). In the 1970s many nations imposed arms and oil embargoes, and sports and cultural boycotts were launched. By the late 1970s some international banks had already reduced lending to South Africa. Sweden banned new investment in 1979.

The most recent wave of sanctions began in late 1984 in response to the uprisings in the townships. The United Nations Security Council approved packages of voluntary measures in 1984 and 1985. The European Community (EC), the United States and the Commonwealth each imposed a set of measures in 1985 and again in 1986. These measures confirmed the oil embargo, further reduced military and nuclear cooperation, limited investment, imposed certain diplomatic sanctions and restricted the sale of sensitive hardware. Imports of gold coins, arms and paramilitary equipment and iron and steel were banned.

BUILDING A WAVE

Most notable about the 1984–7 period was the 'wave' phenomenon. In a space of just over two years most Governments imposed several different sets of measures. Each one drew on the precedents set by others. Thus Sweden banned the import of South African fruit, a measure that had previously been thought to violate General Agreement on Tariffs and Trade (GATT) rules. Ireland then also banned fruit, which dispelled the myth that an individual country could not take action within the EC. Denmark followed with a ban on coal. Once Danish parliamentarians realized what could be done, Denmark became the first industrialized country to impose a total trade boycott. The rest of the Nordic states followed.

Meanwhile the Commonwealth agreed a second package in August 1986. In October 1986 the United States Congress overrode a Presidential veto to pass the Comprehensive Anti-Apartheid Act. It was a stronger package than the Commonwealth one, but legislators openly acknowledged their debt to the Commonwealth for laying the groundwork.

Reinforcing the wave of governmental and inter-governmental action were thousands of local actions. More than a hundred companies pulled out of South Africa. Anti-apartheid movements ran boycott and disinvestment campaigns. Local governments and city councils in many industrialized countries boycotted South African products and refused to deal with companies that had South African links. This in turn prompted more transnational corporations (TNCs) to withdraw from South Africa rather than lose much larger business elsewhere. It also precipitated the decision by United States banks not to roll over loans in 1985, which forced South Africa to freeze payments on its short-term debts. In many ways these financial sanctions imposed by international banks have been among the most effective.

The impact of the nine industrialized countries that made commitments to reduce trade has been impressive. They have cut one third of their trade with South Africa. Their sanctions are equivalent to 12 per cent of all of the world's purchases from South Africa (other than monetary gold) and to 7 per cent of all South Africa's trade (including gold). If these countries had not imposed sanctions, South Africa would be earning 7 per cent more from its exports than it does today.

Table 1. Reduction in trade by nine sanctions-imposing countries
(US$ million)

	Imports from SA			Exports to SA			
	Average 1983–5	1987	Rise/ fall	Average 1983–5	1987	Rise/ fall	Net decrease
USA	2,340	1,420	−921	1,881	1,295	−585	−1,506
Denmark	141	4	−137	60	14	−46	−183
Canada	139	76	−63	134	87	−47	−110
Finland	17	1	−17	73	0	−73	−89
Norway	35	25	−10	75	7	−68	−77
Sweden	49	21	−29	147	108	−39	−68
France	636	583	−54	464	468	4	−50
Australia	104	90	−14	82	57	−26	−40
New Zealand	18	11	−7	16	11	−5	−12
Total	3,481	2,230	−1251	2,931	2,047	−884	−2,135
Total decrease by Sanctions Nine as % share of 1983–5 average of:							
Combined total of Nine			36%			30%	33%
South Africa, excluding monetary gold			12%			7%	9%
South Africa total			7%			7%	7%

Note: Country figures exclude monetary gold, which is not recorded in trade data. This table and all others are based on unrounded data; totals have been rounded for the purposes of these tables.

The nine states are the United States, three Commonwealth countries (Canada, Australia and New Zealand), the Nordic states (Denmark, Finland, Norway and Sweden) and France, which cut its coal imports. Their trade in 1987, compared with that of the pre-sanctions period, is shown in Table 1.

Initial data for 1988 show that sanctions are further squeezing South African exports but that rising mineral prices have compensated. Total non-gold exports were roughly steady; they were up approximately 2 per cent in US dollars and down 2 per cent in SDRs (Special Drawing Rights, an average of the major currencies that may be a more accurate measure because it takes into account the devaluation of the dollar). But base metals exports earned 28 per cent more (in US dollars) because of rising prices, while other exports fell by a comparable amount.

As we note in Chapter 11, other countries have stepped in to fill the gap partially. Nevertheless, South Africa's markets are being restricted, and these states have shown that it is possible to impose effective sanctions. Despite higher minerals prices, South Africa is selling less to the rest of the world, as is shown by comparing percentage changes in South Africa's total exports (including gold), valued in both US dollars and SDRs, in 1987 and 1988 with the 1983–5 average:

	1987	1988 (est.)
US$	+13%	+14%
SDR	−10%	−13%

Thus South Africa's apparent increase in earnings is accounted for by the fall in the value of the dollar. In real terms, as measured in SDRs, South Africa's exports are down by one eighth – a real testament to the success of sanctions.

DIFFERENT SANCTIONS HAVE DIFFERENT OBJECTIVES

A country-by-country review of sanctions is provided elsewhere.[1] Here we detail different classes of sanctions. It is useful to bear in mind the tactical objectives of different classes of sanctions, as set out in Chapter 2. Bans on sales *to* South Africa (Chapter 6) serve two purposes: first, to make it difficult for the apartheid state to obtain strategic goods like arms and oil; second, to raise the cost of sanctions-busting goods sufficiently to impose an economic strain. (Higher costs are related to commissions that must be paid to sanctions-busting middlemen and are a kind of 'apartheid tax'.) Bans on purchases *from* South Africa (Chapter 7) have a largely financial purpose: to cut off South Africa's export earnings. This measure is intended to put severe pressure on the South African economy because the apartheid state will not have money to import essential goods. This, in turn, will have a political impact. Corporate withdrawal (Chapter 9) is intended to stop TNCs from supporting the apartheid economy and repression machine.

People's sanctions (Chapter 10) have three very different objectives. First, they proclaim solidarity with the struggling people of South Africa. Second, they turn personal revulsion into organized positive action, as individuals unite to refuse products and profits tainted with apartheid. Finally, and probably most important in the long run, they put pressure on Governments to take stronger action. Few Western Governments have imposed sanctions on South Africa without pressure from below by anti-apartheid and people's sanctions movements.

6

SALES TO SOUTH AFRICA

The first sanctions imposed by most countries were embargoes on the sale of certain strategic goods to South Africa, particularly arms and oil.

Sanctions are mandatory for the entire international community only if they are imposed by the United Nations Security Council. So far it has only passed one mandatory sanction against South Africa, Resolution 418 of 1977, which bans the sale to South Africa of 'arms and related material of all types, including . . . weapons and ammunition, military vehicles and equipment, paramilitary police equipment, and spare parts'. Also banned are *new* licences and equipment and supplies for manufacturing banned items.

THE SUCCESS OF THE ARMS EMBARGO

Although openly violated by a few countries and narrowly interpreted by many, the arms embargo has been remarkably successful.[1] South Africa has been unable to buy any main weapons systems since 1977. The 1984 Defence White Paper conceded that 'some of the most reliable main armaments are obsolescent'.

South Africa's Navy has lost its deep-sea capability. It has three old French submarines and some newer Israeli fast-attack craft suitable only for coastal patrol. The Air Force is restricted to planes based on pre-1977 designs and licences, and none has been produced since 1982. Its Mirage 2 aircraft are now elderly and out of date by international standards. Despite the fact that it has an aircraft industry, South Africa cannot obtain military air frames or jet engines. The South African military magazine *Paratus* admitted in 1988, 'The programme for modernization of the stock of Mirage 3 models, renamed Cheetahs, does nothing to increase the inventory of air frames, so that any losses in combat or otherwise reflect a permanent depletion.' The Air Force also cannot obtain radars, armed helicopters or the surveillance aircraft that are crucial to command and control in modern warfare. The Army has had particular difficulties with tanks and tracked vehicles as well as anti-tank and surface-to-air missiles. The whole South African military has fallen far behind in the rapidly advancing area of electronic warfare; it lacks modern command, control, communication and intelligence systems, and it does not have the modern electronic counter-measures needed to protect attack aircraft.

The most notable success of the arms embargo was the August 1988 cease-fire in Angola and the subsequent agreement by South Africa to withdraw from Angola and to implement Resolution 435 in Namibia. In July 1987 South Africa had invaded southern Angola in an effort to shore up Unita and to capture the strategic town of Cuito Cuanavale. In previous invasions South Africa had depended on air superiority to limit casualties on the ground. This time, however, the South African Air Force was inferior to the Angolan Air Force and to its anti-aircraft defences, so Pretoria lost a number of planes. Unwilling to risk further aircraft, South Africa put more stress on ground forces. Its sanctions-busting artillery performed well, but the vintage Centurion tanks proved vulnerable. In order to avoid heavy white casualties, South Africa withdrew. Without a decade of the arms embargo, this would have been a very different story.

Another important success of the arms embargo is that it has made it very expensive for South Africa to obtain sanctions-busting weapons. There are large commissions to pay to middlemen for imported hardware, and the cost of locally produced weapons is very high. Thus the arms embargo is increasing the strain on the economy.

This is not to say that the arms embargo has been totally successful. Spurred on by the fear of ever stronger sanctions, South Africa has built up a major arms industry. Armscor (the Armaments Corporation) is one of the largest industries in South Africa, with a turnover of more than US$3 billion per year. About two thirds of Armscor's requirements are met by at least 800 other companies that undertake subcontract work. In other words, much of South Africa's manufacturing industry is involved to some extent in arms production, and various laws ensure that the Government can force any company to do military work.

South Africa has become more or less self-sufficient in the production of light weapons such as rifles, machine-guns, hand grenades, mines, explosives and ammunition. It also produces light vehicles, some of which are exported. South Africa also produces a small range of more sophisticated weapons, but these are all dependent on foreign parts and technology. Beyond that South Africa can only upgrade pre-1977 systems like the old Mirage fighters; even that exercise is highly dependent on foreign expertise and parts.

Another technique that South Africa has used to bypass sanctions has been to increase the portion of apparently civilian items among military equipment. The Ratel armoured personnel carrier is a good example. It is based entirely on European designs and uses standard automotive components, including a locally made diesel engine (itself based on foreign technology).

ARMS-EMBARGO VIOLATIONS

There have been two highly publicized sanctions-busting successes by which South Africa obtained state-of-the-art weaponry. These involved the G5 field howitzer, which has a range of 40 kilometres, and the Valkiri multiple rocket launcher; both are now built in South Africa and exported. In another case South Africa bought submarine-construction plans from West Germany in 1984, but further technical support was halted, and South Africa does not seem to have either the money or the technical capacity to build the submarines – despite having the blueprints. In a second case involving West Germany the export of equipment for a battlefield targeting device was prevented only after extensive publicity by the World Campaign Against Military and Nuclear Collaboration with South Africa.

The United States Department of State reported in 1987, 'Israel appears to have sold military systems and sub-systems and provided technical assistance on a regular basis.' Under United States pressure Israel agreed in 1987 not to sign any new military contracts but refused to terminate existing ones, which means that it is still a major arms supplier in violation of the mandatory United Nations embargo. The United States report also cited companies in France and Italy and, to a lesser extent, West Germany, Britain, the Netherlands and Switzerland. In addition Chile and Taiwan seem to be increasingly important suppliers.

There have been several convictions for illegal arms sales to South

Africa. A Dutch court jailed the head of a shipping company for four months in 1988 for shipping guns to South Africa. In Canada in 1987 two firms were fined for sending night-vision equipment to South Africa. There have been several cases in Britain, although the British Government has been criticized for allowing four South African arms traffickers to leave the country and thus escape imprisonment.

Perhaps more important than direct arms sales has been the sale of components and technical support that allow South Africa to assemble, and sometimes to manufacture, its own weapons. This is often done under the guise of supplying 'dual-purpose' items. Thus a West German firm was able to provide the South African police with helicopters of a type that military forces in several countries have converted to carry missiles. Armscor is dependent on a wide range of private contractors and on normal equipment, such as computers and diesel engines, that have both military and civilian use. (This issue is discussed further in Chapters 16, 20 and 21.) Clearly many countries interpret arms-sales restrictions in South Africa's case very much more leniently than in the case of the socialist countries. Indeed, it seems as if items *are not* sold to the Eastern Bloc if there is a possible military use, while items *are* sold to South Africa so long as there is a possible civilian use.

South Africa is becoming a major arms supplier, although its claim to be selling more than US$900 million per year of weapons to twenty-three countries appears to be exaggerated.[2] Reportedly buyers have included Iran, Iraq, Israel, Chile, Taiwan, Sri Lanka and Morocco. Most sanctions packages, including the EC and Commonwealth measures, include a ban on the purchase of arms and paramilitary equipment, but some countries that claim to abide by these restrictions have appeared at arms-sales shows with South Africa and allow their firms to sell South African weapons to third countries.

Thus the arms embargo, like many others, must be seen as a partly enforced sanction that has been a partial success. Some sanctions busting takes place, but the arms embargo played a central role in forcing Pretoria into genuine negotiations over Angola and Namibia.

THE OIL EMBARGO AND THE 'APARTHEID TAX'

South Africa has no oil supplies of its own and so should be highly vulnerable to a petroleum embargo. The Arab oil embargo was launched in 1973, and it is now endorsed by all the major oil-exporting states. The Organization of Petroleum Exporting Countries (OPEC), the EC, the Nordic states, the United States and the Commonwealth have all imposed an oil embargo.

Despite the embargo South Africa still obtains all the oil it needs. So, in one sense, the embargo has failed. It has succeeded, however, in one very important way: it is costing the apartheid state vast amounts of money to break it. There is, in effect, an extra 'apartheid tax' on every litre of fuel that South Africans use.[3]

In 1986 President P. W. Botha said, 'Between 1973 and 1984 the Republic of South Africa had to pay R22 billion more than it would normally have spent. There were times when it was reported to me that we had enough oil for only a week. Just think what we could have done if we had that R22 billion today.' That R22 billion was equivalent to about US$25 billion at the exchange rates of the time – almost exactly the size of South Africa's foreign debt in 1985, when Pretoria admitted it could not pay its short-term debts. The cost of breaking the oil embargo made South Africa more vulnerable to financial sanctions.

The Shipping Research Bureau estimates that it costs South Africa about US$2 billion per year to break the oil embargo. There is the actual sanctions-busting cost (down from a peak of US$8 per barrel to less than US$2 because of the oil glut), as well as the high cost of storing more than one year's oil supplies. In addition, oil produced from coal in its Sasol plants costs at least three times as much as oil bought on the world market. South Africa is spending more than US$2 billion on the Mossel Bay fuel-from-gas project in an effort to reduce its dependence on imported oil. With the cut-off of foreign investment, South Africa will have to find this huge amount of money from domestic resources or from export credits, which means inevitably that other more useful factories will not be built.

The number of countries still willing to supply South Africa is quite small and thus potentially subject to political pressure. There have been a number of recent victories in the oil-embargo campaign. A notable success in ending sanctions busting occurred in Brunei Darussalam. After reports that some of its oil was going directly to South Africa, in direct violation of the embargo, the Government successfully ended the shipments.

Norwegian ships had been carrying up to one third of the oil to

South Africa. Norwegian as well as Danish firms dropped out of petroleum shipping to South Africa, however, when their Governments imposed stringent rules, which covered not only Norwegian and Danish ships but also any ships controlled or administered by Norwegian and Danish individuals or firms.

In 1987 John Deuss, the oil trader who was probably the biggest supplier to South Africa, declared that he was withdrawing from the trade. His company, Transworld Oil, was based in Bermuda, and he specifically cited Commonwealth sanctions as one reason for ending the trade. Another may have been planned expansion in the United States, where he would have faced very serious anti-apartheid pressure.

BUT THE OIL STILL FLOWS

The oil embargo has imposed a substantial and effective strain on the apartheid economy, and major suppliers and shippers have been forced out of the market. However, the embargo has not yet actually dried up oil supplies.

According to the Shipping Research Bureau, most South African oil now comes from the Middle East, particularly from the United Arab Emirates but also from Saudi Arabia, Oman and Iran. Refined products are obtained from a number of countries, including West Germany and Britain, which do not include refined products in the embargo.

Five of the major transnational oil companies are still active in South Africa, and there is support for projects to open up offshore gas fields and to produce synthetic fuels from gas.

The Shipping Research Bureau also reports that tankers controlled by Greek and Hong Kong shipping companies have taken over the oil trade previously handled by Nordic ships. Many countries impose narrow restrictions, covering only ships with national flags or directly operated ships; ships owned by a national company can still carry oil if they are leased out or flagged elsewhere. Norwegian law still permits the transport of petroleum products from other countries, which continues. (By contrast, Danish law banned trade in oil products as well.)

Table 2 gives a few examples of the considerable variation in the ways that the regulations are implemented.

Table 2. Examples of variations in the oil embargo

	Denmark	Norway	Canada	France	UK
Types of oil exports embargoed					
Crude oil	yes	yes	yes	yes	yes
Refined oil					
Petrol and fuels	yes	yes	yes	yes	no
Feedstocks	yes	yes	yes	no	no
Oil in transit	yes	yes	no	no	no
Are national ships banned from carrying oil to SA?					
Crude oil	yes	yes	no	no	no
Refined oil	yes	no	no	no	no
Is the regulation mandatory?	yes	yes	no	yes	no

THE NUCLEAR BAN

South Africa's refusal to sign the Nuclear Non-Proliferation Treaty (NPT), and the fear that with Israeli help it may have developed nuclear weapons, has led to general sanctions against nuclear-related assistance to Pretoria. Because of Pretoria's failure to sign the NPT, the United States has a long-standing ban on nuclear cooperation; this has been strengthened to include a ban on the 'exports of nuclear goods and technology', as well as items of 'significance for nuclear explosive purposes'.

The EC bans 'new collaboration in the nuclear sector'. This permits France to continue servicing and supplying the Koeberg nuclear reactor in South Africa. The Commonwealth has a ban on 'new contracts for the sale and export of nuclear goods, materials and technology to South Africa'. The Nordic states, Austria and Japan also ban nuclear cooperation. Israel has nuclear capabilities and does not participate in any bans, however.

South Africa remains a member of the International Atomic Energy Agency.

OTHER HIGH TECHNOLOGY

South Africa is heavily dependent on foreign technology, particularly in areas such as computers and electronics (see Chapter 16 for details), and imported technology is essential for the military apparatus of repression and destabilization.

The Nordic states now have total bans on sales to South Africa. These generally include restrictions on technology transfer, including licences.

Most other countries ban some sales to South Africa. In March 1989 Canada announced the broadest national ban of any country that does not have a total embargo. It has a special 'Area Control List' of countries for which a broad range of exports are restricted; currently only South Africa and Libya are on the list. The prohibition on exports to South Africa includes aircraft (and engines and parts), computers and software, electronic and telecommunications equipment, four-wheel-drive vehicles as well as all technology and military hardware on the 'Export Control List' of items banned for sale to socialist countries. The ban covers all would-be buyers in South Africa, both public and private.

The United States has the next most stringent restrictions, with a ban on computers, software and services to the military, police or any agency involved in the enforcement of apartheid; this ban is defined broadly and covers about 30 per cent of former computer sales to South Africa.

The Commonwealth bans 'computer equipment capable of use by South African military forces, police, or security forces'. Austria has a similar ban. The EC bans the sale of 'sensitive equipment' to the military and police. Japan bans computer sales to the military and police.

It is too early to see if these bans have been effective. However, the narrowness of the definitions adopted by most countries other than Canada means that military contractors can still obtain computers and related material. Many countries place no restriction on the inclusion by a third country of a sanctioned item as part of a larger piece of equipment and its sale to South Africa. In some cases computers are simply sent through third countries; Hitachi, for example, is selling computers via Germany. Taiwan is rapidly expanding its computer and electronic sales to South Africa; sales by West Germany, Japan, Italy, France and other states also show increases.

There has been some voluntary restraint. Mitsubishi of Japan pulled out of a US$250 million steel-mill project at the suggestion of the Government. Three Japanese electronic companies are ending sales to South Africa. It is clear too that US firms have reduced machinery and equipment sales to South Africa.

OTHER SALES TO SOUTH AFRICA

There seem to have been few other attempts to restrict sales to South Africa, though Canada has stopped public-sector companies from selling to South Africa, and Italy restricts the sale of civilian aircraft (while Britain and Austria have authorized the sale of aircraft that can be used by the police and military for surveillance).

The Nordic bans also cover servicing and the transfer of production rights and patents, all key elements in technology transfer. Norway's legislation does not allow anyone under its jurisdiction to 'perform any service in South Africa or Namibia or to perform services at the request of persons domiciled in South Africa or Namibia when the request is made by a public authority or is connected with any commercial activity'.

The Commonwealth has a ban on 'government funding for trade missions to South Africa or for participation in exhibitions and trade fairs in South Africa'. The Commonwealth (except for Britain) has extended this ban to include 'all government assistance' to trade with South Africa, and Canada has extended it to cover the funding of trade promotion anywhere by companies that are Canadian-based but majority South African-owned.

7

PURCHASES FROM SOUTH AFRICA

Bans on imports from South Africa are widespread. The Nordic states have a total ban (although Norway exempts manganese). Nearly all nations ban the import of South African gold coins, which halted the production of Krugerrands. Most states also ban the import of military and paramilitary equipment. Table 3 on page 52 gives a rough summary of national and group bans on imports from South Africa.

After the countries with comprehensive trade bans, the United States has the strictest ban, covering iron and steel, agricultural products, textiles, coal, some uranium and products from parastatals. The EC, the Commonwealth, Japan and Austria ban the import of iron and steel. The Commonwealth (except Britain) also bans agricultural products, uranium and coal. Ireland bans fruit and vegetables. Japan bans fresh fruit, will not renew some uranium contracts, will not increase imports of iron ore, sugar and coal (and, in fact, seems to be reducing its imports of these items) and has asked shops to stop selling tinned South African fruit. In France, Britain, Ireland and the Netherlands parastatals do not import South African coal. The Netherlands bans South African uranium for domestic use.

Commonwealth (except Britain) and Irish Governments and government agencies do not purchase South African goods.

As Chapter 5 showed, these bans cover a significant range of South African exports and have had a marked effect on the country's budget. Perhaps most dramatic has been the impact on iron and steel and coal sales, on which a large number of countries have imposed sanctions. Coal sanctions pushed the price down sharply in 1987, when South Africa's coal earnings fell 25 per cent by comparison with those of 1986. This shortfall cost South Africa US$467 million

Table 3. Summary of bans on some South African goods

	Nordic	USA	Comm.[1]	Japan	EC
Iron and steel	T[2]	NT[3]	NT	NT	NT
Uranium	T	P[4]	T	NT	
Agricultural	T	NT	NT	P	
Coal	T	T	T		P
Textiles	T	T			

Notes: [1] Commonwealth except Britain; [2] T is a total ban; [3] NT is a near total ban; [4] P is a partial ban.

and cut 2 per cent off its total export earnings. In the same year earnings from iron and steel sales were down by 27 per cent compared with 1986, costing South Africa US$229 million. Sugar sales are also down, and uranium-production facilities are being closed because of the cutback in sales.

NARROW DEFINITIONS

One of the problems with present import bans is the wide variation in definitions used. This is most obvious in the case of iron and steel. The bans imposed by the Commonwealth countries, the United States and the EC include pig iron, cast iron, ingots, forgings, castings, bars, plates, angles, hoops, strips, rails, etc., but most bans exclude iron ore and ferro-alloys, and over steel items there is inconsistency, as Table 4 shows.

For many countries the term 'agricultural products' excludes inedible farm products like hides, cotton, wool and wood pulp, which together account for one third of South Africa's agricultural exports. It seems anomalous to claim that sugar is an agricultural product while cotton is not, or that the inside of a sheep (the meat) is agricultural but the outside (the wool) is not.

One consequence of these narrow definitions is that they limit the effect of the sanctions to a much smaller range of products than would seem apparent from a general description of the sanction. This, in turn, means that sanctions cover a smaller portion of South African trade than expected. Since Japan imports large quantities of iron ore and less steel, for example, its sanction is less effective than it might be. Similarly, the United States Treasury Department decided that uranium hexafluoride is not an 'ore' or 'oxide' and is not

Table 4. Variations in bans on iron and steel imports

	USA	Australia	EC	Hong Kong	Canada, New Zealand
Iron ore	yes	no	no	no	no
Ferro-alloys	no	no	no	yes	no
Wire	yes	yes	no	yes	yes
Tubes and pipes	yes	no	no	yes	yes
Tanks, drums, vats	no	no	no	no	yes

covered by the United States sanctions law, and it granted licences to increase the import of South African uranium compounds.

TRANS-SHIPMENT

As sanctions tighten, sanctions busting grows. The South African Government has set up a special Secretariat for Unconventional Trade to encourage counter-trade and sanctions busting. Several people, including some with experience of breaking sanctions against Rhodesia, are now involved in sanctions busting on a commercial basis. To make this easier, the South African Government has stopped publishing information about foreign trade and shipping traffic.

Various techniques are used to disguise the South African origin of products. One method is to ship goods first to a country that does not impose sanctions and then to trans-ship them, usually claiming that the goods originate in the intermediate country. In some instances minor modifications can change the official origin of a product. For example, South African coal is sent to Rotterdam, mixed with other coal and sold as 'Dutch blend'. In other cases even this is not done; South African coal imported into Belgium has been sold to France as 'Australian' coal.

A number of places have been suggested as possible intermediate locations where South African goods might obtain false certificates of origin with little or no local processing. These include Mauritius, Montserrat, Uruguay, the Channel Islands and the Isle of Man. A Turkish firm placed an advertisement in a South African business magazine telling South African exporters, 'You will also have the opportunity to export your products to existing markets over Turkey, utilizing the attractive free-trade zones as "Turkish" produce.'[1] An

Israeli firm advertised services such as trans-shipment, reinvoicing and redocumenting: 'Any sanctions impediments can be circumvented through our offices for modest percentages.'

A different trick is used with seafood. The 'country of origin' of seafood is usually the flag of the ship that catches or processes the fish, so South Africans have re-registered their fishing vessels under other flags. They are also transferring fish at sea to non-South African boats. Such sanctions-busting seafood is being sold in the United States and other countries.

Sometimes false customs declarations are made in the importing country. For example, according to Singapore's official trade statistics, it is Mozambique's biggest trading partner. The trade is composed largely of imports of 'Mozambican steel'. Mozambique does not export steel and does not record any such trade with Singapore. One must assume that the steel is South African.[2]

FALSE LABELLING

False labelling seems to be on the increase. For example, 'Botswana grapes' have been sold in England, even though Botswana grows no grapes. 'Swazi apples', 'Swazi wine' and 'Zambian pears' have been sold in Europe. These can easily be identified as fraudulent because these countries do not produce apples, wine or pears.

It is more difficult when the country identified on the label actually produces such goods. Paper has been falsely labelled as from the United States, dried fruit as from Spain, apples as from New Zealand, oranges as from Swaziland and even wine as from France. Another trick is to use a false brand name; the 'Botswana grapes' were sold under an Australian trade name.

Three kinds of false labelling occur. First, goods are legitimately imported as South African, then relabelled. This occurs in the case of South African fruit imported under quota to Europe and then re-labelled to bypass Irish and Danish restrictions or to beat consumer boycotts.

Second, and probably most common, are forged certificates of origin. The goods never even pass through the country alleged to have produced them. A British Sunday newspaper reported that a South African subsidiary of a British firm was willing to sell canned asparagus with false labels and certificates of origin from France, Brazil, Thailand or Israel.[3]

Third, South African goods are imported into a third country, the labels are changed and then the trader obtains a fraudulent certificate of origin from the government. This is particularly common with clothing and commodities subject to preferential treatment.

SPECIAL PROBLEMS FOR BLS

The 'BLS countries' (Botswana, Lesotho and Swaziland) seem to be the main victims of mislabelling. They are three small countries that have long borders with South Africa (Lesotho is surrounded by South Africa). They were tied closely to the South African economy during the colonial era. Because they are landlocked, they export at least some of their goods through South African ports, where it is a simple matter to equip falsely labelled goods with forged certificates of origin. In several countries falsely labelled Swazi citrus and avocados have appeared beside legitimate Swazi produce.

BLS are members of a customs union with South Africa (a relationship also inherited from the colonial era and very difficult to break). The free movement of goods between these three small states and South Africa creates a sanctions-busting channel. For example, a textile firm imported 140,000 finished shirts from South Africa into Swaziland, sewed in false Swazi labels and fooled the authorities into providing a certificate of origin.

It is important to stress that BLS Governments are not conniving at this; the false labels, certificates of origin and customs documents are supplied by agencies inside South Africa. Indeed, these countries are worried that such false labelling will call their own credibility into question and make their products unacceptable in world markets. (This happened when Finnish trade unions boycotted Swazi citrus.)

The Swaziland Chamber of Commerce and Industry told the Expert Study Group that it was concerned about the effect of fraudulent practices on exports of genuine Swaziland-manufactured goods. Because of this it is prepared to overstamp certificates of origin with a Chamber of Commerce stamp when importers request this. 'We can assure you that we only overstamp when we have satisfied ourselves that the goods are correctly described on the Certificate of Origin.' In an effort to prevent fraud the Swazi Ministry of Commerce now puts serial numbers on certificates of origin and code numbers on boxes of Swazi citrus. Botswana has informed foreign customs authorities that it is prepared to re-verify any goods with 'Made in Botswana' labels.

VIOLATIONS

Many countries have reported falsely labelled South African goods, although there have been few prosecutions. India discovered thirteen Bombay-based firms that were trading with South Africa, routeing goods through intermediate countries. The United States, the largest country to impose sanctions, does not give these sanctions priority and investigated only twenty violations in the first year.

The number of violations that are discovered seems to be related to how hard customs officials look for them. New Zealand, one of the smallest countries actively to promote sanctions, uncovered ten violations in two years. In 1988 New Zealand customs officials made one of the largest seizures of banned goods when they found eight containers of falsely labelled South African dried apricots and raisins, worth US$250,000. The importer claimed that the fruit came from Spain and Turkey. Samples were subjected to microscopic analysis and were found to contain pollen that does not occur in Europe. A warrant was issued, and customs officials raided the office and home of the importer. They found documents confirming that the fruit was from the South African Dried Fruit Cooperative.[4] This indicates that enforcement is possible and suggests that falsely labelled South African products may be entering many countries in violation of sanctions.

8

OTHER GOVERNMENT MEASURES

Most Governments have imposed investment bans. The Nordic bans on new investment are very strict and cover leasing as well as licensing and technology transfer, which are not covered by some other bans. Some reinvestment is allowed in order to maintain the commercial viability of an existing operation in South Africa, so long as there is no expansion; Swedish companies require permission to replace worn-out machinery.

Japan has banned investment since 1964 but allows technology transfer. The Commonwealth (except for Britain) bans 'new investment or reinvestment of profits'. The United States bans new investment but allows reinvestment of profits and the purchase of new equipment. The E C has a ban on new investment, which includes establishing or extending branches or establishing new undertakings, but it does not block investments by subsidiaries of European companies outside Europe. Austria and Israel also ban new investment. In several European countries, including the two largest European investors, Britain and West Germany, the ban is voluntary only.

New bank loans to both public and private sectors are banned by the Commonwealth (except Britain), the United States, the Nordic states, Japan and West Germany. The Commonwealth also bans government loans to the Government of South Africa and its agencies (although there seem never to have been many of these). The E C treats most loans for over five years as new investment; the United States appears to treat loans for more than one year as new investment. The rescheduling of existing loans is not normally treated as new lending.

Australia and Japan include trade credits in the loan bans, which means that buyers' credits (bank loans to South African buyers) are prohibited but not suppliers' credits (deferred payment terms). The United States bans both buyers' and suppliers' credits with maturity of over one year (treated as new investment). Belgium and Canada have declared that there should be no increase in trade credits. Hong Kong banks, on the other hand, are providing trade finance for Japanese and other Asian exporters.

Government export credit guarantees and insurance were stopped in the Netherlands, Canada and a few other countries in the 1970s and, more recently, by the entire Commonwealth (except Britain), Ireland and Austria. Italy had previously banned export insurance cover for credits longer than twelve months but recently *raised* the limit to twenty-four months.

Following its debt freeze in 1985, South Africa is considered a bad risk by most countries, and in general the existing bans simply formalize what banks would do anyway.[1] There are a number of loopholes, especially relating to loans that can be guaranteed in some way outside South Africa. For example, there seem to be few restrictions on loans to a TNC for use in South Africa, so long as the loan is not made directly to the South African branch or subsidiary. Similarly, in many cases investments can still be made via third countries. Some loan and investment bans do not include the purchase of South African bonds, shares and other securities.

DOUBLE TAX AND OTHER FINANCIAL MEASURES

The Commonwealth (except for Britain) and the United States have ended double-taxation agreements, though in some countries this curb had little direct effect because of other legislation that permitted taxes paid abroad to be credited against taxes at home. The United States has passed additional legislation to prevent this. The United States also bans its banks (but not their foreign branches) from holding bank accounts of the South African Government and entities controlled by it.

The Commonwealth (except Britain) has a ban on 'government contracts with majority-owned South African companies'. Canada has included grants (such as regional development aid) and sales in the ban. In Australia, however, the Commonwealth ban on 'government contracts with majority-owned South African companies' was interpreted to mean only the national Government. In December 1987 the Western Australian state government went into partnership with the Anglo American Corporation in a gold-extraction project.

AIR LINKS AND TRAVEL

India, the socialist bloc and mainland African countries (except for some southern African states and the Ivory Coast) do not allow South African Airways (SAA) to fly over their countries. The Commonwealth countries (except Britain), the Nordic states, Spain and the United States have cut air links with South Africa. SAA offices have been closed in several countries. Japan does not allow government officials to travel on SAA.

There are still direct flights between South Africa and eleven European countries, three countries in Asia and one in South America. The ban on direct flights to the United States hit particularly hard, but British Airways, TAP, KLM, Lufthansa, UTA and Varig have all run advertising campaigns to attract South Africa–United States travel, thus undercutting the ban. In a similar way several airlines have increased flights to Johannesburg to compensate for the ending of direct flights from the United States, Australia and elsewhere.[2]

The Commonwealth (including Britain) has a voluntary ban on the promotion of tourism. The Nordic states prohibit the organization of travel to South Africa; Denmark even bans the sale of flight tickets and the arrangement of hotel accommodation. Australia and Canada closed the offices of the South African Tourism Board (Satour); it still has offices in twelve countries, including Japan.

Voluntary bans have controlled the promotion of tourism in countries such as Australia and Canada, which make an issue of it, and not in countries such as Britain, which don't. (Britain accounts for nearly one third of visitors from countries other than the neighbouring states.) Air links and press coverage of South Africa seem to be more important than tourism-promotion campaigns in determining whether people visit South Africa. Tourism fell in 1985 and 1986 but rose again in 1987 and 1988. Satour reports that South Africa earns more than US$400 million per year from foreign visitors.

VISAS AND DIPLOMATIC LINKS

Governments have imposed a variety of non-economic measures against South Africa, generally involving diplomatic links and sport and cultural boycotts. Many states have never had diplomatic or consular relations; India, Argentina, Panama, and New Zealand have cut diplomatic links. The EC has agreed that members should recall military attachés from South Africa and not accredit new military attachés from South Africa. Australia has expelled some South African diplomats, and Canada has cancelled the non-resident accreditation of four attachés. Various states have ended cultural and other agreements with South Africa. Canada will not allow government officials to attend certain conferences and meetings in Canada at which South African officials will be present.

Many countries have imposed visa requirements, and South Africans now need visas for all countries except Greece, Israel, Singapore, Switzerland, Britain and some in southern Africa. The Commonwealth (except for Britain) has agreed on 'the withdrawal of all consular facilities in South Africa except for our own nationals and nationals of third countries to whom we render consular services'. Australia and Canada do not issue visas to South Africans in South Africa.

The Nordic states do not issue visas to South Africans wishing to take part in sporting, cultural or scientific activities, and they discourage tourists. The Netherlands, Canada and various other states try not to give visas to South Africans who are violating the cultural and/or sports boycotts. Japan does not issue tourists visas and discourages tourism to South Africa but permits sports, cultural, academic and business travel in both directions.

SPORT

The sports boycott is undoubtedly the most successful non-economic ban. Few South Africans can now play abroad, while any team visiting South Africa (no matter how weak) is front-page news there. South Africa has been banned from an estimated 90 per cent of all world sport and has been expelled from the Olympics and from most international sports organizations. It still retains some international contacts in the case of a few sports, including golf, tennis, boxing, cycling and gymnastics, but its isolation in the context of popular sports like rugby, soccer and cricket is nearly total.[3]

The Commonwealth's 1977 Gleneagles Declaration was one of the first internationally agreed sanctions. It calls on members to take 'every practical step to discourage [sporting] contact or competition'. The EC in 1985 agreed to 'freeze' official contacts and agreements in sport. The South African Council on Sport (SACOS) has promoted the boycott with the slogan 'No normal sport in an abnormal society'.

The sports boycott has had the indirect effect of improving sporting opportunities for black people. In some sports teams have been integrated and major training programmes established; neither would have happened without the boycotts. SACOS's soccer league, the Federation Professional League, however, has been unable to attract sponsorship and funding from business because of its explicitly anti-apartheid line. Furthermore the huge differences in spending on white and black education and recreational facilities means that under apartheid opportunities will never be equal, no matter how many special programmes are established.

CULTURE

Both the EC and the Commonwealth have agreed to discourage 'cultural and scientific events', with certain exceptions. The United Nations Special Committee Against Apartheid publishes lists of sportspeople and entertainers who go to South Africa, and these are used to enforce the boycotts.

The cultural boycott has been effective in stopping most internationally known performers and artists from visiting South Africa, further increasing the sense of isolation. South African performers and groups have also had difficulty in travelling abroad. At the level of books, films, TV and touring exhibitions the boycott is only partly effective. Few British TV programmes are shown in South Africa, but many United States programmes are broadcast. In particular the growth of video recorders means that banned films and TV programmes (whether banned by the apartheid regime or by sanctions) still circulate in pirate form.

Undoubtedly one of the most important results of the cultural boycott has been to stimulate a dynamic local culture, created by black South Africans who have had an opening precisely because South Africa has not been swamped by Western popular culture. Speaking in London in 1987, the ANC president, Oliver Tambo, stressed that a people's culture 'has grown into a mighty stream, distinct from, and in opposition to, the warped and moribund culture of racism'. The people, he said, have created alternative structures. 'Not only should these not be boycotted, but more, they should be supported, encouraged and treated as the democratic counterparts within South Africa of similar institutions and organizations internationally.'[4]

This has led to a modification of the cultural boycott. More than 300 South African artists, performers and other cultural workers met in Amsterdam in 1987 and set down policy guidelines. Their resolution stressed that 'cultural activities and the arts are partisan and cannot be separated from politics'. In particular, cultural workers and academics should not go to South Africa 'except in those instances where such movement, after consultation with the national liberation movement, is considered to be in furtherance of the national democratic struggle'. Similarly, 'South African artists, individually or collectively, who seek to travel and work abroad should consult with the mass democratic movement and the national liberation movement.' However, detentions and bannings make it extremely difficult for the mass democratic movement inside South Africa to make public pronouncements.

Because they have been so strongly applied and have had such an impact in white South Africa, the sports, cultural and academic boycotts are now coming under concerted attack by the apologists of the 'new apartheid'. The South African Government is trying to weaken the boycotts against South African individuals and firms and against holiday travel to South Africa; it is spending millions of dollars promoting the image of a reformed apartheid. Yet individuals who would denounce the 'new apartheid' are detained or banned, while critical books and films are censored. There can be no cultural or academic exchange while the apartheid state itself controls the flow of information.

9

DISINVESTMENT

The withdrawal of private companies has been one of the most significant non-government sanctions, probably second only to the ban on the rolling over of loans by banks. According to the United Nations Economic and Social Council, more than 500 TNCs have sold their holdings in South Africa. More than half the United States firms have left the country. Companies began withdrawing after the Soweto massacre in 1976. Withdrawals slowed down in the profitable period of 1979–80, but increasing numbers of firms were leaving even before the 1984 township uprisings.[1]

The terminology of withdrawal varies from country to country and creates much confusion. We will use 'withdrawal' to signify a TNC's departure from South Africa and 'divestment' to mean people and organizations selling shares in companies with South African links to try to put pressure on them to withdraw. Withdrawal is the act of a TNC, while divestment is a people's sanction against a TNC. 'Disinvestment' we will use to cover the whole process of withdrawal and the exertion of pressure on companies to withdraw.

Besides divestment, the most important pressure on companies to withdraw has been selective purchasing laws, particularly in the United States, which limit local council and other contracts with firms with South African links, Consumer campaigns have also had an impact, most notably on Barclays Bank in Britain.

Many people assumed that when companies withdrew from South Africa, they would cut all links with the country. In practice, this has rarely happened. Most have maintained commercial links, licences, technology-transfer agreements and so on. They continue to provide the products, inputs and services that they supplied before. In the most extreme cases, such as Ford and IBM, withdrawal has had no noticeable effect; the old managers run the old subsidiary and continue to sell the same products supplied by the same former parents. Some firms still obtain raw materials from former subsidiaries.[2]

Withdrawals by United States firms have been promoted by a combination of falling profits and substantial pressure from states and cities with selective investment and buying rules. Some of these regulations applied only to firms with direct investment, but many others are like New Jersey's 1985 law, which applies to 'any company engaged in business in or with the Republic of South Africa'. Clearly, this includes sales, franchises, licences and management agreements. States and cities that formerly had weaker laws are now adopting laws similar to the one in New Jersey.

This change is having an effect, and companies that simply cut equity links have remained under pressure. Motorola, for example, sold out to Altron (see Chapter 14) in 1985 but continued to supply equipment and technology. Under selective buying pressure in the United States, Motorola has been forced to pledge that it will not renew its agreement with Altron when it expires in 1990.[3]

National Governments have had little to say about withdrawal except in Canada. As part of a package of financial assistance for Massey-Ferguson tractors, the Canadian Federal Government and Ontario provincial government acquired shares in the Varity corporation. In 1987 and 1988 both the Federal Government and Ontario provincial government supported shareholder resolutions calling for Varity to withdraw from South Africa.

THE IMPACT ON WORKERS

Sanctions and disinvestment pressure have had mixed effects on workers inside South Africa. In general, companies that were previously foreign-owned and obeyed codes of conduct have been sold to local managers who no longer follow the codes and have reduced their social investment. On the other hand, firms fighting heavy disinvestment pressure have substantially improved wages, working conditions and industrial relations. Shell has perhaps gone farthest, with explicitly political advertising campaigns and financial support for community projects. It is important to note, however, that firms like Shell have made these concessions only in response to international pressure. Also these companies are making no concessions on the central issue of their links with the apartheid state.

Trade unions, in general, have supported corporate withdrawal as a way of putting pressure on the apartheid state. And they point with anger to the foreign companies that claim concern for their black workers while the firms try to stay in South Africa but show no such concern when they decide to pull out. Many withdraw without discussions with the workers and with no provisions or guarantees that improved conditions will be maintained.

Cosatu, at its 1987 Congress, warned, 'Disinvestment, as it is currently being carried out by multinational companies, amounts to nothing more than corporate camouflage which often allows these companies to increase their support for the South African regime.' Therefore 'where disinvestment takes place, companies must give Cosatu notice of their intention to pull out of South Africa so that bona fide negotiations can take place' (corporate withdrawal is called 'disinvestment' in South Africa).

The Chemical Workers Industrial Union (CWIU) has tried to put this provision into effect by demanding that thirty-nine TNCs sign an agreement that they will give one year's notice of intended withdrawal and enter into bona fide negotiations. In the event of disinvestment workers would be guaranteed no worsening of conditions, would be given cash bonuses and would have access to company documents concerning the withdrawal process. Worker trusts would be created with the funds generated by the sale of the company. At first the companies all replied that they would not negotiate, since they had no intention to withdraw. But then one (Sterling Drug) withdrew, sharply underlining the union's demands. In early 1989 twenty-four TNCs agreed to talk to the CWIU about the proposal, although at the time of writing others are still refusing. In the United States the Dellums Bill, approved by the House of Representatives in 1988, would have required United States companies to give ninety days' notice of disinvestment and 'enter into good-faith negotiations with representative trade unions'.

A PARTIAL SUCCESS

Disinvestment must so far be judged a partial success. A majority of foreign firms have probably reduced their links with apartheid. The Financial Rand mechanism, reintroduced in 1985, means that the repatriation of company-sale proceeds does not hit South Africa's balance of payments,[4] but many companies admit that they are paying higher dividends and using the new consultancy and licensing agreements as a way of getting the money out as fees (which are not covered by the Financial Rand system). So disinvestment is a partial success in imposing a strain on the South African economy.

The main goal of disinvestment is usually defined vaguely as to end TNC support for apartheid. Whatever the limitations of the false withdrawals, the psychological impact has been considerable. White South Africa is repeatedly reminded that it is being abandoned by its (largely white) European and North American supporters. This also sets in train an important process within the TNCs concerned; whatever agreements they make when they withdraw, South Africa becomes increasingly peripheral to corporate concerns. A former subsidiary is less important and no longer receives the preferential access to servicing and new technology it once had. Thus the old managers can continue as before, but they are increasingly cut off from foreign technology and support – whatever they may claim.

CODES OF CONDUCT

Codes of conduct for TNCs in South Africa have frequently been put forward as an alternative to corporate withdrawal. The EC, the United States, Sweden, Australia and Canada have codes of conduct for firms in South Africa. Some are voluntary; some cover only majority interests; others also apply to firms with minority interests. These codes generally set levels of minimum pay and call for the recognition of unions and support for education, housing and social facilities for black workers.

Code companies have, in some respects, improved the standards for their workers, but the shortcomings of codes have come in for increasing criticism in recent years. Codes benefit only the tiny proportion of black South Africans who are employed by code firms. Furthermore, these firms tend to provide amenities like housing, which the workers could purchase if they were paid a higher wage, or facilities like education, which the state is not providing because of the apartheid system. The main criticism is that codes cannot tackle the political basis of apartheid. Because of this, in 1987 the Reverend Leon Sullivan ended his support for the United States code named after him and called for companies to withdraw.

The National Union of Metalworkers (NUMSA) worked with the West German trade union IG Metall to draw up a much stronger code, which has been put forward to forty German firms. Under the code South African workers would enjoy the same rights as their German counterparts. Firms would be required to restore union rights removed under the new Labour Relations Act, to take a stand against emergency legislation and to pay the wages of detained workers. Further, unions and shop stewards would be accorded a number of rights that are customary in West Germany but not in South Africa.

10

PEOPLE'S SANCTIONS

Behind all other sanctions lie actions by individuals and groups. People's sanctions have pressured, shamed and forced TNCs and national Governments to take action, and it seems safe to assume that such pressure will continue to be the main force behind the tightening, intensifying and expanding of existing sanctions. It is only right that democratic Governments should respond to strongly felt popular concerns.

Individuals and groups are very limited in what they can do about apartheid directly, but they still have significant power. They can help to support the victims of apartheid and the groups that are struggling to end it. (This is not an issue of this report.) They can impose their own sanctions, and they are probably most powerful in putting pressure on others to cut links with South Africa.

As well as imposing useful economic costs on South Africa, people's sanctions have two functions that should never be underestimated. First, by refusing to be associated with apartheid, people bear witness in a practical way to their abhorrence of a unique evil. Second, people throughout the world are showing solidarity with those in South Africa who are fighting for justice. In these grim times of repression and emergency that solidarity shines as a beacon, telling the oppressed people of South Africa that they are not alone. Thus it is important that people's sanctions should be given wide publicity. Canada, for example, publishes an Anti-Apartheid Register of individuals and organizations who have peacefully demonstrated their opposition to apartheid. The 1988 Nelson Mandela birthday concert was shown on TV throughout the world (except South Africa).

BRINGING PRESSURE TO BEAR

Beacons and witnessing are not enough, however. It will require effective economic pressure to bring about change, and people's sanctions must be judged in terms of practical results as well.

Individuals and organizations are most powerful as consumers; people's individual contribution to sanctions involves not buying South African goods or not buying from firms with South African links. Consumer boycotts against South African goods have occurred in many countries; hundreds of towns, cities, counties, states and provinces refuse to buy South African goods. These include twenty-three states and seventy-nine cities in the United States; in Britain more than seventy local councils are involved (although their action may now be illegal), while more than fifty Dutch councils impose such bans.

In some instances trade unions (particularly in ports and distribution) have refused to handle South African goods. Indeed, in Finland trade unions brought about a total end to trade with South Africa before the Government approved such a ban. Pressure has also been exerted by both consumers and unions on chainstores, and in many countries, from Japan to Ireland, South African goods have been banned from certain shops. South African fruit and clothing have been particularly vulnerable to boycotts, and South African exporters have noticed that sales to the United States have fallen more than would have been expected as a consequence of sanctions alone. This is said to be because 'unofficial sanctions, which are open-ended and subjective . . . [have] affected mainly goods on which, by law, country of origin must be indicated. Retailers are reluctant to display these, as they are afraid of provoking boycotts or demonstrations.'[1]

Increasingly cities and states are refusing to give contracts to firms that still have links with South Africa. This means that TNCs are being excluded from lucrative local tenders, and it has been one of the most important reasons why some United States firms have withdrawn from South Africa. In the United States, the Netherlands and elsewhere some councils give preferential treatment to firms without South African links.

Another important form of action is divestment. More than seventy cities and twenty-one states in the United States have sold US$20 billion in shares held by pensions funds and similar entities in firms with South African links. By now so many investment funds in the

United States are subject to constraints that the share prices of firms with South African links must be somewhat depressed because their market is restricted. This is another form of pressure on management (although it may be less important than the fact that firms with South African links have in recent years performed worse than those without South African links, which suggests that companies that have remained in South Africa are managed worse in other ways as well).

KEEPING SANCTIONS BUSTERS OUT

Another form of people's sanctions is making South Africans un-welcome abroad and restricting those who go to South Africa in violation of embargoes. Many councils bar from local sports grounds and concert halls those who break the sports and cultural boycotts (who are generally identified by the United Nations lists); grants are often denied to those who break boycotts. The city of Hamburg, for example, banned South Africa from its annual tourist fair in 1988.

Sport is generally administered by non-government or quasi-government bodies, which have played a central role in expelling players who go to South Africa and in blocking tours by South African teams. The number of rebel tours is steadily declining because people who go on such tours cut themselves off from other inter-national competition.

Performers and athletes themselves have played a key role in tightening the boycotts. For example, the widespread support for the 1985 record 'I Ain't Going to Play Sun City' sharply reduced the number of musicians willing to play there. Sun City, in a Bantustan near Pretoria, had been regarded by some as acceptable because it was 'outside' South Africa; after the release of the record no one could support that argument.

Many international academic and scientific organizations have expelled South Africa, and some exclude South Africans (other than those linked with the democratic movement) from conferences.

SETTING THE MORAL TONE

People's sanctions have played an essential role: that of setting the moral tone. They have created a climate of opinion in which it is no longer acceptable to deal with apartheid.

United States business executives talk of the 'hassle factor'. They become tired of being challenged at board meetings and shareholders' meetings and by friends at parties; eventually it is easier to get out. Shops cease to stock South African goods because they become tired of protests. But there is more to their action than that: the moral arguments are carrying weight, and they see no advantage in supporting apartheid.

Similarly, Governments faced with conflicting demands for time and resources may be reluctant to take action on South Africa, but it is the moral force of people's sanctions that moves apartheid steadily up the agenda and that is ultimately responsible for the imposition of most of the sanctions described in preceding chapters.

PART III

FRUSTRATING SANCTIONS

11

CHANGING PATTERNS OF TRADE

Sanctions have significantly reduced trade with South Africa, as we showed in Chapter 5, though other countries have moved to fill the gap to some extent.[1] The nine industrialized states that have imposed wide-ranging sanctions have cut their trade with South Africa by between one third (measured in US dollars) and nearly a half (measured in SDRs), while those countries that have not imposed significant sanctions have increased their imports from the apartheid state (see Table 5).

There has also been a significant regional shift in trade. As the United States, the Nordic states and some Commonwealth countries reduce trade, some Asian and European countries are taking their place. West Germany and Japan are now South Africa's biggest trading partners, with substantially more trade (combined imports and exports) than their 1983–5 average. The increases are so large that they cannot be explained by reference to changing rates of exchange.

In Asia, Taiwan and Hong Kong (and probably South Korea) are also significantly increasing their trade with South Africa. In Europe the picture is more complex. Nordic and French total trade is down, but West Germany's trade has increased so much that it is now number one, pushing Britain down to third position. Turkey, Switzerland, Austria, Belgium, the Netherlands, Spain and Portugal all show major increases. It is fashionable to stress the role of Asia in trade with South Africa, but European trade is growing almost as fast – for example, West Germany increased its trade more than Taiwan and Spain more than Hong Kong (value of 1987 combined imports and exports compared to the 1983–5 average (see Appendix 7, Table 1).

South America is a small but growing market for South Africa;

Table 5. Shifting trade patterns: 1987 compared with 1983–5 average

	Imports from SA		Exports to SA		Net change	
	1987[1]	Change[2]	1987[1]	Change[2]		
US$ (billion)						
Sanctions Nine[3]	2.2	−1.3 −36%	2.0	−0.9 −30%	−2.1	−33%
Rest	9.9	2.7 37%	10.3	−0.2 −1%	2.5	14%
Monetary gold	7.1	0.8 12%			0.8	12%
Total	19.3	2.2 13%	12.3	−1.0 −8%	1.1	4%
SDR (billion)						
Sanctions Nine[3]	1.7	−1.6 −49%	1.6	1.2 −44%	−2.9	−47%
Rest	7.7	0.7 9%	8.0	−2.1 −21%	−1.5	−8%
Monetary gold	5.5	−0.6 −10%			−0.6	−10%
Total	14.9	−1.6 −10%	9.5	−3.3 −26%	−5.0	−17%

Notes: [1] The monetary value of 1987 trade. [2] The monetary difference between 1987 and the average of 1983–5 and the change as a percentage of the 1983–5 average. [3] The United States, Denmark, Canada, Finland, Norway, Sweden, France, Australia and New Zealand (see Chapter 5).

Source: Based on the tables at the end of this report and in the companion volume to this report.

Table 6. Trends in regional shares of total trade with South Africa (%)[1]

	1983	1985	1987
Western Europe[2]	49	53	55
East Asia[3]	21	21	28
North America	21	19	13
Nordic states	3	3	1

Notes: [1] Table based on combined imports and exports. [2] EC members plus Austria, Switzerland and Turkey. [3] Japan, Taiwan, S. Korea, Singapore and Hong Kong, including re-exports of the latter two.

sales to Brazil, Argentina and Chile have doubled in the past four years. Some African states have also been slipping and were criticized this year by the Organization of African Unity Liberation Committee for their growing links with South Africa.

We wish to stress, however, that the emphasis should remain on South Africa's traditional trading partners – both the big traders like West Germany and Japan and the traditional second-tier countries like Taiwan and Spain. *Their increases in trade over the past four years have been much larger than the trade with new partners.* The changing pattern of regional trade is shown in Table 6.

THIRD-PARTY TRADE

Some countries appear to be disguising their trade with South Africa by trading through third parties. This is especially easy with precious metals because it is difficult to identify the country of origin. For example, in 1988 Japan's imports fell by 15 per cent (in US dollars) compared with 1987. But the entire decrease was accounted for by a cut in gold and platinum imports; if these are excluded from both 1987 and 1988 figures, other imports actually rose by 6 per cent. Meanwhile Japan substantially increased its imports of platinum and gold from countries that are themselves major importers of precious metals from South Africa.[2]

Similarly, some European countries are importing South African coal through third countries. In 1986 Britain reported that it imported only 300,000 tonnes of South African coal, but European statistics show that 1.1 million tonnes of South African coal was shipped to Britain that year via the Netherlands.[3]

TAKING ADVANTAGE OF SANCTIONS

Published statistics show that importers in some countries have been taking advantage of sanctions imposed by others and increasing their trade in sanctioned commodities. French, Danish and United States coal sanctions should have reduced South African sales by 10 million tonnes; instead they fell by only 3 million tonnes in 1987. Spain, the Netherlands, Portugal and Greece all took advantage of lower South African prices to increase their volume of coal imports.

There is a world surplus of coal, so South Africa cut prices in order to keep its market share. In 1987 its prices fell to less than US $20 per tonne, which is below the cost of production. Since then prices have risen somewhat, but South African prices remain as much as US$5 per tonne lower than those of other countries. This is the discount needed to convince people to buy South Africa's coal.[4] Thus a small volume decrease combined with a large price decrease caused a 25 per cent fall in earnings from coal exports in 1987. Prices rose somewhat in 1988, but the South African discount remained at US$5 per tonne. This 1987 fall in prices benefited importers, but it hurt other coal-producing countries, such as the United States and Australia. They were forced to cut their prices as well, even though they did not need to match South Africa's.

This is also happening with iron and steel. The Swiss Government admitted that Swiss imports of South African steel rose fivefold in 1988: the price of South African steel was low because so many traditional buyers had stopped their purchases.[5] Turkey, China,[6] Argentina and others are increasing their imports of South African iron and steel.

Turkey has become the third largest buyer of South African iron ore and the fourth largest buyer of steel. Concern has been expressed that it is processing this steel in a limited way, then selling it on to other countries as 'Turkish steel' at low prices. A member of Israel's Knesset (parliament) said that an Israeli firm was 'laundering' South African steel; 49 per cent of the firm, Iskoor, is owned by the South African parastatal iron and steel company Iscor.

Such countries are clearly taking advantage of the sanctions imposed by other countries by purchasing South African materials at prices depressed by sanctions. Those countries are likely to use the cost savings to lower the prices of their manufactured goods on the world market, creating unfair competition.

HIDDEN TRADE AND AVOIDING RED HERRINGS

Increasing secrecy is making it harder to detail South African trade. South Africa itself publishes fewer and fewer statistics precisely to frustrate the sort of analysis that we have undertaken. We have worked primarily from data supplied to the United Nations and other bodies by South Africa's trading partners. This, however, is limited because some countries – notably South Korea, certain oil producers and the socialist states – do not report their trade with South Africa.

There is significant illicit and misreported trade (discussed in the following chapters). Nevertheless we believe that less than one fifth of South Africa's commodity trade is secret – primarily that in arms and oil. Indeed, most countries conceal their arms trade, and it is hardly surprising that the oil trade is kept secret. We conclude that reported statistics give an accurate picture of trade in the other items discussed in this report – minerals (other than gold), agricultural products and manufactured goods (other than arms).

It is essential to maintain perspective. Sanctions busting should not be overestimated, nor should the diversion of trade to new partners. Publicly acknowledged, official trade by South Africa's old friends remains much more important. The increase in West German imports of South African fruit, for example, is probably larger than all of South Africa's sales of sanctions-busting fruit.

12

ENCOURAGING SOUTH AFRICAN TRADE

A few countries have directly countered the international sanctions campaign with increased support for South Africa. Taiwan has given fulsome and public support to Pretoria. It doubled its trade in 1987 and doubled it again in 1988, making it South Africa's fifth most important trading partner after the United States. Taiwan has placed more than US$100 million in new investments in South Africa, particularly in small factories in the Bantustans.

Probably the most important government support for trade with South Africa is trade credits and official export credit guarantees and insurance.[1] In Britain the Government is actively promoting trade with South Africa. A headline in the official magazine *British Business* (December 1987) proclaimed, baldly, 'Government Support for SA Trade'. In November 1987 Trade Minister Alan Clark gave a speech in which he stressed the 'exciting opportunities' in South Africa, adding, 'I hope that British companies will continue to be well represented and to keep winning business from our competitors.' Perhaps as a result, British trade with South Africa rose in 1988, after falling in 1986 and 1987.

The British Government is following the precise letter of the Commonwealth ban on 'government funding for trade missions to South Africa', but policy is to offer 'exporters the normal range of assistance apart from those specifically banned'. This includes market reports that promote export opportunities, as well as briefings and other assistance for trade missions, falling just short of actual funding in cash.

The British Department of Trade and Industry (DTI) also appears to be getting close to breaking several other sanctions. For example, the DTI has called for British companies to 'consider establishing own subsidiaries' in South Africa to take on work in the Mossel Bay gas field. It would seem hard to do this without violating the EC ban on new investment, to which Britain subscribes. Furthermore, the Mossel Bay project is designed solely to bypass the oil embargo.

HELPING TO SELL SOUTH AFRICAN GOODS

Not all support for South Africa is so overt, and some even seems unintended and indirect. As sanctions begin to bite, and South Africa finds it difficult to sell its products, it increasingly looks to more covert marketing techniques. One technique is to encourage non-South African companies to do the marketing. (This differs from actual sanctions busting, which usually entails illegal action and was discussed in Chapter 7.) In some cases this involves firms in selling to third countries South African commodities that are banned in their own country.

As most sanctions so far involve South African exports, and as the market for sales to South Africa remains highly competitive, Pretoria is switching increasingly to barter and counter trade. This means that the seller swaps cars or machinery for South African coal or fruit (barter trade), or that the sale is conditional on the seller finding a buyer for the coal or fruit (counter trade). Barter and counter trade are increasingly common in international trade in general, and some TNCs and banks have set up special departments to engage in these. In 1988 there were reports of a dozen counter-trade deals involving South Africa that were worth US$80 million.[2]

Barter trade is also growing in direct sanctions busting, particularly arms-for-oil swaps. South Africa also may offer to swap strategic minerals for oil and push the would-be minerals buyer to break the oil embargo. In some cases firms that want to be involved in the offshore gas project are being asked to find buyers for South African goods. The South African Foreign Trade Organization (Safto) suggests that counter trade would be a good way to maintain access to foreign technology, perhaps in exchange for South African-manufactured goods or tourism deals.[3] Thus in order to sell to South Africa, foreign firms may actually have to promote tours to South Africa or sell sanctioned goods.

South Africa is trying to promote industrialization to increase self-sufficiency, but its market is small, and it tends to be an expensive producer, even with low wages. As foreign exchange is squeezed, foreign firms may increasingly find themselves having to take manufactured goods in exchange. There are already some in-house swaps between subsidiaries of TNCs; for example, at least one German car maker exchanges car parts with its South African subsidiary.

Another technique is joint marketing. For example, in Europe the Bella Nova label is used for joint marketing of Australian, Chilean and South African fruit. This directly undercuts consumer boycotts because it is more difficult to determine the country of origin. Some southern-hemisphere countries use South African firms to market their goods in Europe, particularly fruit. Companies in a number of countries are members of marketing organizations that include South African firms; for example, some companies in countries that ban the import of South African coal are still in the International Coal Development Institute, which includes South African mining companies as members.

Very few countries define sanctions broadly enough to prevent locally registered companies from trading in South African goods in third countries or on the high seas, even in items like coal or oil, which are themselves subject to domestic sanctions. Therefore counter and barter trade and joint marketing are likely to become increasingly important loopholes.

PLATINUM COINS

The success of gold coins produced in competition with Krugerrands has led to the launch of platinum coins by Switzerland, Canada, Australia and other countries. There are also platinum bars, aimed, like the coins, at small investors. Although Canada is a platinum producer and Australia will be, most of the platinum in coins and bars is South African.

After the experience with the Krugerrand, South African producers are encouraging the production of foreign platinum coins but not producing their own. This is because all the foreign coins once boosted the demand for gold and helped to keep the price up – benefiting South Africa.[4] Platinum coins will do the same.

South Africa supplies about 85 per cent of Western platinum consumption. Platinum is the one mineral for which South African supply is genuinely strategic, and this is why it is generally exempted from proposed sanctions. And platinum is an important catalyst in the chemical industry and for auto-exhaust control. However, it is widely predicted that platinum prices will fall sharply in the early 1990s because of increasing production and alternatives for auto-emission controls.[5] Promoting platinum coins and jewellery is seen by South African producers as the way of keeping demand high to ensure restricted supplies and high prices.

Because coins encourage consumption, and hence scarcity, South Africa is the primary beneficiary of platinum coins, no matter whose platinum actually goes into them. Thus Australian and Canadian platinum coins support South Africa's arguments that platinum be exempt from sanctions and push up the price that South Africa earns for its platinum.

13

BLOCKING AND BYPASSING SANCTIONS

A wide range of actions have been taken by Governments and international organizations that reduce the impact and effectiveness of sanctions.

One of the most blatant is the setting of quotas for fruit imports. Despite national bans in Denmark and Ireland and consumer boycotts in several other countries, South Africa retains the same share of the total European market: apples that are not sold in Ireland or Denmark are simply sold elsewhere in the EC, nullifying the effect of the boycott. Fruit imports are regulated partly by the quotas set by the European Commission and partly by 'voluntary' market shares agreed by producers (and mediated by Commission officials),[1] but the effect is that South Africa normally supplies one third of apples imported into the EC. This means that when EC apple imports jumped 70 per cent between 1984 and 1987, South Africa's sales to the EC rose by a similar amount. Thus, despite the fact that two EC member states have barred South African fruit and that there have been repeated anti-apartheid declarations at all levels, South Africa has been permitted substantially to *increase* fruit sales to Europe. Indeed, these are nearly double the value of iron and steel sales lost as a consequence of the EC ban on those products.[2]

HAMPERING PEOPLE'S SANCTIONS

People's sanctions, particularly consumer boycotts and shareholder campaigns, play a central role in mobilizing public opinion against the apartheid state. And, because they demonstrate in a direct way the popular abhorrence of apartheid, they have been an important factor in the decision of companies to cut links with South Africa and of Governments to impose additional sanctions against South Africa. Not surprisingly, Governments and companies that want to continue doing business with apartheid are anxious to limit people's sanctions.

The most effective way to do this is by restricting information, thus making it difficult to organize boycotts. Labels are the key; a survey in Britain showed that 27 per cent of people avoid products labelled 'Made in South Africa'. Sales of South African-made clothing fell by one third between 1985 and 1987 in Britain, in part because of a campaign by the British Anti-Apartheid Movement. But in 1989 Britain withdrew regulations that required country-of-origin labels on clothing and other non-food products in response to a general European change of policy, which will seriously hamper consumer boycott campaigns against growing imports of South African textiles.

Many countries go to great lengths to allow companies to hide trade with South Africa under the general guise of commercial confidentiality. Most countries that subject some South African trade to licensing procedures allow licences to be kept secret. By contrast, Sweden publishes a list of all exemptions to its sanctions, which has discouraged companies from applying for exemptions.

In Britain the Government allows more than 150 firms with politically sensitive subsidiaries, including some in South Africa, to suppress all reference to them in public records.[3] Such companies thus avoid boycotts, as well as circumventing the investment restrictions of ethical investment trusts, and some pension funds, on owning shares in companies with South African links.

Violations of sanctions against South Africa are sometimes kept secret. For example, Britain has a procedure known as 'compounding' under which a firm caught violating customs regulations can admit guilt and receive a secret fine. This has been used at least once to protect a firm that violated the arms embargo.

LOCAL GOVERNMENT AND TRADE-UNION BOYCOTTS

Among the most successful people's sanctions have been actions by local and provincial governments, education boards and so on. In the United States, state and city laws prohibiting contracts with firms that deal with South Africa are the main reason why so many companies have withdrawn from the apartheid state.

The Dutch Government, on the other hand, last year informed local councils that it is contrary to national policy for them to boycott South African products or to refuse to deal with firms, such as Shell, that are active in South Africa. And in Britain new local-government legislation contains a special clause that will prevent local councils from boycotting South African products. These are probably the first actions to protect South Africa against people's sanctions.

Trade-union boycotts of South African goods are another form of people's sanctions. In Finland, for example, it was the trade unionists' refusal to handle apartheid products that stopped trade with South Africa and eventually led to a national ban; in Ireland it was the action of shop workers who refused to handle South African fruit that eventually led the Government to ban it. The United States recognized the importance of trade-union participation in 1962 and, as part of the sanctions imposed against Cuba, encouraged the International Longshoreman's Association to ban all ships participating in the Cuba trade; this ban played a key role in reducing the number of ships sailing from Western countries to Cuba.

Such trade-union bans are legal in some countries and illegal in others. In a few cases individual companies have given employees the right to opt out of trade with the apartheid state. British Airways, for example, allows staff to refuse to work on flights to South Africa.

The problem is that trade-union and local-government boycotts often cut across other types of legislation. Bans on handling South African goods may be seen as prohibited 'secondary boycotts' not linked directly with employer–employee issues. Local councils may be prevented from taking a stand on foreign-policy issues that are the remit of the national Government and may be forbidden to impose 'political' conditions on contracts for goods and services.

In practice, such restrictive laws are already being ignored. In Denmark in 1988 building workers stopped work when they realized that they were constructing a South African consulate. A symbolic penalty was imposed by the Labour Court, but the employers refused to accept the money and the work stoppage continued.[4] In Britain, the National Council of Building Material Producers reported that local authorities were continuing to discriminate against firms with South African links, despite new legislation to prevent this.[5]

National policy in virtually all countries is to oppose apartheid, and citizens should therefore be encouraged to play their part. Thus it would make sense to grant special exemptions to deal with anti-apartheid boycotts. Sweden recognized this in 1985 (two years before it imposed its total ban) and passed a special Act Entitling Municipalities and County Councils to Impose Boycotts Directed at South Africa. The United States Government's General Accounting Office also recognized the importance of local boycotts: 'Our interviews with United States companies that have withdrawn [from South Africa] confirm the importance of state and local selective purchasing laws.'

VOLUNTARY BANS IN PRACTICE

Voluntary bans are, by definition, anomalous, and they are often ignored or interpreted in the most limited way. Japan, Canada and some other countries seem able to make voluntary measures effective: Britain does not. Tourism promotion continues, despite the voluntary ban. Indeed, South Africa was prominent at a major London tourism convention organized with the participation of the Government's own British Tourist Authority.[6] Britain also has a voluntary ban on new investment in South Africa, in keeping with both Commonwealth and EC measures, but the British Anti-Apartheid Movement reports that in the two years from September 1986 nine British firms purchased or set up South African companies, clearly ignoring the voluntary ban.

In a number of cases sanctions have been announced, but laws have never been introduced to make the sanctions mandatory. Such sanctions remain effectively 'voluntary' measures with no enforcement procedures.

WEAKENING EXISTING SANCTIONS

Finally, actions are being taken that may have the unintended side-effect of weakening existing sanctions. For example, the British Government has no ban on South African coal, but the parastatal Central Electricity Generating Board (CEGB) does, which has kept British imports of apartheid coal relatively low. Britain's electricity supply is being privatized, however, which could mean an end to the CEGB ban; two ports are now under construction to allow the import of up to 15 million tonnes of coal a year – much of it likely to be South African. South African firms have also shown an interest in coal mining in Britain.

In Europe a serious problem may arise in 1992, when many internal barriers between countries within the EC will be removed. Goods imported from South Africa into one EC country will have unrestricted access to the rest of the EC. This could make it virtually impossible for individual countries to impose additional sanctions on their own, and it will be hard for Denmark to maintain its total boycott. The issue is not settled, however, and Denmark's strong moral stand and past practical actions do give it some leverage in EC negotiations. Denmark may be able to press for tighter EC-wide sanctions or for the right to maintain its boycott of South African goods.

14

THE ROLE OF SOUTH AFRICAN-OWNED COMPANIES

Two bitterly contested take-over bids in 1988 brought to public attention the role of South African firms abroad. Minorco (owned by Anglo American Corporation of South Africa) attempted to take over Consolidated Gold Fields. Liberty Life tried to assume a more dominant role in the operation of Sun Life. Liberty and Anglo are two South African-based TNCs, while ConsGold and Sun Life are British-registered. The bids marked the acceleration of a process that has been going on for several years and involves two other South African TNCs, Rembrandt and Barlow Rand, as well as several smaller firms, notably Altech and Plateglass.[1]

In part these moves reflect the natural international expansion of large TNCs, but there are three other factors specific to South Africa. First and probably foremost, these companies have been leading the flight and reducing their presence in South Africa. South African companies saw the writing on the wall long before foreign firms did and used the brief period from 1983 to 1985, when it was possible to take money out of South Africa, to set up bases abroad. The Minorco bid for ConsGold shows how priorities have changed. Anglo offered more than US$3 billion in cash to ConsGold shareholders. If that money were invested in South Africa instead, it would make a major contribution to easing the economic difficulties of the apartheid state and would remove some of the pressure of the debt crisis.

Second, South African firms are trying to set up non-South African bases and identities in order to avoid sanctions and the stigma related to South African firms. Several have important British links: Barlow Rand owns J. Bibby, Liberty Life owns the Capital and

Counties property company and Transatlantic Holdings, while Anglo controls Charter Consolidated and other British firms. But the big South African firms prefer companies registered in Switzerland, Luxembourg or offshore islands. It is striking that the controversy surrounding the Minorco bid for ConsGold has not rubbed off on other South African-owned firms, which have been able to act with impunity as if they were European.

Third, South African-owned firms are setting up sanctions-busting channels. Despite its rigid exchange controls, the South African Reserve Bank will still authorize outward investment for this purpose.[2]

Thus South African companies are betting on both sides – they are creating sanctions-busting channels to prop up the regime while removing from South Africa as much money as they can in case the edifice of the apartheid state collapses.

MAJOR FOREIGN INVESTORS

South African TNCs have become major foreign investors. In 1986 more than US$5 billion were invested in Europe and US$4 billion in North and South America, according to the South African Reserve Bank.

Anglo is the biggest foreign investor. Its offshore subsidiary Minorco (based first in Bermuda and, more recently, in Luxembourg) has become one of the major foreign investors in the United States and is expanding in Europe. Minorco's ConsGold take-over proposal involved the sale of all of ConsGold's South African assets and was thus designed precisely to broaden Anglo's base outside South Africa.

As well as controlling the world diamond trade (through De Beers), Anglo also plays a major role in world platinum and gold production, with interests in the United States, Australia, Brazil and elsewhere, and it has a significant interest in oil exploration in Britain, Canada and Indonesia – despite the oil embargo. It is also involved in commodity trading, which is of strategic interest to South Africa, and in a wide range of industries, including railway and mining equipment.

Gencor, South Africa's second largest mining house, works through a Luxembourg company and has interests in North Sea oil, international metals dealing and Brazilian gold.

Rembrandt, the flagship of Afrikaner capitalism and the owner of seventy companies in thirty countries, controls famous brand names like Rothman, Dunhill, Cartier and Piaget. In 1988 it set up companies in Switzerland and Luxembourg to take over its non-South African assets.

Anglo, Liberty and Rembrandt all cooperate with each other and have a number of shared holdings both inside and outside South Africa.

SANCTIONS BUSTING

In 1986 one of South Africa's main electronics and telecommunications firms, Allied Technology (Altron and its subsidiary Altech), declared that its primary technology-development goal was to 'reduce ... vulnerability to sanctions'.[3] In 1988 Altron took over the British Telemetrix computer company, which it holds through a Channel Islands company. Then it sold to Telemetrix its interests in two other European companies and the United States electronic company GTI. Thus these firms all seem like normal British-owned companies.

Altron has taken over the South African assets of a number of firms that have been reducing their interests in South Africa, including Motorola, STC, Rank Xerox and Asea. All agreed to persist with manufacturing licences and to supply products as before (although pressure in the United States has forced Motorola to reconsider its position). In 1988 Altron signed an agreement with a major Taiwanese computer and electronics company. In a similar move the British subsidiary of Barlow Rand bought a United States laser maker, Melles Griot.

South African-based TNCs can arrange for sanctions busting through international intra-company trading, by which a subsidiary in one country sells to a sister company in another. This is difficult for any Government to control. Technology can also be transferred to South Africa within the company. Furthermore, the South African TNCs' heavy involvement in international minerals production and marketing will make sanctions busting much easier, both through market manipulation and by concealing the South African origin of minerals. Iscor, the South African parastatal iron and steel company, for example, works in both directions. Through a Swiss company it owns 49 per cent of the Israeli steel-maker Iskoor. Iskoor provides armour plating for South African tanks, and it markets South African steel.[4] The South African firm Plateglass was caught by the EC dumping South African-made mirrors; they were sold through its British subsidiary at one third less than their price in South Africa.

In fact, many firms can play two games at the same time. As well as engaging in sanctions busting, they may also use transfer pricing to move money out of South Africa: a foreign firm can overcharge for goods it sells to its South African parent or fail to pay for things it buys from the parent. One estimate is that such transfer pricing is costing South Africa 'billions of rands' every year.[5]

ENFORCING THE CONTRACT BAN

The Commonwealth Heads of Government Meeting in London in August 1986 recognized the danger of South African-owned firms. With the exception of Britain, they agreed to 'a ban on government contracts with majority-owned South African companies' and to 'a ban on all new bank loans to South Africa, whether to the public or private sectors'.

There are, however, two serious problems. One is that the long chains and complex linkages of company ownership make it ever harder to pin down overall South African ownership. For example, at least four different Anglo firms have shares in Minorco; together these holdings amount to more than 70 per cent of shares, but no single one is over 40 per cent. Luxembourg is often chosen for registration precisely because ultimate ownership can be concealed. The other problem is that Anglo has become highly skilled at controlling firms while retaining a direct ownership of less than 40 per cent of shares, so that the firms are not considered 'majority-owned'.

These became central issues in the Anglo bid for control of ConsGold. Minorco is technically European, not South African, because it is based in Luxembourg and its assets are outside South Africa. On this ground the Canadian Government said that a loan to help Minorco finance the take-over did not violate the ban. Canada has since reinforced its regulations, but the deal was raised only because Anglo control of Minorco is so well known.

PART IV

VULNERABILITY AND SANCTIONS
POTENTIAL

15

TRADE VULNERABILITY

South Africa is an ideal target for trade sanctions because it is an open economy with a high degree of commercial and financial integration with the Western industrialized countries. South Africa's trade in goods and services is equivalent to between half and two thirds of gross domestic product (GDP). This is a high figure, which has changed little despite the Government's protectionist policies. Indeed, as we show later, attempts to decrease vulnerability have actually increased trade dependence.

It is useful to look at areas where South Africa is most vulnerable to trade sanctions and hence where it might be most effective to widen, tighten and intensify sanctions. Vulnerability should be seen in two ways: ease of applying sanctions and the impact of sanctions if applied.

Several general studies of sanctions point out that it is more effective to target a country's exports than its imports because the competition for export-market share is so intense world-wide. This normally gives an importing country the upper hand in controlling trade, as it can refuse to buy South African goods and be relatively confident that other countries will be anxious to supply them instead. By contrast, if a country refuses to *sell* to South Africa, other suppliers may be less scrupulous.

SOUTH AFRICAN EXPORTS

South Africa's bulk exports are particularly vulnerable in terms of both the impact of sanctions and the ease of their application. There is a world over-supply of coal, most metals, steel and fruit; alternative suppliers are ready and waiting. Because of this surplus South Africa will not easily find alternative buyers. Furthermore, enforcement is easy because bulk commodities are shipped in large volumes and are difficult to disguise. It is possible to fly out millions of dollars' worth of diamonds or platinum without risk of detection, but coal is shipped in bulk carriers. Shipping movements can be followed by satellite and recorded in port reports. It is possible to use chemical analysis to determine the country of origin of crude minerals; South African coal contains an identifiable mix of trace elements such as silicon, potassium and aluminium. Finally, it is easy to require and confirm certificates of origin for entire shiploads of commodities. Thus sanctions busting is hard in the case of bulk commodities.

Mineral dependence of South Africa has been the subject of years of disinformation.[1] Most of South Africa's mineral exports could be replaced very quickly. No country need be dependent on South Africa for coal, iron ore, base metals (copper, lead, tin, zinc, nickel and aluminium), uranium and non-metallic minerals (stone, asbestos, etc.). Because of world surpluses, finding alternative suppliers for these minerals would impose little or no cost penalties.

Much is made of so-called 'strategic minerals', which are important on military and economic grounds and for which there is a significant dependence on South Africa. These minerals are usually defined as platinum and steel additives; sometimes titanium, antimony and andalusite are included. The steel additives are chromium, manganese and vanadium, plus their compounds and ferro-alloys (ferro-chromium, ferromanganese and ferrovanadium); these provide various special properties for stainless and hardened steels. The steel additives, titanium and antimony account for 5 per cent of South African exports. According to studies by the United States Bureau of Mines and others, alternative supplies are available – but sometimes only at a higher price. Andalusite is a refractory (used in furnaces). It could be replaced, but as South African exports of andalusite are only US$5 million per year, it could also be exempted from initial bans on non-metallic minerals. Because of likely world price increases if sanctions were imposed on steel additives, titanium, antimony and andalusite, importing countries might be tempted to break sanctions. Thus South Africa is less vulnerable in relation to these.

Platinum is a special case. It would be possible to do without South African platinum, but it would be very difficult and expensive.[2] If platinum were subject to sanction, South Africa would surely smuggle large quantities of it, and the price would be so much higher

Table 7. Sanctions among countries involved in uranium processing

Oxide to hexafluoride	Enrichment	Sanction?
USA	USA	partial
Soviet Union	Soviet Union	yes
Canada		yes
UK	UK	yes
France	France	no
	Netherlands	no
	West Germany	no
	Japan (under development)	partial

than at present that South Africa would probably earn more from sanctioned than unsanctioned platinum. Thus a sanction would not be useful. Instead it would make more sense to ensure that platinum remains available for strategic uses and that the price stays low.

Uranium is sometimes thought to be 'strategic' but is, in fact, highly vulnerable to sanctions. South Africa produces 13 per cent of the non-communist world's uranium and is second to Canada, which is by far the biggest producer. Because the generation of nuclear electricity has expanded less rapidly than expected, there are world surpluses and large stockpiles; prices are depressed. Cutting off South African uranium would not create shortages.

After uranium has been mined it passes through four processing stages. First, the ore is made into uranium oxide powder (yellowcake). Second, the uranium oxide is converted to uranium hexafluoride gas, which is stored in large drums. Third, the gas is enriched. Finally, it is converted to fuel rods for use in nuclear reactors.

The first stage is relatively simple; it takes place in South Africa, which exports yellowcake. The next two stages are undertaken on a commercial basis in only a limited number of places, as shown in Table 7.

Three of the five countries that can make hexafluoride will not import or process South African uranium, either for their own use or for other countries. This is important, because it is normal practice for countries that do not have processing facilities to buy yellowcake and then have it processed by a country with appropriate facilities. Unfortunately, France and Britain continue to process South African uranium. A total ban on South African uranium could be obtained if these two countries stopped processing it.

The United States ban on uranium covers ore and oxide and is thus interpreted to permit the import of uranium hexafluoride. Consequently, South African yellowcake is now being sent elsewhere to be transformed into hexafluoride and sold to the United States in that form.

PRIORITY EXPORT TARGETS

The following commodities account for 32 per cent of South African exports: agricultural products, iron and steel, iron ore, base metals, uranium, coal and other non-metallic minerals. South Africa is doubly vulnerable in respect of these commodities because as bulk commodities they are relatively simple to control and as world surplus commodities they will find few alternative markets. Therefore they should be the priority targets in any sanctions campaign.

Other manufactured goods (arms apart), including chemicals and petroleum products, account for another 5 per cent of South African exports. These are also vulnerable to sanctions. Although South Africa produces sophisticated equipment in a few areas, such as mining machinery, most of its exports are textiles and other simple manufactures typical of any newly industrializing country (NIC). Its refineries are old-fashioned and produce excesses of some waxes and fuel oils that South Africa does not need, so it exports them. For nearly all chemicals and other manufactured goods there are many alternative suppliers. Consumer goods such as clothing are normally labelled and subject to boycotts.

Thus 37 per cent of South Africa's identified exports are immediately highly vulnerable to sanctions.

Steel additives and ferro-alloys account for 5 per cent of exports and should be targeted later. Some planning would be required, and this should include support for SADCC states to expand alternative production of these minerals.[3]

Gold is high-value, low-volume and easy to smuggle, but it represents nearly half of South Africa's earnings, and a successful sanction against South African gold would have a massive impact. The pro-sanctions World Gold Commission was formed in 1988; it has proposed a promising market-linked ban and other strategies that deserve further investigation.[4]

The remaining two high-value, low-volume commodities, platinum and diamonds, account for 11 per cent of South African export earnings – much less than gold. As they are so easy to smuggle, it would be a waste of effort to try to control them, at least in the early stages of a sanctions programme.

SOUTH AFRICAN IMPORTS: LOOKING FOR CHOKE POINTS

The advantage of sanctions on bulk commodities is that each country that imposes its own measures cuts South African exports – every individual sanction bites. This is not true of the goods that South Africa buys because there are often sellers willing to take part in sanctions busting – for a price. Therefore South African imports will be most vulnerable to sanctions if either one of two conditions is satisfied: there must be a broad international consensus, as with arms and oil, so that there are relatively few rogue suppliers, or the relatively few producers of essential items should agree among themselves to refuse to supply South Africa.

In both cases existing supply limitations should make it possible to identify weak points where particular South African imports could be stopped or sharply reduced. Oil remains the best example; with no oil supplies of its own, South Africa is clearly vulnerable to oil sanctions. Oil-from-coal plants and substantial oil stockpiles have reduced South Africa's vulnerability, but the cost to South Africa of an effective oil embargo would still be enormous because the country remains dependent on imports for two thirds of its requirements.

Countries that are committed to the oil embargo could impose tighter rules on their own companies and put pressure on remaining oil suppliers to do likewise. One useful action would be to extend the already common requirement for 'discharge certificates', which show where oil is unloaded, to try to ensure that oil is not delivered to South Africa.

At the moment the biggest loophole, and the most vulnerable point in the chain of possible action, relates to transport of oil. Some countries, notably the Nordic states, prohibit their ships from carrying oil to South Africa, but many countries that formally abide by the oil embargo do not limit the role of their shipping companies.

The five major oil companies in South Africa (Shell, BP, Mobil, Caltex and Total) are central to both the oil and coal trades. They would be highly vulnerable to any regulations that forced them to choose between their business in South Africa and that elsewhere.

Without them South Africa could still obtain its oil, but with more difficulty and at a higher price.

A BLOCKADE?

Critics of sanctions sometimes argue that comprehensive sanctions would be unenforceable because they would require a naval blockade from Walvis Bay around the Cape to Maputo. This, they claim, would be impossible. In fact, both statements are wrong: a blockade is feasible but not necessary to enforce sanctions.

One of the successes of the arms embargo is that South Africa has been forced to run down its Navy. It now has very little deep-water capacity and is dependent largely on Israeli fast-patrol boats that must remain near the coast. Furthermore, the cargoes that a blockade would need to stop – oil coming in and minerals and agricultural products going out – would all be bulk cargoes carried in large ships. It would not take a very extensive naval force to turn back those ships. South Africa could survive the blockade of all bulk cargoes for only a few months.

This points also to the reason why a blockade is not needed. Bulk carriers and normal commercial freighters are large enough to be identified on satellite photos and by other reconnaissance techniques. Security and intelligence services around the world could monitor South African shipping – and probably already do. If the world were serious about sanctions, pressure could be applied elsewhere. If just one bulk carrier of South African coal were identified and banned, so that no port would accept it, it would be forced to stay at sea like the ships loaded with unacceptable toxic waste. After that few shipping companies would run the risk. Similarly, if pressure were put on the Gulf oil producers, supplies would soon dry up.

A naval blockade would be possible and even practical, but political action would have the same effect.

16

TECHNOLOGY AND SKILLS

White leaders in South Africa often claim that South Africa is sufficiently industrialized to become self-sufficient if sanctions were imposed. Indeed, some business people advocate autarky as a way of stimulating flagging industrial production.

This is nonsense, for two different reasons. First, South Africa is much too small a market to sustain modern industrial production – particularly as under apartheid the earnings of the great majority of the population are so small that they are outside the market for most goods. Second, as a typical NIC South Africa has already passed through the simple import-substitution phase of industrialization, backed by a wall of high protective tariffs.

Despite its pretensions, South Africa is not a major industrial power. It is a middle-sized, middle-income NIC, similar to Algeria and Argentina. Like most developing countries, its exports are raw materials and its imports are machinery and manufactured goods. This means that it is highly vulnerable to a reduction in its supply of manufactures.

MANUFACTURED IMPORTS

South Africa has made major efforts in the past decade to reduce its vulnerability to sanctions by increasing its local manufacturing capacity. The result is somewhat ironic: many things that were imported a decade ago are now produced in South Africa, but import dependence has not decreased.

This is because, first, all sophisticated manufactured goods still contain imported components. The position is demonstrated clearly by South Africa's automobile industry. Under tight government regulations, all cars must have two thirds local content, measured by weight.[1] But a South African government study published in 1988 admitted that the cheapest and heaviest components are made locally to satisfy the rule, but *by value* the local content is only 37 per cent for passenger cars. The study found that South African cars are more expensive than if more components were imported.[2] Japan's biggest exports to South Africa are cars, vehicles and parts (US$985 million in 1987). This is such a large volume that if sanctions were imposed, enough parts could not be smuggled into South Africa and car production would be badly affected.

Second, most machinery is still imported, and the more sophisticated nature of South African industry actually makes it much more vulnerable than Southern Rhodesia was two decades ago. It will not be possible to make spare parts in machine shops and hold equipment together with string, as happened in Rhodesia's less developed industries. South Africa will remain dependent on the outside for spares and servicing.

By now almost anything that South Africa once imported and could be easily and profitably produced locally is being produced locally. Significant further import substitution, and any major move to increase self-sufficiency, will be difficult and costly.

Local manufacturing capacity is not restricted, of course, to physical machinery. It also depends on production processes and knowledge.

There are five different mechanisms for technology transfer: direct foreign investment; licensing agreements; purchase of equipment; purchase of know-how and blueprints; and the experience of skilled people. When TNCs like Ford and IBM withdrew from South Africa they were able to maintain the continuity of their market by establishing sourcing agreements with the nominally independent South African firms. The investment ended, but the other four mechanisms continued. Thus control of the transfer of technology can be successful only if a comprehensive approach is adopted.

The very process of reducing vulnerability to sanctions is itself constrained by sanctions and the threat of their spread because any further import substitution will require imported machinery, computers and other technology. The sales of machinery and spare parts could be halted, however; continued financial and other economic sanctions will make it difficult to find the money to buy foreign technology; and South Africa needs skilled people from abroad.

South Africa is particularly vulnerable to sanctions that would deprive it of the equipment it needs for modernization. This includes computers and sophisticated machine tools. But there is some urgency as South Africa rushes to beat sanctions. In June 1988, for example, Volkswagen announced that it is to build in South Africa a US$18 million plant to make machine tools for its car production. VW South Africa says that it now relies on Japanese and European manufacturers for 70 per cent of the machine tools it needs but that by the end of the century this new facility will make it independent of machine-tool imports.

Computer numerically controlled (CNC) machine tools, robots and other elements of factory automation would also make good targets because such equipment is normally labour-saving. (This is already an area of sanctions busting. For example, a British company was caught in 1985 trying to smuggle computer-controlled milling equipment to a South African arms manufacturer.) Thus a ban on automation technology would directly benefit black workers by reducing the number who are thrown out of jobs by automation.

Although South Africa, like many other countries, assembles computers, it has no real indigenous computer industry and will be unable to develop one in the short term. Local manufacture meets only 25 per cent (in value terms) of South Africa's electronics needs. David Jacobson, a former vice-president of South Africa's Council for Scientific and Industrial Research, notes: 'Even if we design and construct our own hardware in South Africa, the international umbilical cord of component and special material supply cannot be shaken off.'

ARMS AND OIL

Because of the arms embargo South Africa has developed an impressive local arms industry. Nevertheless, few South African weapons are genuinely indigenous; all depend on plans, tools, components and expertise from abroad. Some of these are smuggled in. Others are imported as civilian or 'dual-use' equipment that can be used to make weapons as well as civilian hardware.

South Africa also produces some of its own oil from coal and is developing the Mossel Bay gas field for fuel production.[3] But this requires foreign expertise. The offshore exploration has been undertaken by Norwegian and British companies with North Sea experience, as well as by other European firms. Similarly, about 70 per cent of the technology required to bring the gas ashore will be foreign, including well-drilling equipment, platforms, pipelaying and pipeline control systems. 'This is one of the areas which has been identified as vulnerable to sanctions,' admits Mossgas Director of Projects Ken Graham.[4]

It was concern about precisely this issue that led the Commonwealth Committee of Foreign Ministers on Southern Africa in Toronto last year to invite Governments to consider adopting measures 'to prohibit technology transfer that is designed to enable South Africa to circumvent existing sanctions, particularly in the areas of arms, oil, and computers'.

OTHER IMPORT CHOKE POINTS

As already noted, it will be difficult to block sales to South Africa of many items because of the competition for export markets. Many countries assemble advanced-technology devices of various sorts, and some will sell to Pretoria. South Africa is increasingly turning to Taiwan for its computers, for example.

Nevertheless, sanctions can have an impact because many producers of advanced-technology equipment are themselves dependent on specialized technology that is available from only a few manufacturers. Most personal and small-business computers are based on microprocessor chips that are made in the United States, Japan, West Germany and France. Manufacturers who bought such chips could be required to guarantee that they would not be used in computers to be sold to South Africa. Similar restrictions would have to be imposed on the sale and licensing of chip-making technology. Experience with the Coordinating Committee for Multilateral Export Controls (CoCom) regulations shows that such rules can be enforced where the will exists.

Similarly, many countries manufacture CNC machine tools, but these incorporate control devices made mainly in Japan, West Germany, the United States, Italy and Norway. It is highly likely, for example, that the new Volkswagen machine-tool plant will continue to use imported control devices. Thus South Africa would be vulnerable to restrictions placed on their sale.

THE SKILLS SQUEEZE

Every modernizing country needs a growing corps of skilled people. If South Africa is serious about creating a siege economy that can withstand sanctions, it will need many more skilled people. Cut off from outside technology, it would be forced, in effect, to keep reinventing the wheel: that would require large numbers of scientists, engineers and technicians. But the apartheid education system will ensure that South Africa will remain far short of the skilled people it needs, even without sanctions. This is one of the most important reasons for South Africa's relatively low industrial productivity and for the failure of its attempt at export-led industrialization. Thus the shortage of skilled people may prove to be South Africa's weakest point in any fight against sanctions.[5]

For many years higher education and advanced training have been reserved for whites. This system has never provided enough skilled people, and 25 to 40 per cent of the annual requirement for new higher- and middle-level skilled people has been met by white immigrants. One million Europeans and former colonists emigrated to South Africa between 1945 and 1977.

Following the Soweto uprising in 1976 there was a net emigration in 1977 and 1978, but immigration had returned to the old levels by 1982. In 1985 Barclays tried to recruit 150 white British computer staff for South Africa, promising double their British salaries and 'a lifestyle of your dreams'. But the uprisings and sanctions of 1985 made South Africa seem less appealing; in 1985–7 there was again a net emigration.

The skills crisis has been clear to the business sector for some years and is largely responsible for its pressure to end job reservation and improve black education and training. This pressure has had only a limited effect: black people constituted 23 per cent of students in tertiary education in 1975 and this proportion had risen to no more than 37 per cent by 1986. In 1975 only thirteen out of 908 graduating engineers were black; by 1985 the figure was sixty-six out of 1,542. Since South Africa needs 3,000 engineers a year, the gap remains massive, and the continued failures of the apartheid education system are obvious.

The *Financial Mail* admitted, 'The shortage of skills in the information technology is reaching chronic proportions.'[6] In electronics so many people are underqualified that production standards are falling.

The National Manpower Commission in 1987 warned, 'The management corps has shrunk too low to cope properly with the mobilization of resources and productivity.' This hardly bodes well for any attempts to build a self-sufficient siege economy.

The Big Eight international accounting firms used to send 100 accountants a year to South Africa on two- or three-year contracts, but that has ended. They still try to second staff from overseas offices, but one official admitted, 'It's unusual that they'll stay for longer than three months.'[7]

Increasingly, skilled people will go to South Africa only on flying visits – as trouble shooters, consultants, seconded experts and equipment-servicing staff. Many will be sent by TNCs to present or former subsidiaries or as part of licensing agreements or service contracts. Most engineers who go to South Africa are now recruited by TNCs, and are redeployed by those firms, or recruited for particular tasks via specialist journals. Foreign contractors on big projects like Mossgas will also bring their own skilled staff with them.

It is impossible to stop individuals going to South Africa if they wish, but with most skilled people now going through TNCs as part of technology-transfer packages, it should be possible to impose sanctions with some degree of success. For example, bans on the sale of computers to South Africa could be extended to firms sending people to service or work on computers already in South Africa.

As well as the decrease in immigrants, the post-1976 period has seen a substantial increase in South African emigrants.[8] They are the most skilled and can most easily obtain jobs in other countries. Teachers, doctors, engineers and accountants are leaving in large numbers. Nearly 10 per cent of top computer people leave each year.[9]

Many emigrants are newly trained men who flee to avoid conscription. The change in South African law in 1984 that extended conscription to foreign nationals accelerated the exodus. It also seems likely that many who have other passports do not register as emigrants, and thus emigration is greater than the statistics show.

South Africa's industrial policy is in a state of turmoil. On the one hand, a Government anxious to gain support and funding for its 'repressive reform' policy is advocating the liberalization of the economy, including reductions in local-content requirements, to make industry more efficient and competitive and to spur exports. At the same time the Government is trying to prepare for a siege economy with higher local content and thus less efficiency and reduced international competitiveness. Capital that should go to modernizing industry instead goes to defending apartheid and preparing for sanctions, as well as buying firms from withdrawing TNCs rather than building new factories. The result is confusion and an increasing dependence on imports, especially of technology that could be cut off by sanctions. Meanwhile the apartheid education system has created a skills shortage that makes any industrial policy unworkable, so scarce imported skills become even more vital.

Thus apartheid has created a special vulnerability to technology-transfer sanctions.

17

HOW MUCH PRESSURE IS NEEDED?

The preceding two chapters have shown that South Africa is highly vulnerable to sanctions. Yet it is also clear that the sanctions imposed so far have not been enough: they have helped to push the white regime to the negotiating table over Angola and Namibia but not over ending apartheid within South Africa itself. Earlier we quoted Archbishop Hurley's assessment that 'much stronger pressure is required – pressure that will cause real discomfort to the white community to make it realize that it cannot continue' with apartheid. In this chapter we try to estimate what would be needed to cause that 'real discomfort'.

This requires a more detailed look at the South African economy and at South Africa's debt problem and its 1985 debt freeze. Ironically, the problem dates back partly to the 1980 gold boom, when the gold price touched US$800 per ounce. South Africa assumed that this would reverse its economic decline, and it borrowed heavily abroad. In part the money was intended to pay for major electrification schemes, nuclear power and Sasol oil-from-coal plants, which were needed to reduce the impact of the oil embargo.

In the 1970s some banks had already stopped lending to South Africa, and in the early 1980s more became worried. Debts were still rolled over but for ever shorter periods. By 1985 the debt was US$24 billion, which is not large for a country of South Africa's size, but 60 per cent of it – an unusually large percentage – was due to be repaid in less than a year. In mid-1985 the Government declared its state of emergency. The stock market collapsed and the rand fell. United States banks, faced with growing anti-apartheid pressure and led by Chase Manhattan, refused to roll over the loans any more.

South Africa froze payments and demanded the renegotiation of

US$14 billion worth of short-term debts to international banks. It said that it would continue to repay the other US$10 billion 'outside the net' of the freeze, which consisted of Government-guaranteed trade credits, bond issues and a debt to the International Monetary Fund (IMF).[1]

In 1986 South Africa negotiated a one-year agreement with the banks (the Leutwiler Accord) and in 1987 a three-year agreement (the Stals Accord).

The Leutwiler Accord came only after President Botha announced a series of 'reforms', including partial abolition of the pass laws, on 31 January 1986. This was at a time when various sanctions packages were being imposed, and these 'reforms' seemed designed, at least in part, to meet the banks' demands for tangible evidence of change before they agreed to any rescheduling. The banks, in turn, were looking over their shoulders at their Governments and at anti-apartheid activists.

The Stals Accord came a year later, when general sanctions pressure was easing. Both inside and outside South Africa it was considered generous, both politically and financially. South Africa's repayments were to be a relatively small portion of exports, and Finance Minister Barend du Plessis said that 'not one political demand was made' during the negotiation.[2] The banks agreed to accept slightly higher interest payments and just US$1.4 billion of capital repayments over three years. This represented a mere 10 per cent of the debt that had been due largely in 1985 and 1986.

This agreement expires on 30 June 1990, at which point an estimated US$9 billion will technically be due.[3] Negotiations during late 1989 and early 1990 between the banks and the South African Government will decide both the repayment terms and the time scale. These will be influenced mostly by political considerations but also by the banks' assessment of South Africa's ability to pay. Ironically, if they feel South Africa will be able to pay with little difficulty, they are likely to agree to *easier* terms because some banks may want to renew lending to the apartheid state.

The three-year rescheduling of the Stals Accord was widely seen as offering South Africa a breathing space, 'taking the sting out of the most damaging sanctions yet'.[4] The Commonwealth Committee of Foreign Ministers on Southern Africa specifically called on banks to 'press for rescheduling arrangements which do not extend beyond one year at a time'. This would clearly increase political pressure on South Africa.

THE 1990–91 DEBT BULGE

What makes 1990–91 a critical period for South Africa, however, is not just the renegotiation of the US$9 billion debt. There is also a bunching of nearly US$3 billion in debts 'outside the net' that are due in 1990 and 1991. These are largely bonds, issued by parastatals like Escom, that were purchased in 1980–83 (during and just after the gold-price boom) and have a maturity of between seven and ten years.

Some kind of rescheduling of the US$9 billion frozen debt is likely, but its terms could require more repayments than the Stals Accord. And the US$3 billion in bonds cannot be rescheduled. So if banks are less helpful over the 1990 rescheduling than they were in 1987, South Africa could easily see its repayments double or triple.

The crisis will probably be exacerbated by the lower gold price, which is forecast to remain well below its 1987 peak. The South African-dominated World Gold Council admitted in an internal paper, 'The critical issue facing the World Gold Council is the increasing supply of newly minted gold to the market and the consequent demand shortfall that is anticipated.'[5] Following the 1980 price boom many countries started work on new mines that began production in the mid-1980s. Central banks also realized that it made more sense to sell gold at a rising price. Thus in 1987, for the first time, gold did not rise after a stock-market crash. Prices have declined since then, and many analysts predict that over-supply could keep prices down at least through the 1990–91 debt crisis period and that gold prices will remain below US$400 per ounce and might sink below US$350. Thus Pretoria will have US$1 to 2 billion less each year with which to repay its debts. (Interestingly, the 1985 debt crisis came at a time of a low gold price.)

Finally, many financial commentators noted that some of the economic effects of the 1985–6 sanctions began to show only in 1987–8, when the economy seemed to be recovering because of a higher gold price. In the first half of 1988 a more buoyant economy triggered an unsustainable import boom that was not matched by export growth. Reserves fell, and a balance-of-payments crisis loomed, forcing the Government to adopt deflationary measures, including import surcharges of up to 60 per cent, which truncated economic recovery.

THE HIGH COST OF APARTHEID

The debt bulge comes at a time when the gold price is lower and the economy is already weakened by sanctions and its own failings. GDP per capita has been falling since 1975, and especially since 1981. In the 1980s per capita GDP has fallen at the rate of 2 per cent per year.[6] In other words, the average South African is 15 per cent poorer today than at the beginning of the decade. The late Gerhard de Kock, who until his death in August 1989 was Governor of the Reserve Bank, admitted that there are 'underlying unfavourable trends in the South African economy' and that things were not worse in the late 1970s only because the high gold price provided what he called 'windfall gains'.[7]

The stagnation of the South African economy since 1980 is attributable mainly to the inefficiencies of apartheid and to the actual cost of maintaining white rule, particularly the huge expenses of the military, the police and the apartheid bureaucracy. South African industrialists acknowledge this by being unwilling to invest in their own country. Productive industrial investment has not kept up with depreciation; industrial production in 1989 is lower than it was in 1981.[8] Professor Jan Lombard, then vice-president of the Reserve Bank, noted, 'The stagnation of the industrial sector is totally of our own making. This gives the impression that our country's people are dismantling the South African economy of their own accord.'[9]

Sanctions impose an important extra strain on the economy and increase the cost of maintaining apartheid, but those imposed so far are too limited to account for such a large fall in per capita GDP. Indeed, those who fear that sanctions will wreck a functioning economy ignore the reality that white rule is already destroying that economy. Sanctions represent the only way to force the essential political changes that will halt the downward economic spiral that is already under way.

WHAT VIEW WILL THE BANKS TAKE?

South Africa approaches 1990–91 facing a profound apartheid-induced economic crisis. How it weathers that crisis will depend on two groups of actors – the international banks and the Governments of the industrialized countries. They can use the crisis to apply pressure and force negotiations to end apartheid, or they can provide Pretoria with a lifeline that allows it to restructure and maintain apartheid.

The responses of the two groups are interrelated. International banks are concerned to maximize their profits and protect their loans, but their judgement will be based on a political assessment. If no significant further sanctions seem likely, they will conclude that South Africa is to be protected from sanctions. They will feel that the international community has given its stamp of approval to repressive reform and that economic pressure has been lifted from South Africa. Thus it will seem reasonable to return to business as usual with the apartheid state.

The South African Government hopes that this will happen. South African bankers and high-level government officials are devoting considerable resources to maintaining personal contacts with the international financial community, making regular visits to banks throughout the world.[10] President P. W. Botha visited Zurich in October 1988 to plead for new loans. After his visit South Africa was able to arrange two small syndicated loans worth nearly US$70 million – a drop in the ocean compared with the needed billions. But Escom, traditionally one of South Africa's largest and most trusted borrowers, was told by bankers that there would be no new loans without some political change. This indicates that a few banks may be more sympathetic to Pretoria but that the general lending climate has not really changed.

In an advertisement in London's *Financial Times* in November 1988 Finance Minister Barend du Plessis said, 'I think we shall have the basis for getting back into the world's capital markets, because, quite apart from the perception that there is a prospect of a peaceful political solution in South Africa, the reality will be that that process will, inside South Africa, produce an environment which I am sure will be conducive to our re-entry into the global capital markets.'[11] That somewhat convoluted sentence was preceded by the claim that 'to date we've dealt reasonably successfully with sanctions' and that pressure will not force South Africa to accept 'political solutions' demanded by 'foreign critics'. The need is to 'stabilize the internal political situation', and this will be done through privatization, deregulation and urbanization – in other words, 'repressive reform' and no fundamental political changes.

If, however, 'repressive reform' is not accepted, and if political and economic pressure on the apartheid state is increasing, then international banks will be aware that they cannot return to business as before. And they will realize that tightening sanctions and a low gold price will make it even harder for Pretoria to pay its bills. In those circumstances banks will hardly be willing to make new loans; instead they will put increasing pressure on the regime. They will want either as much money as can be squeezed out of South Africa or significant political changes that will ensure that a South African Government survives to pay the debt eventually.

The outcome of the debt crisis will in turn influence business people and the Government. If white South Africa obtains good terms on its debt renegotiations, and if there are no new sanctions, these will be the signs of international approval. But if the banks impose harsher conditions, and if sanctions further squeeze the economy, then it will be clear that South Africa cannot pursue the policy of apartheid.

HITTING A DECLINING ECONOMY

Having looked at the strains of the South African economy and considered the role of the international banks, it is possible to return to the question of what level of sanctions will produce the 'real discomfort' needed to create a lobby strong enough to initiate negotiations.

South Africans are becoming poorer at the rate of 2 per cent per year. This has caused discontent, but it has not prompted enough white people to question the basis of apartheid. And with good reason: white living standards remain high and would have to fall much more rapidly before most white people felt 'real discomfort'. Considering various studies of the South African economy and the impact of sanctions on other countries, we believe that per capita GDP would need to fall at a rate of at least 5 per cent per year to have a noticeable effect and thus have political impact. (We note that this fall is similar to the economic decline in Rhodesia after 1974, which resulted in Ian Smith's being jeered by white crowds. Sanctions at this level and the growing liberation struggle led to the internal settlement and subsequent discussions at Lancaster House.)

Taking into account the underlying economic decline, this means that sanctions would have to be strong enough to cause the GDP to fall steadily at a rate of 3 per cent per year over several years. Sanctions would ensure this decline by reducing South Africa's ability to import both luxury and essential goods. South Africa has imposed increasingly tight secrecy over its economic statistics, to the point where even South African economists cannot make accurate economic forecasts. We are not able to make specific predictions either, but we are able to reach some fundamental general conclusions.[12]

After a detailed study of the available data we conclude that there is a threshold and that sanctions must be greater than that threshold if they are to have the required impact. *We believe that a sustained cut in South African imports of 30 per cent is the minimum that would produce a fall in GDP that was sufficient to trigger an appropriate political response.*

We note that in 1985 imports did fall by nearly that much and that per capita GDP dropped by more than 4 per cent. Per capita GDP continued to decline in 1986 and 1987, but by 1988 import levels had partly recovered and the per capita GDP decline was temporarily arrested. This in turn was due to the high gold and base-metals prices in 1987 and 1988, as well as to the very easy terms of the Stals Accord. This gives general support to our contention, since the initial GDP fall was in the expected range, but without a sustained cut in imports it was not maintained.

Another way to assess the significance of this kind of import cut is to look at South African estimates of 'essential' imports. The two most widely differing views are perhaps those of Finance Minister Barend du Plessis and Edward Osborn, Nedbank's chief economist, who was in Rhodesia when that country was facing international sanctions. Both referred to the pre-1985 trade pattern. Du Plessis said, 'Our analyses have shown that more than 80 per cent of imports are absolutely essential goods' – these are essential capital and intermediate goods, so only 20 per cent of total imports could be cut. By contrast, Osborn argues that 24 per cent of imports could be substituted by local production in the short term and that another 21 per cent are non-essentials that could be stopped 'without undue loss of public morale' (these include items like coffee, tea, watches, TVs and books) – 45 per cent in all.

Our estimate of a 30 per cent minimum cut falls between these two estimates: the minimum cut in imports that is needed to have a sufficient impact on GDP corresponds, not unexpectedly, to cutting all inessential imports as well as some that will be seen as important by white South Africans.

The most likely sanctions packages will not cut off South Africa's imports directly – it will be hard to stop sales to South Africa. As we have stressed in Chapter 15, it will be more practical to take an indirect route and cut South Africa's exports; if countries stop buying South African goods, it will earn less money and will therefore reduce its imports because it cannot pay.

Because of a sizeable invisibles deficit, the value of imports is equivalent to only two thirds of exports. This implies that a 20 per cent reduction in purchases from South Africa would force South Africa to cut its own purchases by 30 per cent.[13] South Africa might be able to reduce invisibles payments somewhat, but we believe that it is a reasonable approximation to conclude that *to be politically effective, sanctions would need to cut world-wide purchases from South Africa by at least one quarter.*

Is this possible? We noted in Chapter 5 that all of the sanctions regulated by sanctions-imposing countries had cut 7 per cent of all purchases from South Africa. This is only one quarter of what is needed, so it is not surprising that sanctions have only been a partial success. Nevertheless, it shows that even partial sanctions imposed by a limited number of countries can make a significant difference and go a considerable way towards what is needed.

If we follow the guidelines of Chapter 15, with its proposals for tighter and wider sanctions, plus some new actions imposed by most of South Africa's trading partners, then it will be possible to exceed the required threshold of cutting off one quarter of purchases from South Africa. The big step will be to ban the purchase of all South African bulk exports and manufactured goods. This would include coal, fruit and vegetables and base metals. This is reasonable because no action is proposed against precious or strategic minerals, which are more controversial. (This sanction is detailed in Chapter 19 and would affect 37 per cent of 1987 purchases from South Africa.)

Three smaller actions would add to the impact. An end to the production of platinum coins should lead to a fall in platinum prices by 1992; if prices fell by between just 12 and 25 per cent (which is a quite reasonable expectation), this would cut between 1 and 2 per cent of South Africa's total earnings. A five- or three-year phasing-out of trade credits would cost US$600 million or US$1,000 million per year, equivalent to a cut in earnings of 3 to 5 per cent. Finally, to tighten the oil embargo enough to add just US$2 per barrel in sanctions-busting fees – which could be achieved purely by political pressure – would be the equivalent of a 1 per cent cut in purchases from South Africa. Together these measures would amount to 5–8 per cent of purchases.

Table 8. Portion of 1987 imports from South Africa that
would be affected by various factors (%)

Cutting bulk exports	37
Other actions	
Lower platinum price	1–2
Phased-out trade credits	3–5
Tighter oil embargo	1
Impact of a lower gold price	4–10
Total	46–55

Finally, the gold price has fallen from its 1987 average of US$444.50 per ounce. A price of US$400 would cut 4 per cent off the value of total 1987 imports from South Africa. A price of US$350 would be equivalent to a 10 per cent cut. The potential impact of all of these measures taken together is shown in Table 8.

Thus we have put forward a plausible package that, if fully enforced, would be the equivalent of cutting about half of all purchases from South Africa.

But can it be enforced? We expect that the Commonwealth, the United States and other countries that have so far imposed substantial sanctions would support such a package. If so, moral and political pressure might succeed with other countries such as Japan, West Germany, Spain and Turkey, which have increased their trade in recent years but which also profess strong anti-apartheid views.

On the other hand, it must be assumed that Taiwan, Israel and perhaps South Korea may continue to strengthen their links with South Africa. Countries such as the United States are in a position to apply considerable pressure on those states not to increase their trade with South Africa. Together Taiwan, Israel and South Korea have a population of about 70 million and a GDP of US$150 billion, so there is a limit to how much these three can buy from South Africa for their own use; thus they will not be able to be the 'Big Brother' that supports South Africa if they are blocked from becoming third parties in sanctions busting. If they are allowed to become sanctions-busting channels, however, they could seriously weaken the sanctions effort.

Finally, it must be assumed that some of South Africa's important trading partners that have long-standing economic ties and are politically opposed to sanctions will be reluctant, and hence half-hearted, participants. Altogether, then, we could not hope to make the package more than two thirds effective. Nevertheless, that mark would be above the minimum threshold.

THE NEED TO MOVE QUICKLY

Various studies of sanctions applied elsewhere make a central point about the speed with which sanctions are applied. If enforced only slowly, the target is able to adapt; if enforced quickly, the shock reinforces the psychological impact. This view is reinforced by what happened after 1985. Without further sanctions, the South African economy adapted to the 1985 crisis and the per capita GDP decline slowed. Business confidence rose, although the economy remained fragile.

Despite its economic strains, South Africa still has some flexibility. During the 1985 debt crisis, for example, South Africa cut back on oil purchases and ran down its oil stocks, building them up again only in 1987, after the Stals Accord gave it a bit of extra money. It could run oil stocks down again in 1990[14] and gain up to US$1 billion to repay bondholders. So if markedly stricter sanctions are not imposed in 1990, Pretoria could find money for some repayments. This would provide it with surer financial standing, while the lack of sanctions would give it a sounder political foothold and might lead to softer terms demanded by the international banks. This, in turn, would make it much easier for Pretoria to ride out sanctions that might be imposed in 1992 or later, and it might even lead to new loans and investment. Finally, the longer sanctions are delayed, the more time Pretoria has to shift trade to countries like Taiwan and Israel.

On the other hand, the economy has very little space in which to absorb new sanctions, especially in the next two years. If sanctions, the debt bulge and falling gold prices all hit the apartheid state at once, the result could be overwhelming. Hitting South Africa with new sanctions during the 1990–91 debt bulge could have an important multiplier effect, while delaying might make even a larger sanctions package insufficient. Thus it is essential to mount an attack on South Africa during the 1990–91 period.

It is impossible to make detailed economic forecasts about South Africa, but we have made estimates that demonstrate two critical points: first, the present level of sanctions has had an impact but is not enough to cause 'real discomfort', and it is not surprising that it has forced only limited negotiations; second, a reasonable set of sanctions that could be imposed now and that excludes precious and strategic minerals could be expected to have enough impact on the economy and on white morale to have a significant political impact if imposed quickly.

THE WRITING ON THE WALL

Both the Government and the business community have stood by and watched the steady deterioration of the South African economy over the last decade rather than dismantle apartheid. Nevertheless, repeated warnings that sanctions will wreck the economy suggest that there is a limit. In 1985, in the midst of township uprisings, a major financial crisis and a crescendo of sanctions, businesspeople began to talk with the ANC. When repression restored some measure of government control and sanctions pressure eased, business stopped looking for alternatives. We believe that the business community will not allow the economy to be wrecked. Once it sees the writing on the wall, it will put pressure on the Government to settle. Similarly, many other white people will begin to understand that continuing with apartheid is not a viable option. Thus we think it most likely, if a package of sanctions is put in place that is strong enough to cause severe discomfort and to threaten major economic disruption, that negotiations will begin before the sanctions really damage the economy.

Timing is essential. For a limited package like this to have a social and political impact, it must be imposed quickly enough to be felt directly. And for this limited package to have the predicted effect, it must be in place at the same time as the 1990–91 debt crisis – both to discourage bankers from giving Pretoria a better deal and to ensure that financial reserves are stretched beyond the limit.

It would be possible for Pretoria simply to default on its debts. Indeed, du Plessis has threatened this if a new rescheduling agreement is not reached in 1990. If it stopped repayments of capital and interest and also halted foreign payments like dividends and licence fees, South Africa could save between US$3 and $4 billion per year, cancelling out half of the proposed sanctions.

The apartheid state has been wise enough to try to retain a semblance of normality in its relations with the international financial and commercial community because its position is very different from that of other Third World debtors, in that its problems are fundamentally political and not financial. For if Pretoria were to renege on its debts and cut off foreign payments, this would set off the chain reaction that it has been so desperately trying to avoid. TNCs that lost their revenues would no longer be so willing to provide technology and spare parts. Countries that have supported Pretoria because of their high level of economic involvement would lose interest. Banks would no longer be so willing to provide trade credits (as happened for a short period after the debt freeze in 1985). South African assets abroad, including valuable exports, would be seized, making it harder for the country to trade. Political and economic pressure would build as countries began to think the unthinkable. Gold and ferro-alloy sanctions could move to the top of the agenda.

The Government did not consult the business community in 1985, and there is no reason to think that it would this time. But if 1985 caused panic in the business community and a sudden rush to talk to the ANC, then a full renunciation of debts in 1990 or 1991 would cause hysteria. The pressure for a negotiated settlement would be massive.

We cannot be certain about the precise outcome of extended sanctions, but we can be sure of two things. First, sanctions on the level we propose would severely weaken the apartheid state. Second, whether or not South Africa renounced its debts, sanctions at this level would produce a much larger constituency for change. This would happen once it was clear that South Africa was not protected from sanctions, that continued apartheid was not a viable option and that sanctions would cause 'real discomfort'.

PART V

POSSIBLE FURTHER ACTION

18

A STRATEGY FOR ACTION

The white minority is fragmenting. The far right believes that traditional apartheid can be maintained at an acceptable cost. The Government professes to believe that it can hold off sanctions for as long as it will take to carry out its programme of 'repressive reform'. The business community is divided; some call for political change to head off further sanctions, while others back the Government and feel that no serious sanctions are likely. Both camps, however, are investing abroad in readiness for whatever happens.

We are convinced that this growing division within the white minority shows that the Commonwealth Eminent Persons Group correctly identified the central question: Will the white minority come to 'the conclusion that it would always remain protected' from 'effective economic measures'? Pressure for and against change within the white community is directly related to the perception of what the international community will do.

We believe that one of the essential roles of sanctions is to accelerate the fragmentation of the white bloc. Sanctions will support and enlarge a constituency that sees the necessity and value of entering negotiations to lead to majority rule. At the same time effective sanctions should make it clear that international protection against sanctions is ending and that the price of maintaining apartheid is rising.

Both the white minority and the black majority in South Africa now ignore ritual international condemnations of apartheid. Indeed, even the white Government says it is against apartheid as it tries to create new forms of minority rule. And both white and black treat token sanctions as sops to local electoral pressure in the country imposing them rather than as an attempt to put pressure on the apartheid regime.

The EPG was correct in pointing to the need for effective economic measures. In the following chapters we set out a strategy for action, including a series of measures that, we believe, would be effective *if applied quickly enough*. Their effectiveness will be increased by the opportunity created by the 1990–91 debt bulge and by the lower gold price. The same measures, delayed until after 1991, would be much less effective.

A PROGRAMME OF INCREASING SANCTIONS

The Okanagan Statement calls for the 'wider, tighter and more intensified' application of economic and other sanctions. It also stresses:

> While mindful of the widespread view within the international community that comprehensive and mandatory sanctions would be the quickest route to bring Pretoria to the negotiating table, we, with the exception of Britain, believe that, pending the acceptance of such a position by the international community as a whole, genuine efforts should be made to secure the universal adoption of the measures now adopted by most Commonwealth and other countries, including the United States and the Nordic countries.

This points both to a programme of steadily increasing sanctions until genuine negotiations begin and to the routes followed by other states, particularly the Nordic countries, in developing a programme of progressively more stringent economic sanctions.

It is clear that any effective sanctions will require a significant reduction in trade with the apartheid state. *The first step must be for each country to make a public commitment to a steady reduction in trade with South Africa.* Such a pledge would serve as a warning to the apartheid regime and South African business, but it would also give advance warning to those firms that are still trading with South Africa that they should begin now to find other markets and suppliers.

Most countries start with those sanctions that will cost them least. Priority is also given to sanctions that do not need unanimity – where non-comprehensive sanctions will still have an effect. *Thus it is best to start with easier, lower-cost measures which do not need unanimous agreement.*

Coal is a good example of such a sanction. Substituting Australian or Chinese coal for South African coal will carry a cost penalty because South Africa is now forced to sell below world market prices. This extra cost will not be large, however. Furthermore, the extra money will go to countries that may themselves be imposing sanctions, so sanctions will actually be profitable for some. Finally, each country that imposes sanctions will cut South African earnings, so the measures will not need unanimous support to be effective.

As we have seen, *the best candidates for initial sanctions are South African bulk exports of commodities of which there is an ample supply on the world market.* These are coal, iron ore, iron and steel, base metals, non-metallic minerals, uranium, agricultural products, chemicals and other manufactured goods. (Such sanctions are detailed in Chapter 19.) This measure would constitute a widening of United States and Commonwealth sanctions, which already cover a significant part of this group. These commodities alone account for more than one third of South African exports; if sanctions were imposed quickly, cutting off the sale of this group alone would have such economic impact that the political repercussions would be far-reaching.

Cutting off South African exports like ferro-alloys would impose a significant cost penalty; they also account for a smaller proportion of South African exports. In the first phase of sanctions it would be sensible to make a commitment to cut off the purchase of steel additives at a fixed time – say, within three years – if serious negotiations had not begun. This should be backed up by financial and technical support to the SADCC states so that they could develop alternative sources of supply in order to ensure that if and when ferrochromium sanctions were imposed, supplies would still be available.

Trying to block sales to South Africa would require more unanimity and would also involve higher costs for the nations imposing sanctions. Such measures, therefore, could be left to later. Nevertheless, as part of the first phase, with its commitment to reduce trade, we believe that *a few actions should be taken to block sales to South Africa that have a high political profile.* In Chapter 21 we suggest two sanctions that, we believe, would have a significant psychological impact on the white community and would actually benefit black employment.

TIGHTENING THE NOOSE

A significant part of the first phase of sanctions must be the tightening of existing measures, which would involve firmer enforcement and higher penalties. It would mean making some voluntary bans mandatory and rewriting the terms of others to ensure that they were not easily bypassed. It is necessary to close the loopholes, particularly those permitting third-party transactions. Diplomatic initiatives and political pressure are needed to encourage countries with weak sanctions to implement stronger ones. And much more attention will have to be paid to South African companies abroad. (These issues are discussed in Chapter 22.)

Perhaps the most difficult area is technology transfer. *It is important to block South African attempts to increase its self-sufficiency*, which means reducing the flow of technology to South Africa. A key aspect of this was identified by the Commonwealth Committee of Foreign Ministers on Southern Africa when it pointed to the need 'to prohibit technology transfer that is designed to enable South Africa to circumvent existing sanctions, particularly in the areas of arms, oil and computers'. (Detailed proposals are set out in Chapter 20.)

Because the next phase of sanctions would still not be mandatory, some trade would be expected to continue. However, measures should be taken that would discourage such trade without actually banning it. *Here we call on Governments to take actions that would allow market forces to discourage continued links with South Africa.* This would mean giving full publicity to continued trade with South Africa and special legislation, if necessary, to allow local boycotts. (Proposals are detailed in Chapter 24.)

Market forces would include the issue of export credits. Such credits clearly encourage trade with South Africa; cutting them off would encourage firms to search out other export opportunities where credits were available. Credits are South Africa's remaining source of foreign funding and will be used to pay for sanctions-busting projects like Mossgas. (This matter is discussed in Chapter 19.)

We believe that if the preceding measures were all introduced quickly, the political effect would be overwhelming. The pressure within the white community, particularly from business, would be so great that the Government would be forced to the negotiating table.

This view is based on the assumption that all parts of the package would be introduced simultaneously. The economic measures must be strong enough to have a rapid and significant impact on South African GDP. Technology-transfer restrictions must be rigid enough to convince white South Africa that a siege economy is not practical, and psychological measures must be strong enough to create a much keener sense of isolation in the minds of the white minority.

THE NEXT PHASE

Clearly the initial package would distress the white community, but it might not cause the 'real discomfort' that Archbishop Hurley says is needed. We must be prepared for a further phase, with sanctions that have larger direct costs to the sanctions-imposing countries. *This would mean a substantially expanded programme of sanctions, including an end to nearly all purchases from South Africa*. It should be stressed at this point that there are alternative sources of supply or substitutes for all of South Africa's minerals.[1] The problem is cost, but in the case of most minerals the increases would not be large and could be minimized by planning ahead. Canada took a step in this direction when Foreign Minister Joe Clark met Canadian steel producers in February 1989 to suggest that they find alternative suppliers of minerals now obtained from South Africa. A joint Government–industry task force has been established to pursue this proposal.

Ferrochromium presents the most serious problem. The sudden loss of South Africa as a supplier would raise world prices by a significant amount. This, in turn, would cause small but noticeable increases in the prices of consumer goods that use stainless steel. With proper political initiatives this price rise could be made acceptable as a necessary sacrifice to fight apartheid. Furthermore, if actions were taken now to increase Zimbabwean production, the cost of this sanction would be much lower when it was finally imposed. In any case, it must be in the interests of the steel industry to find alternative suppliers. If the initial phase of sanctions did not provoke genuine negotiations, then South Africa would probably descend into the further violence forecast by the EPG. In that case certain mineral supplies would be disrupted by strikes and insurrection.

Diamonds and platinum would be exempted from sanctions because their movements would be too difficult to control at this stage.

It should be noted that South Africa might choose to manipulate platinum supplies to push up its price, which could increase costs. Intergovernmental discussions on a gold sanction would begin.

Eventually, as part of the expanded programme of sanctions, *it may be necessary to follow the Nordic countries' lead and cut off remaining sales to, and purchases from, South Africa.* In some cases there will be alternative markets, particularly for those countries that now buy manufactured goods from South Africa, but some exporting companies will be hurt by such a ban.

At this stage of imposing steadily wider, tighter and more intensified measures, sanctions busting and the few countries that refused to participate would play a much more important role. In particular, it would be hard to stop countries and individual companies selling vital goods to South Africa. The best that could be done would be to *impose restrictions on the re-export of sanctioned goods to South Africa.* This would limit the role that countries like Taiwan and Israel could play because they are dependent on supplies from the United States, Japan and several other major industrial powers. Similarly, *there would have to be effective penalties on countries that refused to participate* in at least the present Commonwealth and United States sanctions, especially those on South Africa's bulk exports. This would need to include very strict bans on the import from third countries of goods that contain South African material. Other penalties, such as those of the United States against taking advantage of sanctions, would need to be broadened and enforced.

COMMITMENT AND POLITICAL IMPACT

Sanctions that have already been imposed have had an initial impact on South Africa. Wider application of United States and Commonwealth sanctions would have a marked economic impact, and the substantially expanded programme of sanctions discussed above would, in the words of the *Financial Mail*, lead to a 'virtual collapse of the economy'. This *would* cause the white community severe discomfort. We do not believe that the business community would allow this to happen – with the support of most whites, it would force the Government to engage in serious negotiations before the economy was allowed to collapse.

The *Financial Mail*, however, declares that it is convinced that such an expanded programme of sanctions 'can be discounted', so Pretoria need not worry about economic collapse. Few South Africans believe that the country's trading partners will make sufficient sacrifices to impose sanctions at that level. If the West made clear that it was prepared to absorb the costs, and if it could convince South Africa of this fact, there would be two results that would tend to reduce those costs.

First, if the South African business community actually believed that, without serious negotiations with representatives of the majority of the population, expanded sanctions would soon be imposed, it would push for negotiation before the 'virtual collapse of the economy'.

Second, by starting now to prepare for wider sanctions the costs to the countries imposing sanctions could be reduced. Companies could plan ahead to find other export markets and other sources of raw materials. If ferro-alloy users were given three years' warning, they would be able to find alternative suppliers; this would entail long-term contracts that would justify the opening of new mines and processing facilities. Prices would be higher than present prices but much lower than the market would set if there were a sudden cut-off due to sanctions or revolution.

Thus a genuine commitment to sanctions would lead to advance planning that would cut costs if such sanctions must be carried out. Such advance planning is prudent in any case, as South Africa is no longer a secure supplier of so-called strategic minerals.

Are expanded sanctions politically realistic and practical? Just five years ago sanctions seemed to be off the agenda. Those who called for a ban on South African oranges were told that this was impossible because of GATT and EC rules. India and most other developing countries had imposed comprehensive sanctions, but such notions were dismissed in Europe. Yet now the Nordic states have comprehensive trade bans; the United States has imposed wide-ranging sanctions; and the Commonwealth has agreed to a significant set of measures. The European Community has imposed limited sanctions, and Japan is publicly committed to trade restraint.

The Okanagan Statement states that 'genuine efforts should be made to secure the universal adoption of the measures now adopted by most Commonwealth and other countries, including the United States and the Nordic countries'. Thus expanded sanctions do now appear to be realistic and practical. We have seen the importance of the lead given at various times by the Commonwealth, by the United States and by the Nordic states. This is a time when another bold lead could be important, when a new and powerful commitment could set the pace. *Therefore the Commonwealth should take the lead and set an example for other states by committing itself now to an expanded programme of sanctions.*

Much has been made of the cost of imposing sanctions – the cost of lost markets and of the higher prices of certain minerals. The cost of not imposing sanctions is incalculably higher – mainly to the people of South Africa but also to other countries, in terms of lost markets and supplies, if South Africa is allowed to descend into violence.

19

TARGETING PRETORIA'S TRADE

In Chapter 18 we stressed that the first priority of any sanctions package must be to stop the purchase of South African bulk exports that could easily be replaced by supplies from elsewhere and could be identified so that sanctions can be monitored. These are agricultural products, iron and steel, non-strategic minerals (including coal and iron ore), chemicals and other manufactured goods. Details of these commodities are included in the tables at the end of this report; Table 9 summarizes the position. As this table makes clear, *one priority must be to encourage all countries to ban South African agricultural products*, which still account for 13 per cent of South African exports. Not only are they inessential but they are also in direct competition with products from other southern-hemisphere producers, including the SADCC states and Commonwealth members.

As Table 9 also makes clear, the present sanctions position is very confused. The Commonwealth, in Nassau in October 1985, agreed to a 'ban on the import of agricultural products from South Africa'. In practice, however, many Commonwealth states ban only *edible* agricultural products. There is no evidence that this limited interpretation was intended when the ban was agreed. We believe that *the ban on agricultural products should follow the GATT definition of 'agriculture'*, as GATT provides an internationally agreed framework, and it would make sense to follow its conventions.[1] The GATT definition – Standard International Trade Classification (SITC) sections 0, 1, 2 (minus divisions 27 and 28) and 4 – encompasses both 'food' and 'raw materials' and effectively includes everything that grows.[2] Thus it includes the following South African products: groundnuts and vegetable oils; cotton and wool; hides and skins; fish and seafood; and wood pulp.

Table 9. Commodities exported in bulk by South Africa

Commodity category	Share of South African exports (%)	Countries that already impose sanctions
Agricultural products, of which:	14	
Fruit, vegetables, grain	6	Comm.,[1] USA, Japan (part)
Meat, fish, dairy	1	Comm., USA
Natural clothing materials	3	USA
Wood, pulp, paper	3	
Miscellaneous farm	1	Comm. (part), USA
Non-strategic minerals, of which:	15	
Coal	7	Comm., USA, some EC
Base metals	4	
Other non-metallic	2	
Iron ore	1	some Comm., USA
Uranium	1	Comm., USA (part), Japan (part)
Manufactured goods, of which:	9	
Iron and steel	4	Comm., USA, Japan, EC
Other manufactures	3	
Chemicals and petroleum products	2	
Total	37	

Note: [1] Comm. = Commonwealth except UK.

The Commonwealth and the United States already ban coal and uranium as well as iron and steel, and sanctions have reduced South Africa's coal earnings from 10 per cent of total exports in 1986 to 7 per cent in 1987. That 7 per cent is important, and there are numerous other coal suppliers who could replace South Africa. Prices would rise somewhat because sanctions-busting coal has kept the world market price artificially low. Uranium and iron and steel are also in surplus on the world market. A high priority, therefore, should be to extend the bans on coal, uranium and iron and steel

South Africa is a major mineral producer, and it is important to distinguish between the few minerals that are strategic and those that are common. South Africa produces most of the base metals (copper, lead, tin, zinc, aluminium and nickel), but it is only a minor world producer of these. It accounts for 3 per cent of world lead and nickel production and only 1 per cent of copper, aluminium, zinc and tin. Internationally, production and consumption often vary by more than that each year.[3] Prices of base metals are often quite volatile – nickel rose fourfold and copper doubled between mid-1987 and mid-1988. Removing South Africa from the market would have less impact than normal annual fluctuation. Users of base metals are accustomed to abrupt price swings and could generally absorb any price changes due to sanctions. Base metals accounted for 4 per cent of South Africa's exports in 1987 and probably double that in 1988 because of rising prices – which reduced the impact of other sanctions. World prices are falling again, but base metals are still important earners of foreign exchange. Because they are major earners for South Africa, while being of no great importance to world markets, base metals are another priority target for sanctions.

Iron ore is not included in many bans on South African iron and steel, but it is another mineral for which there are many other suppliers. South Africa also exports a variety of non-metallic minerals, including building stone, tombstones, asbestos and fertilizer. All of these, except for the refractory andalusite, are widely available.

Thus there are three groups of minerals that could easily be banned now: *base metals* (copper, lead, tin, zinc, aluminium and nickel), *iron ore* and *non-metallic minerals* (except andalusite). They are not strategic; South Africa is not a major world producer; and there is a wide range of alternative (non-communist) suppliers, including Commonwealth members. These minerals account for another 7 per cent of South African exports and could be obtained from other sources. Precious metals such as platinum, and the controversial steel additives and minor metals, are *not* included in this list.[4] However, as we explained in Chapter 12, it is possible to reduce South Africa's earnings as well as to ensure the supply of platinum if *all countries stop the production and sale of all platinum coins and small bars aimed at investors*.

South Africa is trying to expand its exports of manufactured goods and chemicals as a way of expanding industrialization and becoming more self-sufficient in the face of sanctions. Its manufactures are typical of many developing and newly industrialized countries, including some in the Commonwealth. South Africa's textiles, furniture and glassware are in direct competition with products from other N I Cs, and there can be no justification in continuing to buy them from South Africa.

Because the South African market is too small for many high-technology production processes, manufactured exports are essential for many import-substituting industries; there is substantial over-capacity in the chemical industry, for example. Finally, because of the nature of its refineries and the Sasol oil-from-coal plants, South Africa produces a surplus of some kinds of fuel oil and waxes, and it has become a significant exporter; the purchase of these products helps the apartheid regime to break the oil embargo.

The United States bans South African textiles, and many industrialized countries ban South African steel, but there are no other bans that relate specifically to manufactured goods. Thus *an immediate ban should be imposed on South African manufactured goods, including steel, chemicals and petroleum products*. Again, we recommend the use of the GATT convention, which defines 'manufactures' under SITC sections 5, 6 (except division 68), 7 and 8.

TRAVEL

International travel is regarded by white South Africans as one of their most essential links with the 'white' countries of Europe and North America. The tourists who arrive in South Africa, and South Africans' own ability to visit Europe and North America, remain for many the proof that the country is a 'white island just off the coast of Europe' and not really part of Africa.

The psychological impact of international travel is important, but it is not the only issue. The promotion of tourism is manipulated as propaganda. Tourism advertising is aimed increasingly at non-tourists and claims that the foreign press misrepresents a happy and prosperous South Africa. And, indeed, those who do visit, especially on package tours, see little of the misery of South Africa and may come away with a false impression.

Tourism is financially important for South Africa: it earns the country more than US$400 million per year, which is equivalent to 2 per cent of export earnings. Travel out of South Africa is particularly important for the sanctions-busting business community.

Visa restrictions, tourism bans and the ending of direct flights to South Africa are all intended to cut links and intensify white South Africans' sense of isolation – to show them that kith and kin 'at home' do not accept neo-apartheid. *The first step must be to tighten and extend present 'voluntary' tourism-promotion bans*. At the very least this measure should include *the closure of all South African tourist offices abroad and a ban on all advertising that promotes South Africa as a desirable travel destination.* We note that South Africa itself includes business travel in its definition of tourism; we agree and think that business travel should be included in any ban on promotion. Tour operators should be prevented, or strongly discouraged, from offering South Africa as a tour or package destination. Airlines should be prevented or discouraged from promoting South Africa as a destination for business or holiday travel.

The Expert Study Group would not support a ban on travel to South Africa; nor do we feel it feasible to ban directory and other listings of flights, hotels and travel facilities. We do, however, think that it is important actively to discourage travel to South Africa. Therefore we suggest that listings that are exempt from a ban, and tour advertisements and brochures that violate the 'voluntary' tourism-promotion ban, should be required to carry a warning notice similar to those imposed on tobacco advertising. Such a notice might proclaim: 'The Government discourages travel to apartheid South Africa.'

Tourism in the other direction is also important in breaking the isolation of white people in South Africa, so it is important to extend the tourism-promotion ban to include *a ban on the promotion of travel from South Africa.* Governments would be expected to prohibit national companies, and their subsidiaries and agents, from placing advertising in the South African press, promoting package tours and so on.

Finally, the Expert Study Group underlines *the importance of extending the ban on air links to all countries other than the SADCC states.* This ban would cost international airlines very little. They could fly to Gaborone or Harare just as well as Johannesburg. It would be psychologically very important, however, that South Africans had no *direct* access to Europe and that majority-ruled states were their only gateway to the rest of the world. Passing through the SADCC states might dispel a few South African myths about majority rule, and the life of businesspeople and tourists going to and from South Africa would be made a little bit harder.

The air-link ban would also have three financial advantages: South African Airways would lose profitable routes; SADCC airlines and airports would earn money from the transit traffic; and some tourists and businesspeople who might otherwise have gone to South Africa because of better flight connections would change their destinations to the SADCC states.

COUNTER TRADE, MARKETING AND TRANSPORT

We noted in Chapter 12 that South Africa is increasingly using counter and barter trade and that it seems likely to use these as ways of encouraging private companies outside South Africa to do its sanctions busting for it. Companies may be required to sell South African coal, fruit and other sanctioned items in order to obtain a deal that remains legal.

South Africa has also encouraged joint marketing, particularly of products like citrus, for which it has a well-developed marketing infrastructure, which allows it to mix embargoed fruit with fruit from other countries. This occurs because many countries allow their companies to deal in sanctioned goods so long as these goods do not enter the country. Similarly ships often carry sanctioned goods. This seems an excessively narrow interpretation of sanctions, which allows the apartheid state a major loophole. Therefore it is essential that *if a country has imposed a sanction against a South African product or against selling a product to South Africa, nationals of that country, companies based in that country and companies owned or controlled by nationals of that country should not be permitted to transport or trade in that product, or to engage in joint marketing involving that product, even on the high seas or in countries where the product is not banned.* (The term 'controlled' is discussed in Chapter 22.)

CUTTING OFF CREDITS

The initial draft of the report *Apartheid and International Finance* showed that between the debt crisis of 1985 and the time of the report in mid-1988 international banks had refused to give the South African Government new loans. The report concluded that the maintenance and extension of financial sanctions would hobble South African economic growth and maintain the economic pressure on the South African Government to abandon apartheid. Since mid-1988, however, there have been a few small loans, which reinforces the need for the position of the Commonwealth (except Britain), that is, *no new loans to South Africa*, to be adopted by other countries.

At its meeting in Toronto in August 1988 the Commonwealth Committee of Foreign Ministers on Southern Africa recognized that banks whose loans are subject to the South African moratorium and interim rescheduling have no option but to retain their exposure in South Africa or to sell it at a discount to other banks. However, the type of rescheduling accepted by the bank can have a significant effect on the constraints faced by economic policy-makers in South Africa. Ministers agreed to ask banks in their countries to press for rescheduling arrangements which do not extend beyond one year at a time.

We endorse this view and believe that banks should require political concessions even for one-year rescheduling.

TRADE CREDITS

Short-term trade credits are now South Africa's only significant source of foreign finance. These are usually tied to the purchase of particular equipment and are either loans to the buyer (buyer's credits) or delayed-payment terms offered by the seller (supplier's credits), which may itself have obtained a loan from a bank to cover the credit or sold the debt to a bank (discounted trade bills and factoring). South Africa maintains an outstanding trade debt of over US$3 billion. On 6 July 1988 the then Governor of the South African Reserve Bank, Gerhard de Kock, said that in recent months there had been a 'gratifying' increase in trade credits. This, he said, 'serves to ease the balance of payments constraints on economic growth'.

In reports to the CFMSA in 1988 the Expert Study Group and the study on the International Financial System pointed to the importance of export credits. The South African magazine *Finance Week* reacted with concern: 'If Commonwealth and other anti-apartheid lobbyists are able to reduce availability of credits by as little as 20 per cent, it would still have the effect of causing South Africa to repay some US$600 million at least of short-term foreign loans.'[5]

The British Foreign and Commonwealth Office also noted: 'A ban on new export credit, if widely applied, could have a significant impact on economic growth and development in South Africa.' In particular, 'large development projects would be difficult to fund with cash and might have to be cancelled'.[6] Such projects include sanctions-busting ventures like Mossgas. Some countries have banned certain trade credits, but the position is confused. Japan and Australia include trade credits in the ban on bank loans, so buyer's credits are banned but not supplier's credits.

Much of international trade functions on credits of various sorts –

competition depends not on price alone but on credit terms as well. Squeezed by sanctions, South Africa is even more likely to buy from the supplier who can offer the best credit terms. On the other hand, a substantial amount of international trade is based on cash deals with companies or countries that do not have an acceptable international credit rating. Thus if individual countries cut off trade credits, this expedient would not prohibit trade, but it would place certain companies at a disadvantage by comparison with those in countries that still offered credits. The CFMSA recognized this in August 1988, when it agreed only that there should be 'no expansion in trade financing'.

We have looked at this issue in some detail. We have argued that there must be a public commitment to reduce trade with South Africa, and we believe that a reduction in trade credits is in keeping with that recommendation. In Chapter 23 we argue that where there is no ban on trade with South Africa, market forces should be used to discourage trade. A reduction in trade credits would have that effect – firms would increasingly look to other markets where credits made sales easier, while those with a long-term commitment to South Africa who could trade with reduced credits would also be able to continue to trade. As *Finance Week* has pointed out, even a partial reduction in trade credits would have a financial impact.

Therefore, we believe that *Governments should phase out trade credits over several years* (we would suggest three years and certainly no more than five years). This is in keeping with our view that South Africa's trading partners must demonstrate a long-term commitment to reduce trade sharply if South Africa does not move to negotiations. Under this plan trade credits would be cut each year by 33 per cent (if over three years) or 20 per cent (if over five years), either by imposing a ceiling or by steadily reducing the repayment period. It is important as well to define terms so that *trade credits include both supplier's and buyer's credits*. At the same time there should be *a ban on export credit guarantees and insurance*, which would also discourage, but not prohibit, trade.

The concern for Governments imposing sanctions is that if they phase out trade credits but other countries do not, the latter will simply take over that trade and the sanctions will have no impact on South Africa. Clearly this matter will have to be monitored. Publicity remains the strongest weapon. Some Governments may feel the need to follow the United States' lead and enact provisions allowing retaliation against countries that 'take advantage' of sanctions. (This matter is discussed further in Chapter 22.)

HELP FOR THE SADCC STATES

Economic and military help for SADCC is often seen as an alternative to tighter sanctions. We reject this unreservedly. The aid given to SADCC would be small compared with the damage done by the apartheid state, and it would be a much more sensible investment to stop the destruction than to provide bandages for the wounds.

There are, however, four areas in which aid to SADCC would specifically help to enforce sanctions.

The first would be assistance to help SADCC to become an alternative source of supply of South African goods subject to sanctions, such as strategic minerals and agricultural products.

Second, donors could help the SADCC states to find alternative markets and marketing companies for products now sold to, or through, South Africa. Industrialized countries might wish to give preference to SADCC products to help those states to reduce their dependence on South Africa. Where quotas are involved, as with sugar and textiles, it would be proper to assign South Africa's quota to SADCC states.

Third, assistance could be given to allow the SADCC states to buy elsewhere goods that they now import from South Africa. This could involve subsidies to cover extra costs and help to establish import–export agencies.

Fourth, donors should ensure that they purchase supplies from SADCC states rather than South Africa and use SADCC ports when sending assistance to the region.

Clearly, assistance to SADCC should be increased on grounds of general need and to help repair the damage done by South Africa. Such aid cannot be seen as an alternative to sanctions, however.

20

ARMS AND OIL

Discussion of sales *to* South Africa must start with the two long-standing embargoes, arms and oil. The arms embargo remains the only mandatory United Nations embargo. 'The vast majority of the world's oil-producing states prohibit the export of their oil to South Africa,' according to the report of the United Nations Intergovernmental Group to Monitor the Supply and Shipping of Oil and Petroleum Products to South Africa (known as the Intergovernmental Oil Group).

As we noted in Chapter 6, both embargoes have been effective. The arms embargo has prevented South Africa from obtaining new weapons systems and has played a key role in forcing the Pretoria regime to agree to Namibian independence. The oil embargo is costing South Africa at least US$2 billion per year.

Nevertheless, South Africa still obtains arms and oil. Thus tightening the arms and oil embargoes must have a high priority. All efforts to cut sales to South Africa, discussed in this and the next chapter, must always work at two levels: they must block directly the supply of the commodity, and they must prevent South Africa from acquiring the means to produce the embargoed item. The importance of this latter point was recognized by the CFMSA when it called on Governments to 'prohibit technology transfer that is designed to enable South Africa to circumvent existing sanctions, particularly in the areas of arms, oil and computers'.

HOW PRETORIA OBTAINS ITS ARMS

South Africa obtains its arms and military equipment in three different ways:[1] first, through illegal and clandestine deals that involve the smuggling of arms, components, spares and ammunition; second, by importing so-called 'dual-purpose' and 'civilian' equipment that can be turned to military and repressive uses; third, by assembling and manufacturing arms and ammunition, which requires foreign components, designs, technology and expertise.

South Africa has developed a substantial arms industry and become a large arms exporter. Nevertheless, the country is simply too small to be self-sufficient. Virtually every weapon, vehicle or other piece of hardware has imported parts and is based, at least partially, on foreign know-how. This has occurred because the Western industrialized nations have taken an attitude to arms supplies for South Africa that is very different from their view of arms supplies to the socialist countries. This was evident in 1983, when Western security services discovered an attempt to smuggle advanced computers to the Soviet Union via South Africa. The computers were legally exported from the United States to South Africa and were stopped only when they were sent on to Sweden and West Germany in transit to the Soviet Union.[2]

Arms sales controls are codified by most Western countries in an 'export control list', 'security export control' regulations or similar documents. These are based on an agreed list worked out through CoCom, which is an informal grouping of the NATO countries (except Iceland) plus Japan. In general, items on the list cannot be exported to twelve 'proscribed' Eastern Bloc countries. In introducing the 1985 edition of the British list, the then Minister of Trade, Paul Channon, explained, 'We cannot divorce our prosperity from our security, and I believe that the strategic export controls represent a fair balance between our strategic and our commercial interests.'

The list is in three parts: atomic energy materials, munitions and 'dual-purpose' industrial goods with potential military use. (This part of the list is a directory, running to nearly a hundred pages, of dual-use technologies and equipment. It is so comprehensive that under its provisions many common personal computers cannot be taken to Eastern Europe.) Attention focuses on the last group, and Mr Channon stressed that one way to acquire 'advanced technology with military potential ... is through legitimate trade in high technology designed principally for civil use but which could be diverted or applied to military purposes'.

The problem, with respect to South Africa, is that most countries interpret the United Nations mandatory arms embargo in the narrowest sense. They apply only the munitions section of their export control list, while licensing sales of goods on the industrial list. If 'dual-use' items are considered to have military implications for some countries, it is hard to argue that they should not fall under the mandatory United Nations ban.

Clearly in that 'dual-purpose' middle ground there is profitable business that countries will be reluctant to lose, although they accept that they should lose potential sales to countries that are treated as enemies. At the very least, common standards should be applied: nothing that is already embargoed to another country should be sold to South Africa.

In 1989 Canada became the first major Western country to implement a total ban on sales to South Africa of items on its export control list as well as computers and other key technology (see Chapter 6). We commend this action to other countries and urge that *South Africa should not be allowed to purchase any 'dual-use' equipment whose sale is already banned to any other country as part of an export control list or other restriction.*

This is an obvious first step, but it will not be enough. Because South Africa is technically less advanced than the socialist countries, its military and arms industry needs to import many 'low-tech' items that are not considered significant by CoCom. One obvious example is four-wheel-drive vehicles, and Canada has extended its ban to include them. Other countries should follow suit. At its meeting in Harare in February 1989 the Commonwealth Committee of Foreign Ministers on Southern Africa said that the mandatory UN arms embargo should be interpreted to include: articles capable of being converted into arms and implements of war; materials, equipment and technologies of which South Africa has a deficiency and which may be critical to the production of arms, ammunition or implements of war, or their means of utilization or delivery, or counter-measures to them; and goods to assist in the maintenance of repression including aircraft and parts, computers, telecommunications equipment and four-wheel-drive vehicles.

The Expert Study Group strongly supports this view (the full text is given in Appendix 6) – and we warn that some of these items are not covered in various export control lists.

END USERS

One of the most difficult problems of all export controls are third-party transactions, in which an item is sold to one person for a legitimate purpose but is then passed on to someone else for a prohibited use. The United States has imposed very stringent requirements. It has a re-export control system under which a United States export licence is required for items manufactured in other countries that include controlled components either of United States origin or manufactured using United States-origin technology. The United States has used its powers to penalize firms for breaking South African sanctions: in 1982 the British computer company ICL had to pay a United States fine for having sold computers to the South African police containing United States disc drives,[3] and in 1986 the United States Commerce Department fined a British computer company, Systime, US$600,000 for exporting equipment with United States components, without a licence, to countries ranging from Switzerland to Libya.

The more extreme extra-territorial actions by the United States have drawn some protests from Britain, Canada and elsewhere. Nevertheless, they show what is necessary to enforce a wide-ranging arms embargo. We would not advocate such extreme measures at this time. However, we feel strongly that more must be done to limit the re-export to South Africa of strategic goods and technology.

One issue that has been raised in Canada but applies to many other countries is that controlled exports require an end-use certificate that indicates the final destination of the item. Canada and some other countries accept an end-use certificate that declares that an item will be included in some other product, yet do not impose further restrictions on the transformed product. In particular this means that Canadian engines and parts can be included in aircraft that are then sold to South Africa. United States law would not allow this.[4]

Indeed, it appears that embargoed items can be included in goods sold to South Africa. In 1985 Britain maintained that Optima surveillance aircraft could be sold to South Africa, even though its engines were on the export control list, because the entire aircraft was not covered by the regulation. The Expert Study Group believes that *exports of strategic parts and components must have restrictions to prevent these items being used in goods for South Africa; similarly, licensing agreements must contain bans on using the technology to produce strategic goods for South Africa.*

The British House of Commons Trade and Industry Committee, reviewing CoCom and trade with Eastern Europe, made a suggestion

that, we believe, is also appropriate for South Africa.[5] It concluded
that end use was the 'prime consideration' and that exports of
technology should be authorized only if 'the equipment will be so
intimately bound up with other high-value plant as to be virtually
immovable or the recipients agree to a regular inspection by suppliers'
representatives to ensure unchanged use'. It went on to recommend
'on-site inspection of high-technology exports whose diversion to
military use would pose a military threat'. We support this proposal
for South Africa as well and argue that it be made a condition of the
sale of all strategic items for which South Africa claims a purely
civilian use. The Committee makes another suggestion that we feel is
appropriate to South Africa: 'Diversion of spares presents a serious
problem, but this can be overcome by authorizing only a small
holding and making replenishment conditional on the return of
defective items.'

Finally, we feel that the Committee came to two conclusions that
are equally relevant to the sale of strategic goods to South Africa. It
stated, 'We believe that industry supports the CoCom process,' and
it stressed the need for restrictions to prevent technology transfer,
pointing out, 'Equipment and software to assist the design and
manufacture of high-technology equipment is particularly sensitive.'

TURNING OFF THE OIL TAP

No country openly sells crude oil to the apartheid state, yet the
supply of oil has not dried up. There are a number of ways in which
the oil embargo could be tightened to make it harder for Pretoria to
find sufficient fuel. Countries that subscribe to the oil embargo
candidly admit to sending more than US$57 million per year in oil
products, and these are important because some are lubricants and
other products that South Africa cannot easily produce itself. West
Germany, the United States, Britain and Japan are important suppliers: these countries adopt a narrow definition of the oil embargo
that includes only crude petroleum. The British Government actually
opposes a 'comprehensive oil embargo';[6] British regulations do not
include refined oil or non-British Continental Shelf crude oil. Clearly
*the oil embargo should include lubricants and other refined oil
products*.

Another problem is cargoes that are sold at sea, trans-shipped
through intermediate ports and otherwise sent to South Africa in

violation of the embargo. Many countries already require discharge certificates for oil. These list the port of discharge (unloading) and the date and must be submitted to the exporting country after delivery. Because they are already commonly used, *those countries that are serious about imposing the oil embargo will insist on discharge certificates for oil.* The importance of this issue is shown by an incident in which a cargo of North Sea oil was resold several times and ended up in South Africa. The British Government said the embargo had been satisfied because the exporter (Shell) had included a restriction in its contract barring the sale of the oil to South Africa (even though the restriction was violated), while Shell stressed, 'International embargoes are properly a matter of public law, not private contract.' Without a law requiring a discharge certificate it is easy for a cargo to be resold often enough to drift out of the control of the original supplier. *Non-oil producers could also restrict oil movements if they imposed a ban on the use of ports (including free ports) and transit facilities to trans-ship oil to South Africa.*

As it faces the prospect of a tightening oil embargo South Africa has turned to converting coal and natural gas to liquid fuels. This process is expensive and uses techniques not considered commercially viable anywhere else in the world. Furthermore, it produces too much petrol and too little diesel fuel, which means that South Africa will remain dependent on imports.

The central issue, however, is that South Africa depends on foreign technology and machinery for its oil and gas exploration and for the manufacture of liquid fuels. The Mossgas project will cost more than US$2 billion and will provide about 10 per cent of South Africa's need for liquid fuels. It will be dependent on a wide range of foreign technologies and contractors. As well as actual hardware (likely to be provided on trade credits), there will be a need for licences, designs, software and a large number of skilled people. As we have noted, the British Government is already encouraging firms to become involved in this project. Clearly such involvement would undermine the Commonwealth Committee of Foreign Ministers on Southern Africa's proposal for a ban on technology transfer that is intended to circumvent the oil embargo.

Oil technology is not now included in the CoCom industrial list, so it will not be covered by the ban, proposed above, on sales to South Africa of all items on export control lists. *Therefore there is a need for Governments to establish a specific ban on the sale to South*

Africa of technology, equipment, licences, etc., that are intended for oil and gas exploration, production and delivery, and the manufacture of liquid fuels. This ban should also cover contractors, consultants and firms sending people to South Africa to work in these areas.

ARMS AND OIL ARE SIMILAR ISSUES

Many of the problems relating to the implementation of the arms and oil embargoes are similar. For example, some of the countries involved in sanctions busting are well known, and it should be possible to apply international political pressure. At the very least, Governments should take three steps to reduce violations. First, they should *impose stricter end-user requirements on hardware and technology supplies to countries suspected of violating the arms and oil embargoes.* Second, they should *ask security services and trade ministries to take additional steps to identify violations of these embargoes.* Third, they should *publicize all violations of the arms and oil embargoes.*

A related problem has been the unwillingness of Governments to assert control of shipping. Therefore *national bans on the transport of arms and oil must extend to all ships and aircraft owned, leased or in any way controlled by national firms or individuals.*

Another major loophole in both arms and oil embargoes is the role of TNCs in South Africa. The United Nations Intergovernmental Oil Group points to BP, Caltex, Mobil, Shell and Total as companies with subsidiaries that are 'assisting the apartheid regime in the energy field', possibly by importing oil. The experience and international links of these TNCs helps South Africa to break the oil embargo, and their withdrawal would contribute to the effect of sanctions.

The Intergovernmental Oil Group also points to subsidiaries of British, French, Dutch and Belgian firms involved in Mossgas and to local subsidiaries and licensees of TNCs that are involved (often indirectly) in local military production. The regulations proposed in this chapter would impose limitations on the TNCs but would not put a stop to their activities. However, for most firms the South African market is a relatively small one, and they could not afford high extra costs. Therefore *Governments should encourage consumer boycotts directed at firms involved in helping to break the arms and oil embargoes* in the hope that this will put sufficient commercial pressure on the firms to cut their links with South Africa.

There is also the problem that as South African TNCs invest outside South Africa, they are gaining control of possible military contractors and of firms that are involved in oil developments such as those in the North Sea. Therefore *firms that are controlled by South Africa-based companies or individuals should be banned from participating in activities that would be subject to sanctions against South Africa, such as oil and arms production.*

SPECIAL EXPORT CONTROLS

Finally we return to the problems of using export control lists based on the CoCom list. We feel that such lists are a good place to start because they provide at least a partial definition of industrial goods with military application, but there are two reasons why it is important to move on from the CoCom list.

First, there is concern that sanctions against South Africa should not be linked with CoCom because it is closely identified with the security of the Western alliance and with East–West conflicts. Second, the CoCom list is more suitable for industrialized countries, like those of Eastern Europe, than a NIC like South Africa; we noted above that all oil technology and some of the more 'low-tech' arms technology needed by South Africa are not now included in CoCom-based export-control lists. This omission will become more serious in future, as improvements in East–West relations lead to a shortening of the CoCom list. Therefore we would urge that *national legislation should be passed in each country to ban the sale of strategic technology and equipment to South Africa, either directly or through third parties.* This measure will require further study to identify those technologies and equipment that are important to South Africa's efforts to break the oil and arms embargoes but are not now in the various export control lists.

21

CARS AND COMPUTERS

In keeping with our view that it is more difficult to impose sanctions on sales to South Africa than on purchases from it, and that it is important to start with sanctions that are the least difficult to impose, the Expert Study Group recommends only two new sanctions on sales to the apartheid state. Both are practical because they involve only a handful of international suppliers, and both will create and protect black jobs while having a marked psychological impact on the white minority. For this reason we commend these two sanctions especially to those who have voiced concern about black employment and welfare in the context of sanctions (rather than apartheid).

CAR SANCTIONS

Africans in South Africa buy fewer than 1 per cent of all new cars, but they constitute half of the workforce in the local car industry. Thus a sanction that affected new cars without closing down the car industry would be one that preferentially hit the white minority.

High tariffs ensure that most cars are assembled locally rather than imported, and South Africa produces about 200,000 new cars a year. After twenty-five years of steadily enforced increases in local content cars are now 66 per cent South African by weight but only 37 per cent local by value. This local content is less than in many other car-making NICs, ranging from Mexico to Taiwan.

Vehicles and parts are South Africa's largest single import, accounting for 20 per cent of all imports. Japan and West Germany are the major suppliers (their exports are valued at roughly US$900 million per year each), followed by Britain and the United States (about US$200 million per year each).

The seven main car manufacturers are linked with Japanese, United States and West German firms. Britain and Italy have a small presence in the industry. They all import a wide range of components from the parent companies: Honda, for example, imports the entire engine, while Mercedes Benz makes engine blocks in South Africa but imports vital parts like the cylinder head. The South African Board of Trade and Industry admitted in 1988 that 'most of the high-technology developments in automotive-component manufacture in recent years have to a large extent been beyond the capabilities of the South African automotive component industry. The relatively low volumes [of the South African car industry], sophistication of design, patent rights, unavailability of certain raw materials, and severe capital requirements have hindered local high-technology component development.'[1]

Indeed, the internationalization of car production and the very rapid technological changes, especially those involving electronics, are reducing local-content levels throughout the NICs. Taiwan, for example, has actually lowered its local content required from 70 per cent to 50 per cent. South Korea produces 100 per cent local-content cars for domestic consumption, but 25 per cent of the value of its exported cars is imported high-technology components, such as automatic transmissions and emission controls, because it cannot meet the high standards demanded internationally with local parts.

Could car sanctions be imposed effectively? The vital high technology in modern cars is produced only in Japan, the United States and Western Europe (or under licence from producers in those countries) and thus would be relatively easy to cut off if those countries agreed to impose sanctions. Clearly the West German and Japanese car makers, which dominate the market, would object vociferously to any sanction, and the South African market is important for these companies. For Toyota, for example, South Africa is the second largest foreign market after the United States. Toyota's United States operation is four times as large, however, and its Canadian operation is only slightly smaller than its South African one. Thus if it were forced to choose, by either government or consumer pressure, it would reluctantly withdraw from South Africa.

What would happen if sanctions were imposed on vehicle and vehicle part sales to South Africa? It seems clear that South Africa could produce a car with nearly 100 per cent local content. It might have help from motor manufacturers in Taiwan and South Korea and would still be able to smuggle in from the West some small but expensive components; nevertheless a nearly 100 per cent South African car would probably be 'reminiscent of today's passenger vehicles of Eastern Europe – outdated, unsophisticated and inhibitingly expensive'.[2]

A sanction on vehicles and parts would have three indirect effects. It would affect spares, which would make it much more difficult to maintain existing cars. The fuel consumption of locally made cars would be much higher, since one aspect of high-tech design is fuel-saving technology, and this would interact with the oil embargo. Finally, the sanction would make it more difficult for South Africa to manufacture its military vehicles, which are still partly dependent on imported 'dual-use' components.

The main impact would be on car workers and car buyers. A jump from 37 per cent to nearly 100 per cent local content, even for fewer cars, would create jobs in the depressed motor industry. Skilled workers would be needed to make even the least sophisticated engines, transmissions and other parts. Thousands would be employed in workshops throughout the country to make spares in an effort to keep old cars running. Thus a car sanction would create jobs and would probably provide a small boost to the local economy.

For white car buyers it would be a shock comparable with, perhaps greater than, that of the sports boycott. They have become accustomed to modern cars and frequent model changes. With the imposition of a car sanction the price of apartheid would be visible constantly on the road.

COMPUTERS AND AUTOMATION

South Africa is computerizing its industry. As we noted in Chapter 16, it is dependent almost totally on imported equipment, technology and people to undertake this task.

The Commonwealth (including Britain) already has a ban on the 'sale and export of computer equipment capable of use by South African military forces, police or security forces'. The United States bans the export of computers and software to entities of the South African Government that are engaged in the enforcement of apartheid. But there is a wide variation in interpretation. The British Department of Trade and Industry encourages computer sales to the

Council for Scientific and Industrial Research (CSIR). But CSIR is at the heart of South Africa's military research establishment and is one of the agencies on the United States banned list.

In any case present bans on sales to the military, police and apartheid-enforcing agencies are empty; modern telecommunications and networking technology mean that those agencies can easily use computers that they do not own or control. Armscor, the state armaments company, reports that it uses 700 South African private-sector subcontractors. Their use of computers and other technology in work for Armscor cannot be regulated. The United States does post-shipment checks on computers, but the General Accounting Office admitted, 'It is possible for the military or police to use a United States-made computer remotely by modem or off-site terminal without detection by a post-shipment check.'[3]

Thus the Commonwealth phrase 'capable of use by South African military forces . . .' should cover nearly all computers because of the close links between industry, Government and the military in South Africa. In fact, it seems to have been interpreted much more narrowly. If countries were to follow the Canadian lead and ban all items on the export control list, this would stop the sale to the apartheid state of most modern computer technology. The export control list is very broad in this area; it includes, for example, common microcomputers containing the standard Intel 80386 microprocessor chip.

South Africa has increasingly turned to Taiwan as a source of electronics and computers. Taiwanese electronics sales to South Africa doubled in 1987 compared with 1986 and looked likely to double again in 1988. Public statements by South African industry sources make clear that they are hoping that Taiwan will be a safe sanctions-busting source.

Two sets of components are central to computer technology: microprocessors, which drive personal computers, and dynamic random access memories (DRAMs), which are essential for all computers.[4] These are made by a small number of manufacturers on licence from an even smaller number. (For example, of one megabit DRAM chips 88 per cent are made in Japan and the rest in the United States, South Korea and West Germany.) It would be practical to restrict the re-export of these microprocessors and DRAMs to South Africa and even to control Taiwan and others who might help South Africa. Therefore *tighter controls should be imposed on micro-processors and DRAMs to ensure that they are not exported or re-exported to South Africa as part of computers and electronic equipment.*

Automation, rather than sanctions, has been the main cause of job losses in South Africa and is likely to remain so in the next few years. Farm mechanization has thrown many thousands of farm workers out of work and into starvation, and a ban on the import of vehicles and parts would also protect jobs by slowing further agricultural mechanization.

Computers are the building blocks of both office and factory automation, and computer numerically controlled (CNC) machine tools are now at the heart of factory automation and the South African arms industry. CNC mechanisms are also the 'brains' inside machining centres, robots, automatic testing equipment and modern flexible manufacturing systems.

Not only are CNC machine tools important for reducing labour (saving about one job per machine tool on average), but they are also essential for meeting rising quality standards. Quality is becoming an important issue in South Africa because the country is pressing to increase local industrialization in order to beat sanctions. It also hopes to export some of its production to offset high costs and can do this only if the quality of its manufactures is competitive with other world producers.

A restriction on factory automation would be a particularly good target for international action. First, it is essential to curb sanctions busting as part of South Africa's quest for self-sufficiency in arms and other industries. Second, South Africa is still entirely dependent on foreign suppliers, and the gap created by the withdrawal of suppliers could not easily be filled by countries willing to break sanctions, so the sanction could be enforced. Finally, it would be a job-creating sanction.

CoCom recognizes the military importance of factory automation, and export control lists already include CNC machine tools and industrial systems as well as the technology, software and components for them. Thus any ban based on existing export control lists, as already proposed, would also cover this area.

However, because end-use certificates are sometimes required only for delivery to intermediate manufacturers and because of likely reductions in the scope of the CoCom list as part of improved East–West relations and because CNC devices are normally included in machine tools and other equipment, we suggest special attention be paid to *a ban on the sale of* CNC *devices to South Africa, including strict controls to ensure that* CNC *devices are not included in any equipment sent to South Africa.* We commend this measure especially to those who are worried about the impact of sanctions on black jobs because it will protect jobs rather than destroy them.

22

ENFORCEMENT

As sanctions intensify, so do South Africa's efforts to counter them. Thus the issue of enforcing regulations has become increasingly important. This is a complex issue involving conflicting goals and priorities: for example, we are asking customs officials to interdict falsely labelled South African fruit at the same time as we are requesting them to seize narcotics, which may be seen as a higher priority.

Some sanctions busting and smuggling is inevitable, but the goal must be to increase the likelihood, and raise the cost, of getting caught. This means that sanctions busters will inevitably charge more for their efforts, which will increase the 'apartheid tax' that South Africa will have to pay on sanctions-busting trade. *An important step will be to increase the penalties for sanctions busting.*

The United States Comprehensive Anti-Apartheid Act of 1986 sharply increased the penalty for mismarking South African goods or giving false information to customs authorities. The mismarking of goods from most other countries will carry only a fine, whereas the mislabelling of South African goods can entail a ten-year prison sentence. Canadian sanctions come under the Act designed for strategic trade covered by CoCom; the penalties rise to C$25,000 and five years in jail. The effect is to discourage businesspeople from dealing in sanctions-busting goods; they may be willing to risk a small fine but not jail. Such a change in law imposes no extra cost on the Government.

STRICTER CUSTOMS PROCEDURES

Countries that have imposed sanctions will want to tighten their own customs procedures in order to limit sanctions busting. For imports this will involve much closer scrutiny of goods that could be mis-labelled. *One step would be to require certificates of origin for goods subject to sanction. Such certificates would need to show country of production rather than port of embarkation.* This would make it more difficult to hide the origin of commodities like coal by trans-shipping them via intermediate ports.

The United States General Accounting Office noted that United States Customs' highest priorities are 'narcotics, fraud, controls on high-technology exports to the Soviet bloc, financial incidents and pornography'. United States Customs has not received additional resources to deal with South Africa and has not established an independent informer network.[1] By contrast, however, when the United States imposed sanctions against Cuba it increased the funding and staff of the Bureau of Customs.[2] The Dellums Bill, which passed the United States House of Representatives but not the Senate in 1988, called for the establishment of a 'Coordinator of South African Sanctions'.

Governments should create special customs units to deal with South African sanctions busting. Such units already exist to deal with drugs, transfer pricing and various other customs matters, The sanctions-enforcing unit could be small, but it is important that at least a few customs staff should have South Africa as their top priority.

Links would need to be established with South Africa's neighbours, who are often victims of the false identification of goods, so that a quick check could verify labelling. These countries would probably need assistance in setting up a verification system, but they would want to cooperate because false labelling is creating unfair competi-tion for their products.

Special attention would have to be paid to goods from free ports to ensure that they were not trans-shipped South African goods or, as in the case of coal, mixtures of South African and non-South African products. Customs officials would perhaps also need to conduct regular chemical checks on imported goods like coal, which are sometimes given false certificates of origin. Checks would also need to be made on oil, arms and other embargoed goods being sent to free ports to ensure that they were not trans-shipped to South Africa.

THE ROLE OF THE SECURITY SERVICES

The participation of intelligence and security services in the detection and prevention of sanctions busting would be essential. When the United States imposed sanctions against Cuba it enlisted all arms of government to enforce them – the Central Intelligence Agency (CIA), the State, Treasury and Commerce departments and embassies abroad. It was thus able to identify inadmissible trade and to bring political and other pressure to bear in order to stop it; the measures were also clearly successful in sharply curtailing Cuban trade with non-socialist countries. The CIA has played a central and publicly acknowledged role in enforcing the CoCom provisions.

Leaving the investigation of sanctions busting to under-funded non-government organizations would obviously be less effective and would indicate a lack of seriousness. The South Africans would take their cue from the degree of enforcement.

CONTROLLING SANCTIONED INPUTS

Consideration will need to be given to goods that are made from South African raw materials but satisfy normal rules of origin (typically 20 to 50 per cent local content). Clearly it cannot be acceptable for Turkey to import cheap steel billets from South Africa, roll them into simple products and then sell these items to countries that are boycotting South African iron and steel – even if the finished products qualify technically as having been 'made in Turkey'. At the very least such goods should not qualify for entry under special quotas, such as exist for textiles and steel. *It would be best to ban the import from third countries of goods that contain South African materials already subject to sanction.* Admittedly this ban would be difficult to enforce, and some exceptions would need to be made for South Africa's neighbours, but the United States' sanctions against Cuba have demonstrated that such rules can be made to work. The United States was anxious to prevent the sale of Cuban nickel, for example, so it required Governments and firms to ensure that there was no Cuban nickel in any stainless steel. Similar techniques were used to keep Rhodesian chromium out of stainless steel. It was such a nuisance for companies to separate Cuban from non-Cuban nickel and Rhodesian from non-Rhodesian chromium that they simply did not buy the embargoed goods. Both sanctions were highly effective.

COUNTERING OPPORTUNISM

We have shown that some countries have increased their trade with South Africa, reducing the effectiveness of sanctions. *One way to stop this is to take measures against countries that take advantage of sanctions imposed by other states.* The United States sanctions law has a specific provision under which 'the President is authorized to limit the importation into the United States of any product or service of a foreign country to the extent to which such foreign country benefits from, or otherwise takes commercial advantage of, any sanction'. So far the President has not acted. But press reports indicate that one reason for Japan's restraint in its trade with South Africa is fear that the United States will enforce this provision against it. Countries that have already taken measures should also adopt a provision like the United States one and should use it.

When one computer company expands to fill the gap left by another that has withdrawn from South Africa it is clearly taking advantage of an anti-apartheid action. Similarly when a country buys more South African coal or steel because of lower sanctions-induced prices, it is taking advantage of those sanctions. Where appropriate, action might be taken against individual companies, but in many cases, such as Turkey and steel or Spain and coal, it would only be sensible to take action against the country. This would smack of extra-territoriality and would worry some Governments, but such action should be considered in the light of the unfair advantage taken by certain countries. There is in international trade a long history of retaliation against countries that take unfair advantage, and this seems a clear case of that.

SOUTH AFRICAN-CONTROLLED COMPANIES

The issue of South African-controlled companies has become increasingly important, both because of their sanctions-busting potential and because they are subject to sanctions themselves. It is often very difficult to identify the true owners of a firm, however, because Luxembourg, Switzerland and many islands allow ownership to be concealed. Indeed, when the United States Congress wanted to require foreign investors to disclose their holdings if these represented more than 5 per cent of any United States business, British and other TNCs made such an outcry that the legislation was dropped.

We appreciate that it will be difficult to propose general regulations concerning the identification of foreign-owned firms; we argue, therefore, for regulations specific to South Africa. In particular, *national legislation should be passed to make it permissible, in a wide range of circumstances, to demand a declaration that a company is not ultimately owned, controlled or managed by a South African company or individuals. There should be large penalties for false declarations.* At the very least, such declarations would be required from firms seeking government contracts, grants, etc. They should also be required from firms working in sanctioned areas, such as computers, and could be required by local councils and other bodies that might want to refuse to deal with South African-controlled firms. This would not violate considerations of commercial confidentiality, corporate secrecy and so on because companies could continue to hide their true ownership; they would have to reveal South African links only if they wanted certain sorts of contract.

We have also noted the potential of South African-controlled companies for sanctions busting in the fields of technology transfer, finance and exports. One way to limit this would be to require that *all sanctions imposed on South Africa should also apply to South African-controlled companies.*

Ownership and 'control' need to be clearly defined. Anglo American has shown itself adept at controlling firms with as few as one third of the shares, or by means of long chains of shareholdings (often each involving a minority) or by holding smaller percentages of shares through several different intermediates. Thus the Commonwealth sanction on government contracts with 'majority-owned South African companies' is much too narrow.

United States law uses a variety of definitions of control that are helpful. The State Department describes control as 'authority to manage, direct or administer the affairs' of a firm. Other United States regulations declare that control is presumed in any of these cases: ownership of 25 per cent of the outstanding voting shares when no other person owns an equal or larger percentage; having a majority on the board of directors; operating the firm on a management contract; or having the right to appoint a majority of the board of directors or the firm's chief operating officer.[3] This sort of definition is clear and should be adopted in the context of sanctions.

Such a definition must also be applied to any chain of commercial interest: if A controls B and C, and together B and C control D, then

A controls D. This issue became very clear when Canadian and United States banks were involved in funding the Minorco take-over bid of Consolidated Gold Fields. Minorco is based in Luxembourg and is technically a European firm; furthermore, it was not directly 'majority-owned' by any single company because 39 per cent of its holdings were owned by one firm in the Anglo group, 21 per cent by another and 11 per cent by two others. The *ultimate* control and ownership of the firm were quite evident, however.

OTHER TNCS

Dealing with South African-controlled companies is difficult enough; dealing with other TNCs will be even harder. TNCs are probably the main channel for technology transfer, particularly to present and former subsidiaries in South Africa. There are also some financial transfers in the form of loans and internal trade credits (although, on balance, transfer pricing is probably taking money out of South Africa).

Swedish legislation concerning Swedish-based TNCs is very strict and is framed to ensure that Swedish regulations extend to Swedish-controlled firms outside Sweden. In particular a Swedish parent company has an obligation actively to supervise its subsidiaries' operations in order to prevent the infringement of sanctions legislation.

Different countries have different legal traditions, but they will all need to take special care to ensure that any regulations clearly apply to transactions that take place within a TNC.

23

INFLUENCING MARKET FORCES

Our model of incremental sanctions implies that some trade with South Africa will continue. Furthermore, sanctions cannot be watertight. Therefore other mechanisms should be developed that would lead companies to feel that it is in their own interest not to deal with apartheid even if they are legally allowed to do so. The concept of 'market forces' has gained renewed strength in recent years, and we believe that it is important to try to use market forces to reduce trade with South Africa.

There are two related issues. First, it should be in the commercial interest of firms not to trade with apartheid. Second, voters, consumers and workers should be able to use the marketplace to express their abhorrence of apartheid in a small but practical way and to reduce their personal connections with South Africa.

PUBLICIZING LINKS WITH SOUTH AFRICA

Consumer pressure can be enough to show firms that it is in their commercial interest not to deal with South Africa and is clearly behind the decision of many companies to withdraw from South Africa and of many banks to end loans to South Africa. Consumers can exert pressure, however, only if they are informed. Unfortunately, in some countries firms are allowed to conceal their South African ownership, the fact that they have South African subsidiaries or have been issued export licences to send goods to South Africa and similar information.

It seems perverse that companies should be allowed to hide behind claims of commercial confidentiality because they know that their local business would be hurt if consumers knew they had South

African links. Publicity is an important weapon. Many companies are clearly embarrassed about their continuing South African links and go to great lengths to hide them. In part they fear consumer reaction if these connections became known, and their executives are aware that they would be criticized by their friends if it were known that they were continuing to deal with the apartheid state. To allow market forces to operate, *it seems to us essential that the maximum amount of information about company links with South Africa must be published.*

The first step should be to give maximum publicity to violations of both voluntary and mandatory sanctions. A public statement by the Canadian Government criticizing a firm that made an investment in South Africa in spite of a voluntary ban seems to have discouraged other firms from making investments. By contrast, Britain's unwillingness to publicize violations of the voluntary tourism ban has been taken as a licence to continue promoting tours to the apartheid state.

The next step should be to publicize trade that does not yet violate sanctions, which would entail the publication of all permits, licences, waivers, etc., allowing trade with South Africa. This is already done in the Nordic states, but in other countries such permits are normally kept secret as a matter of general policy in relation to commercial confidentiality. We would argue that South Africa is a special case and that it should be made clear to firms, when they apply for licences or permits, that these will be published.

The importance of this measure should not be underestimated. Norway's oil-transport legislation allows ships to carry oil to South Africa in certain circumstances, but it requires that each case be reported to the Government and that some information in the report should become public. It was thought that shipping companies would take advantage of this loophole, but fear of publicity seems to have stopped them from doing so.

ENCOURAGING PEOPLE'S SANCTIONS

There should be stricter legislation requiring country-of-origin labels on agricultural and manufactured products. This would allow consumers to impose their own sanctions by refusing to buy. In the Nordic countries consumer boycotts were already reducing South African sales before the Government imposed more general sanctions.

Legislation clarifying the right of workers to refuse to handle South African goods is another avenue. In Finland trade unions were able to halt South African trade long before the Government imposed a ban, and the United States used dockworkers' unions to enforce its Cuba boycott (though in several countries such boycotts are illegal).

An especially important provision would be to permit local boycotts. In most countries there is a need for legislation clarifying the right of local councils, schools, public institutions and the like to refuse to use South African goods or to deal with firms active in South Africa.[1] In some circumstances public bodies must now accept lowest tenders even if these benefit the apartheid system. Waiving this requirement with respect to South Africa would allow local bodies to impose their own sanctions and to absorb the costs if they wished to do so.

Sweden introduced such legislation in 1985, before it imposed comprehensive sanctions. In introducing the legislation Foreign Trade Minister Mats Hellström noted, 'If it is to be possible for municipalities and county councils to participate in demonstrations of solidarity against apartheid in South Africa, then special legislation must be enacted.' He stressed, 'This is a special measure dictated by the unique conditions of South Africa'; hence it would not serve as a precedent for overriding basic principles enshrined in a wide variety of existing legislation.

COMMERCIAL AND FISCAL DISINCENTIVES

Governments can take actions that will encourage firms to reduce their dealings with South Africa without actually forcing them to stop. The reduction in trade credits proposed in Chapter 19 would do this. Another technique was proposed in the Dellums Bill, by which firms that were involved in the South African oil trade or had investments in South Africa would not be able to obtain oil or other mineral licences in the United States. This would have hit particularly the transnational oil companies, like Shell, that are active in South Africa. The intention was that firms would then respond to market pressures and decide whether their interests lay in the United States or in South Africa.

The decision by the Commonwealth (except Britain) to terminate double-taxation agreements is a similar technique designed to make South Africa less attractive to private business. It has proved less effective than expected because of provisions in the tax law of some countries, which continued to permit firms to claim a credit for taxes paid in South Africa. The United States recognized this problem, and the adoption of the so-called 'Rangel Amendment' on 1 January 1988 has meant that companies can no longer offset South African taxes against United States taxes due. It is estimated that United States firms are now paying one third more United States tax on their South African earnings, which makes South African investments much less attractive. In 1989 Mobil gave this as its main reason for withdrawing from South Africa.

To carry out the intent of the decision to end double-taxation agreements, *special legislation will be needed in some countries to ensure that companies may not offset or credit South African tax against tax due in another country.*

ACTION ON GOLD

Gold is so fundamental to the South African economy that some action should be taken. Jewellery would be a good place to start because it is normally made of newly mined gold and because jewellery gold is classified as 'non-monetary' gold and is listed in trade statistics. (By contrast, monetary gold is not listed in trade statistics, and much monetary gold was mined many years ago.) *We suggest, therefore, that when new gold jewellery is sold, the source of the gold should be identified.*

Ample non-South African supplies are available for jewellery – indeed, this measure might put a tiny price premium on non-South African gold. Because of the amount of gold in circulation and the stocks held by jewellers and dealers, as well as the fact that the trading network is not geared to identifying the source of gold, it would be reasonable to allow two or three years for the measure to take full effect.

This sanction would not have a financial impact on South Africa because it would not reduce the total demand for gold, but it would identify gold with apartheid in the public mind and would allow consumers to avoid jewellery made with South African gold. This, in turn, would raise the profile of the gold issue, leading to more discussion about a possible gold sanction against South Africa. Research is already under way that has suggested some promising routes to gold sanction; this should be pursued.

PART VI

SUMMARY AND CONCLUSIONS

24

PROPOSED ACTIONS

The Commonwealth Eminent Persons Group, Archbishop Hurley, and others whom we have quoted in this report use phrases like 'effective economic measures', 'much stronger pressure' and 'pressure that will cause real discomfort'. What is common is the demand for measures that will have a direct economic and political impact on South Africa rather than mere token measures that express continued displeasure with apartheid and repression.

There is a realization that continued opposition by some Governments means that comprehensive, mandatory sanctions cannot be put into place in the near future. On the other hand, the 1990–91 window of opportunity calls for rapid action. Thus the need is for a package of measures that would be effective and, if it were imposed quickly by many Governments acting individually or in groups, would exert the required pressure to propel Pretoria into genuine negotiations.

THE TOP PRIORITY:
SANCTIONS MUST REFLECT COMMITMENT

It is clear from our analysis that sanctions will not be effective if they are imposed piecemeal over decades. It is also clear that the white minority sees the slow and reluctant imposition of sanctions as *de facto* support for the reformulation of apartheid and continued white rule.

An energetic sanctions effort is needed in the next two years, when South Africa will be most vulnerable. This should be an essential part of diplomatic efforts in the region, not an alternative to them. It would create a larger lobby for negotiations and would mean that

Pretoria would be forced to negotiate an end to apartheid rather than use false negotiations to prolong it.

Therefore we believe that the following measure should be an essential part of the diplomatic effort and the starting point of the whole process:

1. Governments must make a public commitment to a steady reduction in trade with South Africa, setting a date to end trade with the apartheid state if no progress is made towards a negotiated settlement.

This would give notice to the apartheid regime and to businesspeople and others within South Africa. It would also give ample warning to businesses within states that impose sanctions of the need to find new markets and new sources of raw materials.

Progress towards a negotiated settlement should be measured against the five steps in the Commonwealth Accord on Southern Africa, agreed at Nassau (see Chapter 2 and Appendix 2). If Pretoria were to agree to these five steps, no new sanctions would be imposed while genuine negotiations continued; this would be a strong incentive to remain at the conference table once talks had started. Existing sanctions should not be lifted, however, until a negotiated settlement, acceptable to all parties, is reached.

The public commitment to end trade need not be enshrined in law, but it must be firmly stated government policy backed up by a programme of ever tighter sanctions. We would hope that Governments would set a date to end trade no more than five years from now – that is, by 1994 – if no progress is made towards dismantling apartheid.

TOWARDS REDUCING SOUTH AFRICA'S INCOME

Our investigation has made clear that it is absolutely essential to reduce South Africa's income sharply. This means a large reduction in export earnings and an end to remaining loans. As we have stressed in this report, we have targeted for initial actions a practical set of commodities that excludes the precious and strategic metals that many countries would have difficulty in banning initially.

Most sanctions entail some cost to countries imposing them, so it makes sense to start with the least expensive ones and with those sanctions that are easiest to enforce. Historically it has proved easier to sanction a country's exports than its imports. Therefore the first target must be South African bulk exports for which there are many other suppliers. Of these there are two main categories:

2. *The importation of all South African agricultural products should be banned. 'Agriculture' should follow the GATT definition and should include everything that grows.*

3. *The importation of all non-strategic South African minerals should be banned. These would include coal, base metals (copper, lead, tin, zinc, aluminium and nickel), iron ore, uranium and non-metallic minerals.*

Ferro-alloys and steel additives, as well as andalusite, could be exempted.

Similarly there is no reason to import any South African manufactured goods, including clothing, chemicals, petroleum products, furniture, etc.

4. *The importation of all South African manufactured goods should be prohibited. 'Manufactures' should follow the GATT definition and include chemicals and steel.*

Many countries, among them the Commonwealth and the USA, already ban some of these products, including edible agricultural products, coal, uranium and steel. In their case this proposal should be seen as a widening of existing measures. For some European and Asian countries, however, these will be significant new sanctions.

We do not propose a ban on South African precious metals at this time, but it is important not to increase artificially either their consumption or their price.

5. *The production and sale of all platinum coins and small bars for investors should be prohibited.*

Where Governments have already produced platinum coins for collectors they should offer to buy them back but otherwise ban their trade.

The purpose of most economic sanctions is to reduce the amount of money available to the apartheid state. Bans on loans and investment have the same goal. Most Governments restrict investment and longer-term loans. This leaves trade credits as the major remaining source of foreign funds.

6. *Trade credits for sales to South Africa, including both buyers' and suppliers' credits, should be phased out over three to five years. Any remaining guarantees and insurance should be ended immediately.*

Although the main goal of this sanction is to cut the flow of funds to the apartheid state, ending trade credits will also have the effect of discouraging trade with South Africa. This is in keeping with our first recommendation. The phasing out will reflect the commitment to end trade within a given period of time.

In the rest of this summary we make a number of additional recommendations for action. They cannot be seen as alternatives to our first six. *We stress that an effective sanctions package must include our first six recommendations.* Without them any other actions would simply be tinkering with existing measures and would not have the necessary political impact.

TIGHTENING THE ARMS AND OIL EMBARGOES

We do not call for large-scale new bans on sales to South Africa at this time. These would be more costly to the countries imposing sanctions, and more difficult to enforce, than bans on purchases from South Africa. However, it is essential to tighten the existing bans on sales to South Africa, which cover arms, computers and oil.

7. *The United Nations mandatory arms embargo should be interpreted broadly to include any goods that could be converted into arms or used either for arms production or to maintain and intensify repression.*

The first step would be to follow the Canadian lead and ban the sale to South Africa of all items on the export-control list.

8. *South Africa should not be allowed to purchase any 'dual-use' equipment that has possible military applications and of which the sale to any other country is already banned.*

Most countries have some restrictions on the sale of computers to the military, police and/or apartheid-enforcing agencies. Unfortunately, such bans are meaningless because telephone linkages and the networking of computers make it possible for the Government and for military contractors to use virtually any modern computer in South Africa. Therefore we recommend that Governments follow Canada's example and impose a blanket ban.

9. *The sale of all computers, software and electronic and telecommunications equipment to South Africa should be banned.*

The oil embargo, as imposed by some countries, contains a number of loopholes that should be closed.

10. *The oil embargo should include refined oil products. Oil producers should require discharge certificates for all oil. Ports and transit facilities should not be allowed to handle oil for South Africa.*

The Commonwealth Committee of Foreign Ministers on Southern Africa has already accepted a proposal contained in our interim report:

11. *Technology transfer that is designed to enable South Africa to circumvent existing sanctions, particularly in the area of arms, oil and computers, should be prohibited.*

In the case of oil this would mean a ban on the sale of technology, equipment, licences, etc., to South Africa for oil and gas exploration, production, delivery and conversion into other liquid fuels. A specific measure would be contingent on this ban on technology transfer:

12. *There should be a voluntary ban on recruitment for, and dispatch of skilled people to, South Africa to take part in any activity that would help South Africa circumvent any sanction.*

This would necessarily include a ban on recruitment advertising and on the seconding of staff to South Africa for activities that would help circumvent sanctions.

One of the biggest loopholes in the arms and computer bans, even in some countries with rigorous restrictions, is that banned items can be purchased by a third party and incorporated in equipment that is then sent on to South Africa.

13. *Tighter restrictions should be imposed on the re-export to South Africa of strategic goods and technology, either directly or included in other products.*

CARS, COMPUTERS AND JOB CREATION

Although we are not calling for an immediate end to all sales to South Africa, we have identified two sanctions that would have a marked political effect. These have been identified particularly for those countries that are concerned that sanctions will harm the black majority; both will create jobs for black people while adversely affecting the white minority.

14. *The sale of all vehicles and vehicle kits and parts to South Africa should be banned.*

In order to allow some old-fashioned cars to be built locally, and thus to protect jobs in the car industry, this measure would be phased in over two or three years.

We have already called for a ban on the sale of computers on military grounds. The ban is also important as part of an effort to halt computers for automation and hence to stem job losses.

15. *Strict controls should be placed on the export and re-export to South Africa of microprocessors, dynamic random access memories, and computer numerical control devices.*

SPREADING THE NET

As tougher sanctions are imposed by a growing number of countries, it will become increasingly important to close off ways of bypassing those sanctions. Both South African companies and companies of sanctions-imposing countries are a burgeoning sanctions-busting conduit.

16. *All sanctions imposed on South Africa should also apply to South African-controlled companies.*

Because of their potential for sanctions busting, South African-controlled companies should not be permitted to be involved in areas subject to sanctions, such as arms, computers and oil. Similarly bans on loans and investment should apply to South African-controlled companies as well as to South Africa itself. Limits should be imposed not just on 'majority-owned' South African companies but also on the much larger group companies controlled from South Africa.

In countries where ultimate ownership and control are not always public, extending sanctions to South African-controlled companies would require regulations that made permissible the demand for a declaration that a company is not controlled from South Africa. There should be a substantial penalty for false declarations.

It seems shortsighted for a country to impose a sanction but still allow companies to deal in the sanctioned product in third countries or on the high seas. This has become an important loophole in sanctions regulations.

17. *Governments should ensure that their nationals and companies do not transport or trade in sanctioned goods anywhere in the world.*

In particular this would mean that if a country supported the oil embargo, then shipping companies registered in that country could not carry oil to South Africa. Similarly if a country banned the import of South African coal and steel, then nationals and companies of that country could not trade in South African coal and steel anywhere in the world.

As sanctions become tighter and more sophisticated, so it will become more important for South Africa to break sanctions. Thus better enforcement will become more urgent. Because customs officials have so many duties, it is important that one person or a small group should have South African sanctions as a priority. Furthermore, penalties for sanctions busting should be sufficiently punitive to dissuade companies and individuals from incurring them.

18. *Special sanctions-enforcement units should be established. The penalties for South African sanctions busting should be increased to include possible jail sentences.*

The Commonwealth might wish to establish a small unit to assist cooperation over South African sanctions enforcement between member-state customs agencies.

Some countries will inevitably take advantage of sanctions imposed by others. This abuse cannot be prevented, but it can be reduced.

19. *Action should be taken against countries and companies that take commercial advantage of sanctions that have been imposed against South Africa.*

A MORE INTENSIFIED APPLICATION OF SANCTIONS

Some existing sanctions are in danger of being relaxed, have still not been imposed by a few countries or have had less impact than was intended. Financial sanctions have been particularly effective and will play a central role in creating the economic window of opportunity in 1990–91, so it is essential that Pretoria should have no access to new funds.

20. *All countries should prohibit all new loans to, and investment of any sort in, South Africa.*

For some countries this would mean making voluntary bans compulsory. Many others would need to tighten the terms of their investment bans.

The rescheduling of South Africa's debt is probably inevitable, but this must be used to extract political concessions. Banks have commercial priorities and will be more concerned with repayment and interest rates than with political gains, so Governments will need to force the banks to take apartheid into account.

21. *Banks with loans subject to the South African freeze should not be permitted to reschedule those loans for more than one year unless Pretoria accepts the five steps set out in the Commonwealth Accord on Southern Africa, adopted at Nassau.*

Banks should also be pressed by Governments to put political pressure on Pretoria as part of annual rescheduling negotiations.

Some double-taxation agreements have already been rescinded in order to make South Africa less attractive for business. This measure has not always been effective, and special legislation or regulations may be needed.

22. *Companies should not be allowed to offset or credit South African tax against tax due elsewhere.*

Cutting air links with South Africa has had an important psychological impact on white South Africans.

23. *The ban on air links with South Africa should be extended to all states other than those in the SADCC region.*

Since the Expert Study Group proposes a steady reduction of trade with South Africa rather than an immediate ban, and because sanctions enforcement cannot be watertight, it is important to influence market forces so that businesses discover that it is in their own interests to reduce their dealings with apartheid.

24. *Maximum publicity should be given to all continued economic links with South Africa. This includes the publication of all violations of voluntary bans, as well as of all permits and exemptions which allow dealing with South Africa.*

Because of the importance of the arms and oil embargoes and because a number of countries still violate these long-standing sanctions, more should be done to expose violators.

25. *Governments should publicly identify companies and countries that help to break the oil and arms embargoes. Consumer boycotts and people's sanctions against perpetrators should be encouraged.*

In many countries traditional laws and practices limit the ability of workers, trade unions, local councils and other bodies to boycott South African goods and South African-linked firms. These principles need not be breached in general, but it is important to recognize South Africa as a special case.

26. *Where existing law would prohibit such action, special laws or regulations should be approved to permit workers to refuse to handle South African goods and to permit councils and other local bodies to boycott South African goods and South African-linked firms.*

PREPARING FOR THE NEXT PHASE

Our targeted programme of sanctions includes only some of South Africa's trade. We hope that this will be sufficient, but, in keeping with the commitment to end trade if Pretoria fails to begin genuine negotiations, it is essential to prepare now for further sanctions. We identify three areas where more study will be needed to develop effective sanctions.

Gold is South Africa's most important export, but there are a number of difficulties that lead us to not include it in the first targeted package. However, recent research suggests that a practical gold sanction could be developed. We feel that it is important to raise gold as an issue and to put a gold sanction on the agenda.

27. Investigations into the possibility of a sanction against gold should be expanded. New gold jewellery should identify the source of the gold as a way of publicizing the issue of South African gold.

Tighter control will be needed over products that may contain sanctioned South African goods, such as steel and agricultural products.

28. Legislation should be developed to ensure that goods from third countries do not contain significant amounts of inputs from South Africa that are subject to sanctions.

This might involve changes in certificate-of-origin legislation.

Although the use of existing export-control lists is a good start in tightening the arms embargo, such lists do not include oil technology or some of the lower-level military technology that South Africa needs. Furthermore, export-control lists restrict only hardware, not licences and the movement of people, which are both important for technology transfer.

29. National bans should be developed to prohibit the transfer of strategic goods and technology to South Africa.

Such legislation would be independent of, or would expand on, export-control lists. Developing such regulations would require the identification of technologies needed by South Africa to break the arms, oil and computer bans. More detailed study is needed of how to ban licences, the movement of personnel and so on.

The Expert Study Group was given wide terms of reference, which meant that it looked at many areas. It has produced a list of twenty-nine recommendations, but it is anxious that this is not seen as a menu from which a few items may be chosen. *Recommendations are listed in order of priority. The first six must be accepted if the package is to be effective.*

The remaining recommendations try to close the gaps in present sanctions and would play an important role in tightening and intensifying the existing measures; they also look forward to a second phase of sanctions. They would be effective, however, only if accompanied by the widening of sanctions called for in the first six recommendations.

If enough countries adopted this proposed package, it would have a considerable economic, psychological and political impact on South Africa. Sanctions would help to create a much larger constituency pressing for genuine negotiation and should push Pretoria to the conference table.

The Commonwealth can take the lead, not only through practical example but also by putting pressure on other countries to impose similar sanctions. Therefore we make one final recommendation.

30. *After they have set an example by imposing wider and tighter sanctions against South Africa, Commonwealth states should launch a major diplomatic effort to encourage other industrialized countries to adopt similar measures.*

25

SANCTIONS ARE A LIFE-AND-DEATH ISSUE

It is twenty-nine years since the Nobel Prize winner Chief Albert Luthuli first called for economic sanctions. At that time he said: 'The economic boycott of South Africa will entail undoubted hardship for Africans. We do not doubt that. But if it is a method which shortens the day of bloodshed, the suffering to us will be a price we are willing to pay. In any case, we suffer already. Our children are undernourished, and on a small scale (so far) we die at the whim of a policeman.'

There are those who still say that the way to end apartheid is through increased trade and investment and by using moral suasion to try to influence the white leaders of South Africa. After three decades of pursuing that policy a new generation of children is undernourished, death at the whim of the police is no longer on a small scale and suffering has increased manyfold. Those who oppose sanctions are effectively arguing that South Africa should be treated differently from Argentina, Libya and other countries against which sanctions have been imposed. They are arguing that a policy that has allowed so much suffering for three decades should be allowed to continue.

The mood in southern Africa *is* changing, however, and there is new international potential for negotiation. At the same time there is ferment among the white minority and a growing constituency for negotiation. These developments offer an opportunity that should not be ignored. Neither should it be exaggerated. The white leadership has not changed its goal of maintaining white hegemony. Little progress has been made on any of the five steps set out in the Commonwealth Accord on Southern Africa. Pretoria still looks to a false negotiation as a means of maintaining and restructuring apartheid rather than to a genuine negotiation to end apartheid.

Sanctions are the way to force Pretoria to enter into genuine negotiations. Sanctions are necessary to take advantage of the opportunity now available. *Sanctions are an essential part of negotiations, not an alternative to negotiation.*

In 1986 the EPG concluded that the South African Government was 'in truth not yet prepared to negotiate fundamental change'. In an open letter to Christians in Britain seventeen southern African bishops confirmed that the position has only worsened since the EPG mission. The bishops wrote:

> We believe that it is not enough to condemn the racist policies of the South African regime. Words, alone, will not deter the South African Government from the pursuit of its repressive and undemocratic policies. In a situation of civil war, drastic strategies for peace are necessary. Do not be deceived by certain changes which have been made in South Africa. The constitution is fundamentally racist. The Government continues to 'rule by clampdown' and detentions. There is no meaningful freedom of speech nor opportunity for effective peaceful protest and democratic political organization. The family life of countless blacks has been shattered and communities continue to be uprooted. The situation is an affront to humanity. Much greater pressure is needed from the outside world to pull us back from ever-worsening conflict and war.[1]

The message is resounding and clear from those black leaders inside South Africa who are still free to speak out. 'The question of mandatory and comprehensive sanctions against the South African apartheid system has become a life-and-death issue, so as to reduce the number of fatalities in this struggle to end apartheid,' declared Frank Chikane, General Secretary of the South African Council of Churches.

Existing measures against South Africa have had an impact, albeit a limited one. They played a key role in forcing South Africa to negotiate over withdrawal from Angola and Namibian independence. Increasingly, white businesspeople are saying that political change is the only way to avoid further sanctions.

The Expert Study Group believes strongly that a practical sanctions package, excluding controversial items such as gold and ferro-alloys, could be effective in forcing Pretoria to the conference table – but only if it is imposed quickly. Because of the urgency, it makes sense for individual countries and groups of countries to impose their own sanctions packages. This will create a momentum, as happened in 1985–6, resulting in a wave of sanctions. The wave would amplify the economic crisis anticipated in South Africa in 1990 and 1991 because of a debt bulge and lower gold prices. Many white people, especially those in the business community, would finally realize that it is just too expensive to maintain apartheid.

A storm looms on the horizon. Will apartheid be helped to ride out that storm? People are waiting to see what the foreign opponents of apartheid will do. Inside South Africa the white minority wonders if the international community will allow it to continue with repressive reform. The international banks are asking if the pressure will be lifted, making it safe for them to grant new loans. The TNCs that have remained in South Africa are asking themselves if the worst is over and whether profitability will return with an easing of sanctions. Pretoria's international allies want to know if their shoring up of apartheid will continue to be profitable. And the majority wonders whether Chief Luthuli's call for an economic boycott of South Africa will be ignored for another thirty years.

We wish to underline the urgency of this matter. We have tried to determine what action would be an effective support for genuine negotiation, and we conclude that it will require a significant and immediate increase in pressure but one that is within the reach of the Governments of the industrialized world – given the political will to contribute to the ending of apartheid.

The package we propose involves a significant widening and tightening of existing sanctions, and it entails some cost. The cost is small, however, compared with that being paid by the people of South Africa, and it is also small by comparison with that of the much larger sanctions package that would be needed later to have the same impact.

If this opportunity is missed, the limited sanctions package proposed here may not be sufficient. If Governments merely tinker with existing sanctions, or if new measures are imposed only after 1991, then the white minority will feel, justifiably, that it is being protected from sanctions. It will conclude that no fundamental change is needed.

For the white minority negotiating fundamental change and giving up a monopoly on power will be a long, difficult and worrying process. It is a road that will be taken only when it is the only one available. Sanctions are essential to demonstrate that the option of reforming apartheid is too expensive and is internationally unacceptable. Sanctions are necessary to push Pretoria down the demanding path to genuine negotiation.

We can only restate the question asked by the EPG: 'Is the Commonwealth to stand by and allow the cycle of violence to spiral? Or will it take concerted action of an effective kind? Such action may offer the last opportunity to avert what could be the worst bloodbath since the Second World War.'[2]

APPENDICES

APPENDIX 1

THE EXPERT STUDY AND ITS TERMS OF REFERENCE

THE EXPERT STUDY GROUP

At their meeting in Vancouver in October 1987 Commonwealth Heads of Government (with the exception of Britain) agreed to 'evaluate on a continuous basis the application of sanctions in order to assess their impact' under the Okanagan Statement and Programme of Action (see Appendix 5). At its first meeting in Lusaka in February 1988 the Commonwealth Committee of Foreign Ministers on Southern Africa, established at Vancouver to provide high-level impetus and guidance in furtherance of the Okanagan Statement's objectives, approved the terms of reference of a study and requested the Commonwealth Secretary-General to arrange for it.

The Commonwealth Secretary-General accordingly commissioned an Independent Expert Study on the Evaluation of the Application and Impact of Sanctions Against South Africa. A group of nine people, with expertise in various areas of sanctions, was formed. Dr Joseph Hanlon was appointed coordinator. In addition, twelve other researchers and institutions contributed to the work of the group.

The members of the Expert Study Group are as follows.

DR JOSEPH HANLON, the study coordinator, is a writer on southern Africa. He is the author of two books on Mozambique, *Mozambique: The Revolution Under Fire* (1984) and *Mozambique: Who Calls the Shots?* (forthcoming); two books on destabilization, *Apartheid's Second Front* and *Beggar Your Neighbours* (both 1986); a study of sanctions, *The Sanctions Handbook*, with Roger Omond (1987); and two Economist Intelligence Unit Special Reports on SADCC (1984 and 1989).

DR MARTIN BAILEY is a reporter for the London *Observer*. He has been a consultant to the United Nations on sanctions against South Africa and is the author of *Oilgate: The Sanctions Scandal* on the Rhodesia oil embargo.

MS JOANNA CHATAWAY is a researcher at the Open University, having received an M.Phil. from the Institute of Development Studies. Her main areas of research include technology choice and transfer.

MR AURET VAN HEERDEN is a founder member of the Community Resource and Information Centre (CRIC), Johannesburg. At CRIC he did research and leadership training on behalf of trade unions, including a study on economic and employment conditions related to sanctions. Currently he is with the Equal Rights Commission of the International Labour Organization.

MR RICHARD MOORSOM is a research fellow at the Chr. Michelsen Institute, Bergen, Norway, and has written extensively on economic issues concerning southern Africa, including a series of Catholic Institute for International Relations publications: *The Scope for Sanctions, Namibia: Transforming a Wasted Land* and *Namibia: Exploiting the Sea*.

MR PETER ROBBINS has been a dealer in base and precious metals for more than twenty years. He is the founder of the Minor Metals Traders Association and author of several books on metals markets. He has been a consultant to the United Nations on metals marketing and is the chairman of the World Gold Commission.

DRS PETER SLUITER is a political scientist with long experience of research and lobbying on sanctions against South Africa. He currently coordinates the South Africa desk of the Association of West European Parliamentarians for Actions Against Apartheid (AWEPAA).

MR COLIN STONEMAN is an economist at the Centre for Southern African Studies at the University of York. He has worked on the SADCC region for more than a decade and is author of *Zimbabwe's Inheritance* (1981) and *Zimbabwe's Prospects* (1988).

DR NICOLA SWAINSON is a political economist who has done research and teaching at universities in Africa, North America and

New Zealand. During part of this study she was southern Africa desk officer at the Catholic Institute for International Relations.

Additional research was done by:

Mr George Crown	Dr Tom Lodge
Ms Sandra Ferguson	Dr Tessa Marcus
Dr Paul Goodison	Dr Donna Rich
Dr Tom Hewitt	Ms Kate Targett
Ms Ruth Jacobson	Mr Jon Walters
Ms Jodie Lewis	Mr Jaap Woldendorp

The Catholic Institute for International Relations.

The Secretary-General also constituted an Advisory Group to assist the Expert Study Group in the preparation of the study. It met twice in London, in July 1988 and March 1989, to offer advice and comment. The Advisory Group's members were:

Dr Martin Bailey[1]
Ms Phyllis Johnson
Mr David Martin
Mr Moloetsi Mbeki
Mr Richard Moorsom
Mr Vella Pillay
Mr Colin Stoneman[2]
Mr Bernard Wood[1]

The Experts began their work in April 1988 and submitted an interim report to the CFMSA meeting in Toronto in August 1988. They completed their report in May 1989.

Responsibility for the contents of the study rests with the Expert Study Group.

TERMS OF REFERENCE FOR A STUDY ARISING FROM THE OKANAGAN STATEMENT (PARAGRAPHS 7–11)

Introduction

With the exception of Britain, Commonwealth Heads of Government at their Vancouver meeting agreed that economic and other sanctions have had a significant impact on South Africa and that their wider,

[1] Were able to attend only the first meeting.
[2] Participated in the second meeting only.

tighter and more intensified application must remain a part of the international community's response to apartheid. In this context, they agreed to evaluate on a continuous basis the application of sanctions in order to assess their impact; and also committed themselves to continuing efforts to secure a more concerted application of a global sanctions programme.

2. In order to assist in the fulfilment of the above decisions of the Heads of Government, the study will review the scope of the existing sanctions by the Commonwealth and non-Commonwealth governments, voluntary bodies and private sector, examine their implementation and evaluate their impact not only in economic terms but also in terms of the morale of the Pretoria regime and the political processes in South Africa.

3. The study will also identify efforts to frustrate sanctions and the manner and the extent to which the impact of sanctions is weakened as a result. In examining what action can be taken to strengthen the impact of sanctions, it will consider the scope for further concerted efforts by the Commonwealth and the wider world.

Possible Outline of Study

4. The areas of enquiry for the study may be set out as follows:

A.   Review of Current Sanctions

Scope and legal status of sanctions adopted by country or group of countries, by major category of sanctions; the status of various United Nations measures (mandatory or non-mandatory) and their implementation; measures by voluntary groups and the private sector; dates of adoption and implementation; monitoring mechanisms and provisions of penalties against offenders.

B.   Efforts to Frustrate Sanctions

Efforts by South Africa to frustrate sanctions by category of measures; the role of governments, organisations and groups outside South Africa in frustrating sanctions; South Africa's policies towards its neighbours in frustrating sanctions.

C. Strengthening Existing Measures

Scope for making existing measures more effective through a wider, tighter and more intensified application:

(i)   Economic Impact of Sanctions
      Impact on credit and investment flows to South Africa; on the cost and supply of oil; on exports and imports in terms of volume and unit values. Economy wide impact in terms of capital formation; access to technology; employment and growth of GDP; and on the confidence of the business community.

(ii) Impact on Military Capability
      Impact on access to security/military related technology and on the availability of armaments; on the military capability of South Africa.

(iii) Political Impact
      Impact on the Pretoria regime and its willingness to negotiate, on the political perceptions of the business community and on the White electorate in general. Impact in terms of South Africa's isolation in the international community and its ability to conduct external relations.

D. Areas of Vulnerability

Areas, economic or otherwise, in which South Africa is particularly vulnerable to sanctions. Measures that will have a significant impact when applied (a) concertedly or (b) bilaterally. A prioritisation of possible measures.

E. Possible Further Action

Possible further action given South Africa's vulnerability in particular areas.

Time-frame and Modalities

5.   An initial study concluded within a period of, say, not more than six months could be followed up by updating and extending the enquiry to further areas, as the situation evolves, at periodic intervals.

The Secretary-General in consultation with the Chairman will arrange for the study to be undertaken in a manner that would *inter alia* permit the issue of interim reports or segments of the Study to members of the Committee from time to time.

Commonwealth Secretariat
Mulungushi Conference Hall
Lusaka

2 February 1988

APPENDIX 2

THE COMMONWEALTH ACCORD ON SOUTHERN AFRICA

1. We consider that South Africa's continuing refusal to dismantle apartheid, its illegal occupation of Namibia, and its aggression against its neighbours constitute a serious challenge to the values and principles of the Commonwealth, a challenge which Commonwealth countries cannot ignore. At New Delhi we expressed the view that 'only the eradication of apartheid and the establishment of majority rule on the basis of free and fair exercise of universal adult suffrage by all the people in a united and non-fragmented South Africa can lead to a just and lasting solution of the explosive situation prevailing in Southern Africa.' We are united in the belief that reliance on the range of pressures adopted so far has not resulted in the fundamental changes we have sought over many years. The growing crisis and intensified repression in South Africa mean that apartheid must be dismantled now if a greater tragedy is to be averted and that concerted pressure must be brought to bear to achieve that end. We consider that the situation calls for urgent practical steps.

2. We, therefore, call on the authorities in Pretoria for the following steps to be taken in a genuine manner and as a matter of urgency:

(a) Declare that the system of apartheid will be dismantled and specific and meaningful action taken in fulfilment of that intent.
(b) Terminate the existing state of emergency.
(c) Release immediately and unconditionally Nelson Mandela and all others imprisoned and detained for their opposition to apartheid.
(d) Establish political freedom and specifically lift the existing ban on the African National Congress and other political parties.

(e)   Initiate, in the context of a suspension of violence on all sides, a
      process of dialogue across lines of colour, politics and religion,
      with a view to establishing a non-racial and representative
      government.

3.   We have agreed on a number of measures which have as their
rationale impressing on the authorities in Pretoria the compelling
urgency of dismantling apartheid and erecting the structures of
democracy in South Africa. The latter, in particular, demands a
process of dialogue involving the true representatives of the majority
black population of South Africa. We believe that we must do all we
can to assist that process, while recognising that the forms of
political settlement in South Africa are for the people of that country
– all the people – to determine.

4.   To this end, we have decided to establish a small group of
eminent Commonwealth persons to encourage through all practicable
ways the evolution of that necessary process of political dialogue.
We are not unmindful of the difficulties such an effort will encounter,
including the possibility of initial rejection by the South African
authorities, but we believe it to be our duty to leave nothing undone
that might contribute to peaceful change in South Africa and avoid
the dreadful prospect of violent conflict that looms over South
Africa, threatening people of all races in the country, and the peace
and stability of the entire Southern Africa region.

5.   We are asking the President of Zambia and the Prime Ministers
of Australia, The Bahamas, Canada, India, the United Kingdom and
Zimbabwe to develop with the Secretary-General the modalities of
this effort to assist the process of political dialogue in South Africa.
We would look to the group of eminent persons to seek to facilitate
the processes of dialogue referred to in paragraph 2(e) above and by
all practicable means to advance the fulfilment of the objectives of
this Accord.

6.   For our part, we have, as an earnest of our opposition to
apartheid, reached accord on a programme of common action as follows:

(i)   We declare the Commonwealth's support for the strictest en-
      forcement of the mandatory arms embargo against South
      Africa, in accordance with United Nations Security Council

Resolutions 418 and 558, and commit ourselves to prosecute violators to the fullest extent of the law.

(ii) We reaffirm the Gleneagles Declaration of 1977, which called upon Commonwealth members to take every practical step to discourage sporting contacts with South Africa.

(iii) We agree upon, and commend to other governments, the adoption of the following further economic measures against South Africa, which have already been adopted by a number of member countries:

(a) a ban on all new government loans to the Government of South Africa and its agencies;

(b) a readiness to take unilaterally what action may be possible to preclude the import of Krugerrands;

(c) no Government funding for trade missions to South Africa or for participation in exhibitions and trade fairs in South Africa;

(d) a ban on the sale and export of computer equipment capable of use by South African military forces, police or security forces;

(e) a ban on new contracts for the sale and export of nuclear goods, materials and technology to South Africa;

(f) a ban on the sale and export of oil to South Africa;

(g) a strict and rigorously controlled embargo on imports of arms, ammunition, military vehicles and paramilitary equipment from South Africa;

(h) an embargo on all military co-operation with South Africa; and

(i) discouragement of all cultural and scientific events except where these contribute towards the ending of apartheid or have no possible role in promoting it.

7. It is our hope that the process and measures we have agreed upon will help to bring about concrete progress towards the objectives stated above in six months. The Heads of Government mentioned in paragraph 5 above, or their representatives, will then meet to review the situation. If in their opinion adequate progress has not been made within this period, we agree to consider the adoption of further measures. Some of us would, in that event, consider the following steps among others:

(a) a ban on air links with South Africa;

(b)   a ban on new investment or reinvestment of profits earned in
      South Africa;
(c)   a ban on the import of agricultural products from South Africa;
(d)   the termination of double taxation agreements with South
      Africa;
(e)   the termination of all government assistance to investment in,
      and trade with, South Africa;
(f)   a ban on all government procurement in South Africa;
(g)   a ban on government contracts with majority-owned South
      African companies;
(h)   a ban on the promotion of tourism to South Africa.

8.   Finally, we agree that should all of the above measures fail
to produce the desired results within a reasonable period, further
effective measures will have to be considered. Many of us have either
taken or are prepared to take measures which go beyond those listed
above, and each of us will pursue the objectives of this Accord in all
the ways and through all appropriate fora open to us. We believe,
however, that in pursuing this programme jointly, we enlarge the
prospects of an orderly transition to social, economic and political
justice in South Africa and peace and stability in the Southern Africa
region as a whole.

Lyford Cay, Nassau
20 October 1985

APPENDIX 3

COMMONWEALTH HEADS OF GOVERNMENT REVIEW MEETING, LONDON, 3–5 AUGUST 1986 COMMUNIQUÉ

1. As agreed at Nassau last October, our Meeting was held in the special context of the crisis in Southern Africa. At the outset of our discussions we specifically reaffirmed our commitment to the Commonwealth Accord on Southern Africa which, with our other colleagues, we had concluded at Nassau. We reaffirmed, in particular, the united belief we expressed in the Accord that 'apartheid must be dismantled now if a greater tragedy is to be averted, and that concerted pressure must be brought to bear to achieve that end'.

2. At our request the Co-Chairmen of the Commonwealth Group of Eminent Persons (EPG), General Olusegun Obasanjo and Mr Malcolm Fraser, introduced the report of the EPG and answered the many questions we put to them. Sir Geoffrey Howe, the British Foreign Secretary, who undertook a mission to Southern Africa in his capacity as President of the Council of Ministers of the EEC, also briefed us on the results of his mission.

3. The Report of the EPG, Mission to South Africa, was the central document at our discussions. That unanimous Report has commanded attention worldwide as pointing the way forward for South Africa and for the world in relation to South Africa. We warmly commend the Group's work which has made a positive and enduring contribution to the efforts to end apartheid and establish a non-racial and representative government in South Africa. We particularly commend the EPG's 'negotiating concept' and deeply regret its rejection by the South African Government.

4.   At Nassau, the Commonwealth unanimously adopted a common programme of action which included a number of economic measures against South Africa. It was our collective hope that those measures and the efforts of the EPG to promote a process of dialogue in South Africa would, within six months, bring about concrete progress towards our objectives of seeing apartheid dismantled and the structures of democracy erected in South Africa.

5.   As envisaged in the Accord, we have reviewed the situation. We are profoundly disappointed that the authorities in Pretoria have taken none of the five steps which at Nassau we called on them to take 'in a genuine manner and as a matter of urgency'. Nelson Mandela and other political leaders remain in prison. A new and more widely repressive emergency has been imposed and political freedom more rigorously curtailed; the ANC and other political parties are still banned. Beyond these, however, it has been a matter of deep concern to us that the EPG after its most patient efforts has been forced to conclude that 'at present there is no genuine intention on the part of the South African Government to dismantle apartheid' and 'no present prospect of a process of dialogue leading to the establishment of a non-racial and representative government'. We had looked at Nassau for the initiation by Pretoria of a process of dialogue in the context of a suspension of violence on all sides. Instead, as the EPG found, the cycle of violence and counter-violence has spiralled.

6.   We receive the Group's findings with disappointment, and deplore the conduct of the South African Government whose actions, including the raids on neighbouring countries at a crucial moment of the EPG's work, terminated its efforts for peaceful change. We continue to believe with the EPG that the cycle of violence in South Africa must end. It is clearly established that the situation in South Africa constitutes a serious threat to regional peace and security.

7.   It is thus clear to us that since our meeting in Nassau there has not been the adequate concrete progress that we looked for there. Indeed, the situation has deteriorated.

8.   Accordingly, in the light of our review and of our agreement at Nassau, we have considered the adoption of further measures against the background of the EPG's conclusion that the absence of effective economic pressure on South Africa and the belief of the South

African authorities that it need not be feared are actually deferring change. We acknowledge that the Commonwealth cannot stand by and allow the cycle of violence to spiral, but we must take effective concerted action.

9. We are agreed that one element of such action must be the adoption of further measures designed to impress on the authorities in Pretoria the compelling urgency of dismantling apartheid and erecting the structures of democracy in South Africa.

10. In doing so, we have looked particularly at the measures listed in para 7 of the Accord which some of us at Nassau had already indicated a willingness to include in any consideration of further measures. But we have looked as well to other measures under consideration elsewhere. In deciding on the adoption of further measures, we recognise that if they are to have maximum effect they should be part of a wider programme of international action.

11. The British Government's position is set out in paragraph 12. The rest of us have agreed as follows:
(a) The adoption of further substantial economic measures against South Africa is a moral and political imperative to which a positive response can no longer be deferred.
(b) We ourselves will therefore adopt the following measures and commend them to the rest of the Commonwealth and the wider international community for urgent adoption and implementation:
  (i) All the measures listed in paragraph 7 of the Nassau Accord, namely:
    (a) a ban on air links with South Africa,
    (b) a ban on new investment or reinvestment of profits earned in South Africa,
    (c) a ban on the import of agricultural products from South Africa,
    (d) the termination of double taxation agreements with South Africa,
    (e) the termination of all government assistance to investment in, and trade with, South Africa,
    (f) a ban on all government procurement in South Africa,
    (g) a ban on government contracts with majority-owned South African companies, and

     (h)   a ban on the promotion of tourism to South Africa, and

  ii) the following additional measures:

     (i)   a ban on all new bank loans to South Africa, whether to the public or private sectors,

     (j)   a ban on the import of uranium, coal, iron and steel from South Africa, and

     (k)   the withdrawal of all consular facilities in South Africa except for our own nationals and nationals of third countries to whom we render consular services.

(c)   while expressing both concern and regret that the British Government does not join in our agreement, we note its intention to proceed with the measures mentioned in paragraph 12 below.

(d)   We feel, however, that we must do more. We look beyond the Commonwealth to the wider international community. We will, therefore, immediately embark on intensive consultations within the international community with a view to securing concerted international action in the coming months, our emphasis being on those countries that presently sustain a significant level of economic relations with South Africa.

12.   The British Government, while taking a different view on the likely impact of economic sanctions, declares that it will:

  (i)   put a voluntary ban on new investment in South Africa,

 (ii)   put a voluntary ban on the promotion of tourism to South Africa, and

(iii)   accept and implement any EEC decision to ban the import of coal, iron, and steel and of gold coins from South Africa.

13.   As a further element of our collective commitment to effective action, we have requested the Secretary-General, with assistance from our Governments, to co-ordinate the implementation of the agreed measures and to identify such adjustment as may be necessary in Commonwealth countries affected by them.

14.   We renew the call we made at Nassau on the authorities in Pretoria to initiate, in the context of a suspension of violence on all sides, a process of dialogue across lines of colour, politics and religion with a view to establishing a non-racial and representative government in a united and non-fragmented South Africa. If Pretoria responds positively to this call and takes the other steps for which we

called in paragraph 2 of the Nassau Accord, we stand ready to review the situation and to rescind the measures we have adopted if appropriate; and to contribute, in all ways open to us, to an orderly transition to social, economic and political justice in South Africa and to peace and stability in Southern Africa as a whole.

15. On the other hand, we are equally mindful of our further commitment at Nassau that if in a reasonable time even these further measures have not had the desired effect, still further effective measures will have to be considered. We trust that the authorities in Pretoria will recognise the seriousness of our resolve. Acts of economic or other aggression against neighbouring states by way of retaliation or otherwise will activate that resolve.

16. Regretting the absence of full agreement but recognising that the potential for united Commonwealth action still exists, we agree that the seven Governments will keep the situation under review with the view to advising whether any further collective Commonwealth action, including a full Heads of Government Meeting, is desirable. We are conscious that the situation in South Africa may evolve rapidly and dangerously. We believe the Commonwealth must retain its capacity to help to advance the objectives of the Nassau Accord and be ready to use all the means at its disposal to do so.

17. Meeting in London at a time of heightened strains within our association, we take the opportunity to renew our own firm commitment to the future of the Commonwealth and to the aims and objectives which have guided it over the years. We are fortified in this renewal by the spirit of frankness in friendship which characterised our discussions and our belief that they have helped to light a common path towards fulfilment of our common purpose, namely, the dismantling of apartheid and the establishment of a non-racial and representative government in South Africa as a matter of compelling urgency.

5 August 1986

APPENDIX 4

EXCERPTS FROM THE OKANAGAN STATEMENT AND PROGRAMME OF ACTION ON SOUTHERN AFRICA

7. With the exception of Britain we believe that economic and other sanctions have had a significant effect on South Africa and that their wider, tighter, and more intensified application must remain an essential part of the international community's response to apartheid.

8. We realise that if the sanctions and other measures we have adopted are to have maximum effect, they must be part of a wider programme of international action. While mindful of the widespread view within the international community that comprehensive and mandatory sanctions would be the quickest route to bring Pretoria to the negotiating table, we, with the exception of Britain, believe that, pending the acceptance of such a position by the international community as a whole, genuine efforts should be made to secure the universal adoption of the measures now adopted by most Commonwealth and other countries including the United States and the Nordic countries. We commit ourselves to continuing efforts to secure a more concerted application of a global sanctions programme.

9. Further, in the interest of greater effectiveness, we have decided to continue co-ordination by the Secretariat of the implementation of measures as agreed by each member and to identify any efforts to frustrate them.

10. With the exception of Britain, we agree to evaluate on a continuous basis the application of sanctions in order to assess their impact. Moreover, given the significance of South Africa's relationship with the international financial system and the need for a better understanding of developments and possibilities in this sphere, with the exception of Britain we will initiate an expert study, drawing on independent sources, to examine this aspect of the South African economy.

11. Finally, mindful of our commitment at Nassau which we reaffirm here in Vancouver, we agree that we will continue to take further action individually and collectively as deemed appropriate in response to the situation as it evolves until apartheid is dismantled; in the case of all but Britain that includes sanctions.

Lake Okanagan
16 October 1987

APPENDIX 5

EXCERPTS FROM THE CONCLUDING
STATEMENT OF THE
COMMONWEALTH COMMITTEE OF
FOREIGN MINISTERS ON SOUTHERN
AFRICA

SECOND MEETING: TORONTO, 2–3 AUGUST 1988

2. Sanctions

The Committee had before it two Reports prepared pursuant to its decisions at Lusaka.

A. Impact of Sanctions

The first was an Interim Report on the Evaluation of the Application and Impact of Sanctions against South Africa prepared by an Expert Study Group pursuant to Terms of Reference agreed by the Committee at Lusaka with a view to widening, tightening and intensifying economic and other sanctions. The Committee noted the conclusions of the Interim Report that trade sanctions are having a discernible impact on South Africa, that its economy is coming under pressure and that the impact of sanctions will be enhanced if the sanctions themselves are more widely adopted and their application intensified and tightened. Within this context, the Committee agreed on an action plan of individual and concerted *démarches* on countries which have so far not adopted Commonwealth measures, or whose trade practices in relation to South Africa are tending to diminish the impact of Commonwealth sanctions.

With a view to intensifying and tightening the application of sanctions already agreed, the Committee invited Commonwealth and other Governments to consider adopting the following measures as recommended in the Interim Report:

(a)   to press other countries to adopt the Commonwealth trade bans, priority attention being given to coal;

(b)   to implement procedures for stricter customs scrutiny and give higher priority to investigating sanctions violations;

(c)   to provide, where necessary by legislation, for heavier penalties for those violating sanctions, including publicising of violations and the consequent penalties;

(d)   to prohibit technology transfer that is designed to enable South Africa to circumvent existing sanctions, particularly in the areas of arms, oil and computers;

(e)   to clarify the definition of agricultural products in order to reinforce the scope of the ban of agricultural products from South Africa;

(f)   to undertake to increase publicity and information about companies which continue to trade with South Africa, in violation of agreed sanctions; and

(g)   to permit orderly actions of local authorities, private sector groups and individuals in demonstrating their abhorrence of apartheid.

Additionally, the Committee asked the Secretary-General to publish the statistical tables on South Africa's trade prepared by the Expert Study Group. The Committee looked forward to the early submission of the experts' final report in the New Year.

B.   Financial Links

The second Report was that prepared on behalf of the Committee by officials of the Governments of Australia, Canada, and India on South Africa's relationship with the international financial system with a view to exploring the possibilities of effective action against South Africa in this area. The Committee's conclusions on this Report are set out in the Annex to this Statement which was separately released by the Committee during its Meeting. The Committee agreed that in the light of its conclusions it would be desirable to make the Report available to all Commonwealth Governments and to the wider international community.

C. *Propaganda Against Sanctions*

The Committee recognised that Pretoria's fear of sanctions was leading to a concerted campaign supported by massive financial resources to convince Western countries that black South Africans were opposed to sanctions. The Committee recognised that this was itself an admission by Pretoria of the effectiveness of sanctions. Its deliberations also confirmed throughout the Committee's view that black South Africans continued to look principally to sanctions as the international community's most necessary form of pressure on Pretoria for peaceful change. The Committee, therefore, believed it to be a paramount need to counteract South African propaganda that sanctions are opposed by blacks because it hurts them. In this regard, it agreed that it was specially important for the authentic voices of black South Africans, particularly of black trade unionists, to reach the outside world.

APPENDIX 6

COMMONWEALTH COMMITTEE OF FOREIGN MINISTERS ON SOUTHERN AFRICA

STATEMENT ON THE ARMS EMBARGO AGAINST SOUTH AFRICA

1. At Toronto, the Commonwealth Committee of Foreign Ministers on Southern Africa invited Commonwealth and other Governments to consider prohibiting technology transfer that is designed to enable South Africa to circumvent existing sanctions, particularly in the areas of arms, oil and computers. The intent of the existing UN and Commonwealth arms embargo is not only to deny South Africa a military capability but also to increase the cost of maintaining apartheid. The World Campaign Against Military and Nuclear Collaboration with South Africa Report makes clear that the most substantial loopholes in the UN arms embargo derive from differing interpretations of the embargo, more specifically, of what exports should be banned.

2. With a view to tightening the mandatory UN arms embargo against South Africa and in order to ensure that there is no misunderstanding about the Commonwealth ban, or the Commonwealth's interpretation of the UN ban, the Committee commends the following clarification of what exports should be banned as 'arms and related material' by way of supplement to the suggestions made in Security Council Resolution 591.

(i)   Arms, ammunition, implements or munitions of war, or any articles deemed capable of being converted thereinto or having a strategic or tactical value or nature. Materials, equipment and technologies which are designed or used for the development, production or utilisation of arms, ammunition or implements of war. Materials and equipment incorporating unique technology, the acquisition of which by South Africa may reasonably be expected to give assistance to the development and production of arms, ammunition and implements of war, of their means of utilisation or delivery, or counter-measures to them. Materials, equipment and technologies of which South Africa has a deficiency, and which may be critical to the production of arms, ammunition or implements of war, or their means of utilisation or delivery, or counter-measures to them.

(ii)   'Strategic or tactical nature or value' to be considered to include goods which assist in the maintenance of repression in South Africa: specifically exports of high technology including aircraft, aircraft engines and parts thereto, data processing equipment and software, electronic and telecommunications equipment; and also exports of four wheel drive vehicles.

The Committee calls for the above provisions, in conjunction with those contained in Resolution 591, to be made mandatory by the Security Council.

3.   The Committee also urges that:
  (i)   a Monitoring Unit be established at the United Nations in order to assist the UN 421 Committee. The Unit would, inter alia, investigate alleged breaches and publish its findings regularly;
 (ii)   measures be considered for preventing foreign technology and expertise from assisting the internal armaments industry of South Africa; and for subsidiaries in South Africa of overseas companies being prohibited from manufacturing or supplying any items having a strategic or tactical value which would enhance the capability of the military and security forces; and
(iii)   the provision in the Resolution 418 (1977) (mandatory arms embargo) relating to licences be strictly applied with a view to all licences being terminated.

4.   The Committee further calls for a mandatory embargo on the import of South African arms and military goods to complement the embargo on the export of arms and, in particular, for the Security Council to make its resolution on the import of arms mandatory.

5. The Committee encourages all Commonwealth members to provide the Secretary-General with details about how they have implemented the UN arms embargo as well as the further measures to strengthen that embargo which have been adopted by the Commonwealth.

Harare, Zimbabwe
8 February 1989

APPENDIX 7

TRADE STATISTICS

Tables 1–17 look at trade with South Africa in 1987 and compare that with 1986 and with the average of 1983–5. It is difficult to select a single 'normal' year to use as a basis for comparison, so we have instead used this average of three years as a way of taking into account the wide changes caused by the debt crisis and drought.

Tables 18–22 look at the limited data available for 1988 and compare them with similar periods in 1987.

In an attempt to give as complete and accurate a picture of trade flows as possible we have looked at data supplied by South Africa's trading partners instead of by South Africa itself. South Africa's published trade returns were always inadequate for this purpose because they lacked detailed commodity breakdowns. In any case the South African Government progressively suppressed the publication of even routine trade statistics, finally ceasing publication completely.

Therefore for tables 1–17 we started with partner-country trade returns as supplied to the United Nations world trade database. All members have reporting obligations to the United Nations, so this database maintains by far the most complete world-wide coverage of inter-country commodity flows. Countries report in terms of a single standard commodity code, the SITC, removing at least some of the many code and category variations between national publications. Most partners supply the United Nations with information on their trade with South Africa, and Governments often supply data on computer tapes to the United Nations well before they are able to publish full returns in their national series.

None the less, problems do remain. Several significant trading partners do not report their South African trade. For several major and sensitive commodities (notably diamonds, uranium, arms and petroleum) a number of key trading partners suppress details. The UN Statistical Office's practice of organizing its trade data in terms of customs zones also poses a problem because even where partner countries differentiate its members in their national publications, the UN aggregates data for the whole of the Southern African Customs Union (SACU – South Africa plus Botswana, Lesotho and Swaziland).

We have therefore modified the data by taking account of information from several other sources:

1. official SACU customs returns, plus the South African Reserve Bank's national accounts entries for merchandise imports and exports and for net gold exports;
2. official trade statistics of Botswana, Lesotho and Swaziland (BLS);
3. published national trade reports of partner countries;
4. reference publications of the principal international agencies monitoring trade flows (IMF, OECD, EC);
5. industry sources for particular commodities, notably coal, uranium and diamonds;
6. independent research by institutions with specialist knowledge of particular commodity flows, especially the Shipping Research Bureau for petroleum.

The data were checked for anomalies and certain corrections made; notably, Hong Kong's 1985 imports from South Africa were revised downward by US$100 million. Re-exports, where reported, were excluded for all countries except Singapore and Hong Kong.

Special explanations are needed for the data relating to five areas or countries.

Singapore The figures supplied by the United Nations, as reportedly supplied to them by Singapore, have an implausible commodity composition and are quite out of line with official national statistics, so were excluded. From 1986 Singapore's published data specify nearly all African countries. In the residual category 'other countries of Africa' the only possible partners of any significance excepting South Africa were Swaziland and Zimbabwe. Trade with Singapore identified in the returns of these two countries was therefore deducted. In addition, since nearly all the commodities attributed to

Mozambique in Singapore's imports are neither made in Mozambique nor exported via Mozambique from neighbouring countries, they were reclassified as of South African origin and included. The resulting figures specify Singapore's trade at the three-digit level for 1986–7.

South-east Asia (other). As analysed above, Singapore's published trade indicates a large flow of re-exports that we believe to be exports from other countries in South-east Asia to South Africa, via Singapore.

East Asia (other) Re-exports from Hong Kong.

South Korea Data submitted to the United Nations for 'SACU' are clearly for BLS only. South Africa published data on trade with South Korea up to 1984, and these were converted, where it was possible, to correlate with SITC categories or to identify more detailed categories from the general commodity structure of South African trade and were extrapolated. For coal and some minerals industry sources were used.

Taiwan Because it is not a member, the United Nations does not distribute Taiwanese trade data as a matter of policy. However, the national trade publications contain full details of Taiwan's trade with South Africa, and these were integrated after the necessary checking and conversion.

At the time of writing 1988 data were not yet available from the United Nations. Therefore tables 18–22 are based on OECD data and national sources and may not be directly comparable with tables 1–17. In Tables 4–7, 10–13 and 19–21 'total' refers only to the total of the listed entries (and not to the total trade with South Africa in that category), while in other tables this is called 'sub-total'. We apologize for this inconsistency. Note that data for 'South Africa' always include Namibia because it is impossible accurately to dis-aggregate Namibia.

More detailed trade statistics and more information on method-ology are contained in the companion volume to this book, *South Africa: The Sanctions Report – Documents* (James Currey, London, 1989).

Table 1. Recent changes in trade of US$50 million or more: 1987 compared with the 1983–5 average

	Imports from SA			Exports to SA	
	US$ (m)	%		US$ (m)	%
Increases					
Japan	574	34	West Germany	552	28
West Germany	283	30	Japan	334	22
Taiwan	241	115	Taiwan	213	102
Switzerland[1]	183	218	East Asia (other)[2]	80	172
Italy	166	10	Belgium/Luxemb'g	66	30
South Korea	159	74	Switzerland	53	24
Spain	147	86	Netherlands	50	21
Turkey	135	159			
Hong Kong	93	40			
Belgium/Luxemb'g	67	21			
Netherlands	50	36			
Israel[3]	50	29			
Decreases					
France	−54	−8	Norway	−68	−91
Canada	−63	−45	Finland	−73	−100
UK[1]	−118	−10	USA	−585	−31
Denmark	−137	−97			
USA	−921	−39			

Notes: [1] Reflects large shifts in the diamond trade. Excluding diamonds, UK imports decreased only US$20m and Swiss imports increased by US$59m. [2] Re-exports via Hong Kong. [3] Figures available for SACU only.

Sources: UN Statistical Office; OECD; national trade reports.

Table 2. Imposing and undermining sanctions: trade trends 1983–7 (value)

	Imports from SA			Exports to SA			Total change
	Average 1983–5	1987	Rise/fall	Average 1983–5	1987	Rise/fall	
All trade, in US$(m)							
Sanctions Nine[1,2]	3,481	2,230	−1,251	2,931	2,047	−884	−2,135
Rest[2]	7,278	9,938	2,660	10,445	10,293	−152	2,508
Monetary gold	6,374	7,130	756				756
Total	17,133	19,298	2,165	13,375	12,340	−1,036	1,129
All trade, in SDR (m)							
Sanctions Nine[1,2]	3,360	1,725	−1,635	2,829	1,583	−1,246	−2,881
Rest[2]	7,036	7,688	652	10,066	7,963	−2,103	−1,451
Monetary gold	6,135	5,516	−620				−620
Total	16,532	14,929	−1,603	12,895	9,546	−3,349	−4,952
Trade excluding gold, diamonds, platinum and oil, in US$ (m)							
Sanctions Nine[1]	2,209	1,349	−861	2,893	2,035	−857	−1,718
Rest	5,723	6,932	1,209	7,183	8,425	1,242	2,451
Total	7,932	8,281	349	10,076	10,460	384	733
Trade excluding gold, diamonds, platinum and oil, in SDR (m)							
Sanctions Nine[1]	2,136	1,043	−1,093	2,793	1,575	−1,218	−2,311
Rest	5,529	5,363	−166	6,917	6,517	−399	−565
Total	7,665	6,406	−1,259	9,709	8,092	−1,617	−2,877

Notes: [1] The USA, France, Canada, Australia, New Zealand and the Nordic countries. [2] Including non-monetary gold and oil.

Table 3. Imposing and undermining sanctions: trade trends 1983-7 (%)

	Imports from SA			Exports to SA			Total change
	Average 1983-5	1987	Rise/fall %	Average 1983-5	1987	Rise/fall %	
All trade, in US$ (m)							
Sanctions Nine[1,2]	3,481	2,230	-36	2,931	2,047	-30	-33
Rest[2]	7,278	9,938	37	10,445	10,293	-1	14
Monetary gold	6,374	7,130	12				12
Total	17,133	19,298	13	13,375	12,340	-8	4
All trade, in SDR (m)							
Sanctions Nine[1,2]	3,360	1,725	-49	2,829	1,583	-44	-47
Rest[2]	7,036	7,688	9	10,066	7,963	-21	-8
Monetary gold	6,135	5,516	-10				-10
Total	16,532	14,929	-10	12,895	9,546	-26	-17
Trade excluding gold, diamonds, platinum and oil, in US$ (m)							
Sanctions Nine[1]	2,209	1,349	-39	2,893	2,035	-30	-34
Rest	5,723	6,932	21	7,183	8,425	17	19
Total	7,932	8,281	4	10,076	10,460	4	4
Trade excluding gold, diamonds, platinum and oil, in SDR (m)							
Sanctions Nine[1]	2,136	1,043	-51	2,793	1,575	-44	-47
Rest	5,529	5,363	3	6,917	6,517	-6	-5
Total	7,665	6,406	-16	9,709	8,092	-17	-17

Notes: [1] The USA, France, Canada, Australia, New Zealand and the Nordic countries. [2] Including non-monetary gold and oil.

Appendices

Table 4. Imports from South Africa by country (US$ million)

Trading partner	1986	1987	% change on 1983–5 1986	% change on 1983–5 1987	% change 1987 on 1986	Rank 1983–5	Rank 1987
Japan	2,248	2,280	32	34	1	2	1
Italy	1,914	1,791	18	10	−6	3	2
USA	2,520	1,420	8	−39	−44	1	3
West Germany	1,255	1,242	31	30	−1	5	4
UK	1,227	1,089	2	−10	−11	4	5
France	488	583	−23	−8	19	6	6
Taiwan	319	451	53	115	41	10	7
Belgium/Luxemb'g	361	385	13	21	7	7	8
South Korea	369	375	71	74	2	9	9
Hong Kong	348	325	50	40	−7	8	10
Spain	286	319	66	86	12	11	11
Switzerland	87	267	3	218	207	18	12
Israel[1]	203	221	18	29	9	12	13
Turkey	202	219	138	159	9	17	14
Netherlands	195	189	40	36	−3	15	15
Austria	95	107	17	32	13	19	16
Australia	97	90	−7	−14	−7	16	17
Mauritius[1]	68	76	66	85	12	22	18
Canada	230	76	65	−45	−67	14	19
Portugal	60	73	58	91	21	23	20
Brazil[1]	60	71	86	119	18	27	21
Singapore	47	69	−13	29	48	20	22
Sri Lanka[1]	60	NA	162			29	23
Greece	53	58	44	56	9	24	24
Réunion	35	38	17	27	9	28	25
Venezuela	NA	NA				25	26
Chile[1]	35	NA	53			30	27
Argentina[1]	31	NA	71			32	28
Norway	26	25	−27	−28	−1	26	29
Sweden	21	21	−59	−58	0	21	30
Peru	13	NA	29			35	31
Ireland	22	12	15	−35	−44	31	32
New Zealand[1]	15	11	−15	−38	−27	33	33
Thailand	10	NA	59			37	34
Ecuador[1]	NA	NA				36	35
Denmark	102	4	−28	−97	−96	13	36
Finland	1	1	−96	−95	19	34	37
Total	13,102	11,887	18	7	−9		

Note: [1] Figures available for SACU only.

Sources: UN Statistical Office; OECD; national trade reports.

Table 5. Imports from South Africa by country (SDR million)

Trading partner	1986	1987	% change on 1983–5 1986	% change on 1983–5 1987	% change 1987 on 1986	Rank 1983–5	Rank 1987
Japan	1,916	1,764	16	7	−8	2	1
Italy	1,631	1,385	4	−12	−15	3	2
USA	2,148	1,098	−5	−51	−49	1	3
West Germany	1,070	961	15	4	−10	5	4
UK	1,045	842	−10	−28	−19	4	5
France	416	451	−32	−27	8	6	6
Taiwan	272	349	35	73	28	10	7
Belgium/Luxemb'g	307	298	0	−3	−3	7	8
South Korea	315	290	53	41	−8	9	9
Hong Kong	297	251	32	12	−15	8	10
Spain	244	247	46	48	1	11	11
Switzerland	74	207	−8	155	179	18	12
Israel [1]	173	171	4	3	−1	12	13
Turkey	172	170	108	105	−1	17	14
Netherlands	166	146	24	9	−12	15	15
Austria	81	83	3	5	2	19	16
Australia	82	69	−18	−31	−16	16	17
Mauritius [1]	58	59	46	48	1	22	18
Canada	196	59	46	−56	−70	14	19
Portugal	51	56	40	53	10	23	20
Brazil [1]	51	55	64	75	7	27	21
Singapore	40	53	−23	3	34	20	22
Sri Lanka [1]	51	NA	131			29	23
Greece	45	45	27	25	−1	24	24
Réunion	30	30	3	2	−1	28	25
Venezuela	NA	NA				25	26
Chile [1]	30	NA	35			30	27
Argentina [1]	26	NA	52			32	28
Norway	22	20	−36	−42	−10	26	29
Sweden	17	16	−63	−67	−9	21	30
Peru	11	NA	14			35	31
Ireland	19	9	1	−48	−49	31	32
New Zealand [1]	13	8	−25	−51	−34	33	33
Thailand	8	NA	42			37	34
Ecuador [1]	NA	NA				36	35
Denmark	87	3	−36	−97	−96	13	36
Finland	1	1	−96	−96	8	34	37
Total	11,167	9,195	4	−14	−18		

Note: [1] Figures available for SACU only.

Sources: UN Statistical Office; OECD; national trade reports.

Table 6. Imports from South Africa by country, excluding precious minerals
(US$ million)

Trading partner	1986	1987	% change on 1983–5 1986	% change on 1983–5 1987	% change 1987 on 1986	Rank 1983–5	Rank 1987
Japan	1,529	1,479	16	12	−3	1	1
UK	962	1,017	−10	−5	6	3	2
West Germany	982	965	13	11	−2	4	3
USA	1,339	603	22	−45	−55	2	4
Italy	552	567	9	12	3	6	5
France	444	532	−27	−13	20	5	6
Taiwan	317	448	53	117	42	10	7
South Korea	369	375	71	74	2	8	8
Spain	280	312	65	84	11	12	9
Hong Kong	313	288	49	37	−8	9	10
Belgium/Luxemb'g	264	268	−1	1	1	7	11
Israel[1]	203	221	18	29	9	11	12
Turkey	202	219	138	159	9	17	13
Netherlands	193	187	41	36	−3	15	14
Austria	93	101	33	44	8	18	15
Switzerland	70	88	50	89	26	21	16
Australia	87	76	−14	−26	−13	16	17
Mauritius[1]	68	76	66	85	12	22	18
Canada	226	76	63	−45	−67	14	19
Portugal	60	73	58	91	21	23	20
Brazil[1]	60	71	86	119	18	27	21
Singapore	47	69	−13	29	48	19	22
Sri Lanka[1]	60	NA	162			29	23
Greece	53	58	44	57	9	24	24
Réunion	35	38	17	27	9	28	25
Venezuela	NA	NA				25	26
Chile[1]	35	NA	53			30	27
Argentina[1]	31	NA	71			32	28
Norway	26	25	−27	−27	−1	26	29
Sweden	20	21	−59	−58	3	20	30
Peru	13	NA	29			35	31
Ireland	22	12	15	−35	−44	31	32
New Zealand[1]	15	11	−16	−39	−28	33	33
Thailand	10	NA	60			37	34
Ecuador[1]	NA	NA				36	35
Denmark	102	4	−28	−97	−96	13	36
Finland	1	1	−96	−95	18	34	37
Total	9,083	8,281	15	4	−9		

Notes: Gold, diamonds and platinum are excluded from the data. [1] Figures available
for SACU only.

Sources: UN Statistical Office; OECD; national trade reports.

Table 7. Imports from South Africa by country, excluding precious minerals
(SDR million)

Trading partner	1986	1987	% change on 1983–5 1986	% change on 1983–5 1987	% change 1987 on 1986	Rank 1983–5	Rank 1987
Japan	1,303	1,144	2	−10	−12	1	1
UK	820	787	−21	−24	−4	3	2
West Germany	837	747	0	−11	−11	4	3
USA	1,141	467	7	−56	−59	2	4
Italy	470	438	−4	−11	−7	6	5
France	379	412	−36	−30	9	5	6
Taiwan	270	347	35	74	28	10	7
South Korea	315	290	53	41	−8	8	8
Spain	239	242	45	47	1	12	9
Hong Kong	266	223	31	10	−16	9	10
Belgium/Luxemb'g	225	207	−12	−19	−8	7	11
Israel[1]	173	171	4	3	−1	11	12
Turkey	172	170	108	105	−1	17	13
Netherlands	165	145	24	9	−12	15	14
Austria	79	78	17	15	−2	18	15
Switzerland	60	68	32	51	14	21	16
Australia	74	59	−24	−41	−21	16	17
Mauritius[1]	58	59	46	48	1	22	18
Canada	193	59	44	−56	−70	14	19
Portugal	51	56	40	53	10	23	20
Brazil[1]	51	55	64	75	7	27	21
Singapore	40	53	−23	3	34	19	22
Sri Lanka[1]	51	NA	132			29	23
Greece	45	45	27	25	−1	24	24
Réunion	30	30	3	2	−1	28	25
Venezuela	NA	NA				25	26
Chile[1]	30	NA	35			30	27
Argentina[1]	26	NA	52			32	28
Norway	22	20	−35	−42	−10	26	29
Sweden	17	16	−64	−66	−6	20	30
Peru	11	NA	14			36	31
Ireland	18	9	1	−48	−49	31	32
New Zealand[1]	13	8	−26	−52	−35	33	33
Thailand	8	NA	42			37	34
Ecuador[1]	NA	NA				35	35
Denmark	87	3	−36	−98	−96	13	36
Finland	1	1	−96	−96	7	34	37
Total	7,742	6,406	1	−16	−17		

Notes: Gold, diamonds and platinum are excluded from the data. [1] Figures available for SACU only.

Sources: UN Statistical Office; OECD; national trade reports.

Table 8. Imports from South Africa by commodity group, 1987 (US$ million)

Value	% of total	Commodity group and item
8,742	45	Gold [1] of which:
		1,612 Non-monetary gold
1,569	8	Platinum group metals
1,408	7	Coal
1,075	6	Fruit, vegetables, grain of which:
		Fruit and veg., including:
		176 Preserved fruit and juice [2]
		135 Apples [2]
		115 Pears, avocados, etc. [2]
		92 Oranges [2]
		60 Grapes [2]
		32 Grapefruit [2]
		24 Raisins [2]
		10 Other citrus
		Other:
		227 Maize
		110 Sugar and honey
		26 Vegetables
		13 Groundnuts and oil
		10 Coffee and tea
1,041	5	Ferro-alloys, associated ores of which:
		652 Ferro-alloys
		251 Chromium
		79 Manganese
		47 Molybdenum, tungsten, etc.
769	4	Iron and steel of which:
		255 Pig iron, steel ingots
		209 Universals, plates, sheets
		156 Bars, rods, angles, shapes
		39 Tubes and pipes
		34 Iron and steel scrap
		24 Wire (not insulated)
		16 Simple steel manufactures [2]
725	4	Base metals of which:
		263 Copper [3]
		139 Aluminium
		118 Nickel
		59 Lead
		18 Zinc
569	3	Natural clothing materials of which:
		390 Wool, mohair, yarn [2]
		92 Hides, leather articles [2]
		35 Cotton and yarn [2]
		28 Vegetable tanning extracts [2]
		22 Furskins [2]
547	3	Diamonds

Table 8 (cont.).

Value	% of total	Commodity group and item
532	3	Manufactured goods of which:
		122 Machinery
		65 Electrical and electronic goods
		58 Cars, trucks, parts
		53 Clothing and footwear
		31 Glass and glassware
		30 Furniture
		19 Synthetic yarn
		15 Cloth
493	3	Wood, pulp, paper of which:
		216 Pulp and pulpwood
		196 Paper and paperboard
		18 Plywood, panels, board, etc.
339	2	Chemicals of which:
		188 Inorganic chemicals
		78 Organic chemicals
		39 Resins and plastics
337	2	Other non-metallic minerals of which:
		70 Granite
		67 Fertilizer
		59 Asbestos
		30 Quartz, mica, felspar
223	1	Iron ore
197	1	Uranium, radio-active material
163	1	Meat, fish, dairy of which:
		85 Fish
		52 Crustaceans
150	1	Miscellaneous farm products of which:
		57 Animal feedstuff[2]
		31 Tobacco[2]
		24 Cut flowers[2]
114	1	Silver, precious ores, jewellery
97	1	Petroleum products
76	0	Unspecified
19,165	99	Sub-total
19,298	100	Total[4]

Notes: Includes all countries with imports above US$10m in any one year 1983–7. All commodity items above US$10m in 1987 are listed. 'Unspecified' includes SITC 911 (post) and 931 (special transactions), residuals under SITC 9 and differences between the country total and the sum of its listed commodities. For several countries only SACU data are available. The aggregates given here are thus slightly overstated. [1] Net gold exports. [2] For these commodities, figures are available for SACU only. The corresponding group aggregate is for South Africa. [3] Includes copper-nickel matte. [4] Reported partner-country trade plus net gold exports. Uranium understated.

Sources: UN Statistical Office; OECD; national trade reports.

Table 9. Imports from South Africa by commodity group: 1987 compared with 1983–5 average and 1986 (US$ million)

Commodity group	1986	1987	% change on 1983–5 1986	% change on 1983–5 1987	% change 1987 on 1986
Meat, fish, dairy	188	163	21	5	−13
Fruit, vegetables, grain	1,015	1,075	26	34	6
Natural clothing materials	511	569	−12	−2	11
Wood, pulp, paper	448	493	59	75	10
Miscellaneous farm products	130	150	−9	5	16
Iron ore and powder	250	223	−11	−20	−11
Ferro-alloys, associated ores	989	1,041	7	12	5
Iron and steel	934	769	67	37	−18
Gold [1]	7,370	8,742	−8	9	19
Diamonds	465	547	27	50	18
Platinum group metals	1,213	1,569	41	83	29
Silver, precious metal ores	136	114	−41	−50	−16
Coal	1,877	1,408	15	−14	−25
Crude and refined petroleum	123	97	35	7	−21
Base metals	650	725	−14	−4	12
Uranium, radio-active material	394	197	8	−46	−50
Other non-metallic minerals	334	337	11	12	1
Chemicals	338	339	26	27	0
Manufactured goods	578	532	65	52	−8
Unspecified	61	76	−22	−3	24
Sub-total	18,001	19,165	6	12	6
Total [2]	18,113	19,298	6	13	7
– coverage (%)	99	99			

Notes: Includes all countries with imports above US$10m in any one year 1983–7. 'Unspecified' includes SITC 911 (post) and 931 (special transactions), residuals under SITC 9 and differences between the country total and the sum of its listed commodities. For several countries, only SACU data are available. The aggregates given here are thus slightly overstated. [1] Net gold exports. [2] Reported partner-country trade plus net gold exports. Uranium understated.

Sources: UN Statistical Office; OECD; national trade reports.

Table 10. Imports from South Africa by commodity group and country (US$ million)

Commodity group and country	1986	1987	% change on 1983–5		% change 1987 on 1986
			1986	1987	
Agricultural products					
Edible meat, fish and dairy products					
Japan	34	35	23	25	2
Italy	17	22	48	83	24
Spain	14	20	210	337	41
France	13	20	37	103	49
Australia	20	13	−1	−32	−32
Réunion[1]	11	12	34	49	11
Hong Kong[1]	12	11	41	37	−3
USA[1]	40	2	−5	−94	−94
Total	161	135	22	3	−16
Fruit, vegetables and grain					
Japan	223	252	111	138	13
UK	204	202	−1	−2	−1
West Germany	125	156	38	72	25
France	70	115	47	144	65
Taiwan	47	59	209	285	25
Belgium/Luxemb'g	29	39	41	88	33
Switzerland	27	32	12	32	18
Netherlands	23	27	−8	8	18
Austria	24	26	46	64	12
Hong Kong	18	22	−4	14	19
South Korea	NA	NA			
Israel	15	20	31	75	34
Italy	9	15	68	159	54
Spain	12	12	39	38	0
Singapore	8	11			36
Venezuela	3	NA	−74		
Canada	25	1	−8	−96	−96
Sweden	0	1	−99	−95	804
USA	72	0	−10	−100	−100
Total	934	990	27	34	6

Table 10 (cont.)

Commodity group and country	1986	1987	% change on 1983–5 1986	% change on 1983–5 1987	% change 1987 on 1986
Agricultural products related to clothing					
Italy	110	125	−12	0	14
UK	80	92	−21	−9	16
Japan	70	89	4	33	28
West Germany	67	80	−8	8	18
France	48	55	−28	−17	16
Spain	19	21	−21	−13	10
Taiwan	13	19	42	101	42
Hong Kong[1]	10	15	55	149	61
Belgium/Luxemb'g	10	11	−18	−12	8
Portugal	7	11	−30	3	48
USA[1]	27	8	−26	−77	−69
Canada[1]	10	8	33	−3	−27
Netherlands	2	3	−73	−58	54
Total	474	538	−14	−2	14
Wood, pulp and paper					
Japan	94	96	29	31	1
USA	65	72	76	94	10
UK	53	63	−10	8	20
Taiwan	26	34	51	97	30
Italy	27	25	463	419	−8
West Germany	16	24	188	327	48
France	15	21	226	349	38
Singapore	15	20			29
Hong Kong	18	19	30	41	8
Venezuela	12	NA	60		
Thailand	12	NA	468		
Australia	9	9	−3	−3	−1
Total	365	384	55	63	5
Miscellaneous agricultural products					
West Germany	43	52	−10	7	20
Netherlands	27	26	52	48	−3
UK	9	15	8	82	69
Italy	4	12	127	574	197
USA[1]	11	5	−36	−72	−56
Hong Kong[1]	2	3	−81	−77	24
Total	96	112	−9	6	16

Table 10 (cont.)

Commodity group and country	1986	1987	% change on 1983–5 1986	% change on 1983–5 1987	% change 1987 on 1986
Iron, steel and related products					
Iron ore and powder					
Japan	140	136	−15	−17	−2
UK	27	33	79	122	24
Turkey	33	21	101	26	−37
West Germany	27	14	−49	−73	−47
Italy	9	10	−5	13	19
Austria	10	7	252	155	−27
France	0	0	−100	−99	100
Total	246	222	−9	−18	−9
Ferro-alloys and associated ores					
UK	198	225	−10	2	14
Japan	234	221	6	0	−6
USA	196	178	31	19	−9
West Germany	105	127	9	31	20
France	57	74	−5	23	30
Spain	35	43	47	82	23
Italy	42	39	−7	−15	−8
Canada	15	19	1	23	21
Taiwan	14	17	85	131	25
Turkey	8	15	51	188	91
Belgium/Luxemb'g	7	14	−18	56	91
Sweden	9	11	−38	−22	26
Australia	10	9	23	7	−13
Norway	22	8	28	−54	−64
Total	953	1,000	7	12	5
Iron and steel					
Taiwan	55	124	67	277	126
Hong Kong	129	109	155	116	−15
Japan	127	91	184	104	−28
Turkey	81	87	94	108	7
Israel	55	52	42	35	−5
West Germany	44	45	45	49	3
UK	38	32	66	42	−15
Sri Lanka	31	NA	236		
Singapore	21	30			45
Greece	30	26	141	102	−16
Argentina	17	NA	187		

Table 10 (cont.)

Commodity group and country	1986	1987	% change on 1983–5 1986	% change on 1983–5 1987	% change 1987 on 1986
Iron and steel (cont.)					
Portugal	16	12	16	−7	−20
Spain	17	12	60	15	−28
USA	184	5	4	−97	−97
Canada	10	0	86	−95	−98
Total	855	626	72	26	−27
Precious metals and stones					
Non-monetary gold and coin					
Italy	1,357	1,222	22	10	−10
Japan	366	231	252	122	−37
West Germany	212	122	279	118	−42
France	22	23	44	54	7
Austria	1	6	−86	−45	297
USA	79	0	−78	−100	−100
Total	2,038	1,604	23	−3	−21
All gold	7,370	8,742	−8	9	19
Diamonds and precious stones					
Switzerland	3	131	−66	1,324	4,066
Belgium/Luxemb'g	91	111	91	135	23
USA[1]	360	87	−3	−77	−76
Hong Kong[1]	36	35	58	55	−2
UK	222	23	83	−81	−90
Japan	23	19	32	10	−17
West Germany	11	8	34	−2	−27
Total[*]	745	415	25	−31	−44

[*] Most BLS diamonds are attributed to South Africa. Namibia is also a major exporter.

Platinum group metals					
USA	742	729	44	42	−2
Japan	330	552	26	110	67
West Germany	50	147	79	422	192
UK	38	46	381	479	20
Switzerland	13	46	−54	68	263
France	21	27	91	144	27
Australia	9	13	414	680	52
Total	1,203	1,560	41	83	30

Table 10 (cont.)

Commodity group and country	1986	1987	% change on 1983–5		% change 1987 on 1986
			1986	1987	
Silver and precious metal ores					
UK	126	100	−42	−54	−20
West Germany	2	7	−59	18	188
Total	128	107	−43	−52	−17
Mineral fuels					
Coal					
Japan	401	312	8	−16	−22
Italy	214	171	4	−17	−20
South Korea	204	168	80	48	−18
Spain	146	132	104	84	−10
West Germany	172	94	55	−16	−46
Belgium/Luxemb'g	97	89	−3	−11	−8
Taiwan	77	76	68	67	0
Hong Kong	94	74	28	1	−21
Israel	95	71	32	−1	−25
Netherlands	62	59	101	92	−5
France	95	50	−57	−78	−48
Turkey	22	35	188	359	59
Portugal	15	25	545	1,020	74
Switzerland	14	18	254	359	30
Greece	5	13	−54	8	132
Austria	3	12			244
UK	8	3	−31	−75	−63
Denmark	93	0	−28	−100	−100
USA	52	0	54	−100	−100
Total	1,868	1,401	16	−13	−25
Crude and refined petroleum					
USA	47	27	72	−2	−43
Spain	14	24	98	244	74
Italy	3	10	2	247	240
West Germany	11	9	67	33	−20
Japan	23	3	10	−83	−85
New Zealand	0	0	−99	−99	7
Total	97	73	39	5	−25

Table 10 (cont.)

Commodity group and country	1986	1987	% change on 1983–5		% change 1987 on 1986
			1986	1987	
Other minerals					
Base metals					
West Germany	160	136	−16	−29	−15
Japan	54	121	−50	12	122
USA[1]	125	98	−1	−22	−21
Italy	56	69	4	28	23
Taiwan	30	64	−34	41	114
Belgium/Luxemb'g	72	54	−20	−40	−24
UK	40	49	57	92	23
Turkey	16	38			130
Austria	29	27	6	2	−4
France	24	25	−28	−24	5
Hong Kong[1]	7	4	−25	−55	−40
Venezuela[1]	0	NA	−100		
Total	614	686	−14	−4	12
Uranium and radio-active materials					
France	80	159	−34	31	99
West Germany	12	25	−74	−45	109
Canada	32	6	−8	−82	−80
USA	272	0	67	−100	−100
Total*	394	191	8	−48	−52

* Understated: many importers conceal their trade. The UK is a major importer and toll processor, especially for the USA and Japan. Namibia accounts for some 40 per cent of 'South African' exports.

Commodity group and country	1986	1987	% change on 1983–5		% change 1987 on 1986
			1986	1987	
Other non-metallic minerals					
West Germany	66	57	78	56	−13
Japan	49	54	−7	3	11
USA	40	41	−17	−15	2
Italy	29	37	8	37	27
Belgium/Luxemb'g	22	28	141	209	29
France	16	18	−12	−3	11
UK	19	16	28	5	−18
Netherlands	9	13	6	56	47
Spain	10	11	34	51	13
Turkey	18	6	258	21	−66
Australia	5	4	−55	−64	−19
Thailand	0	NA	−91		
Total	285	287	16	17	1

Table 10 (cont.)

Commodity group and country	1986	1987	% change on 1983–5 1986	1987	% change 1987 on 1986
Miscellaneous					
Chemicals					
USA	46	54	19	41	18
Brazil	29	34	168	221	20
Japan	51	33	−4	−38	−35
West Germany	30	27	22	12	−8
Netherlands	20	24	−1	22	23
UK	20	23	22	39	13
Taiwan	19	18	49	40	−6
Turkey	19	14	185	116	−24
Hong Kong	9	13	13	59	40
Austria	10	11	31	45	10
Belgium/Luxemb'g	10	9	20	8	−10
Australia	9	9	−20	−23	−4
Total	271	269	24	24	−1
Manufactured goods					
UK	129	145	−6	6	13
USA	132	95	64	19	−28
West Germany	49	67	195	302	36
Australia	20	21	−22	−16	7
Canada	113	21	725	55	−81
Japan	17	20	578	710	19
Israel	9	20	−7	103	119
France	11	18	88	208	64
Italy	9	15	109	228	57
Netherlands	15	15	93	87	−3
Belgium/Luxemb'g	10	14	102	170	34
Hong Kong	13	12	65	63	−1
Taiwan	6	12	504	1,036	88
Total	534	477	68	50	−11
Unspecified					
USA[1]	32	26	−21	−36	−18
Israel[1]	4	25	−79	43	592
Total	35	51	−39	−12	45

Notes: Includes all countries with imports above US$10m in any one year 1983–7. 'Unspecified' includes SITC 911 (post) and 931 (special transactions), residuals under SITC 9 and differences between the country total and the sum of its listed commodities. [1] Figures available for SACU only.

Sources: UN Statistical Office; OECD; national trade reports.

Table 11. Imports from South Africa by country and commodity group (US$ million)

Country and commodity group	1986	1987	% change on 1983–5 1986	% change on 1983–5 1987	% change 1987 on 1986
Japan					
Platinum group metals	330	552	26	110	67
Coal	401	312	8	−16	−22
Fruit, vegetables, grain	223	252	111	138	13
Non-monetary gold and coin	366	231	252	122	−37
Ferro-alloys, associated ores	234	221	6	0	−6
Iron ore and powder	140	136	−15	−17	−2
Base metals	54	121	−50	12	122
Wood, pulp, paper	94	96	29	31	1
Iron and steel	127	91	184	104	−28
Natural clothing materials	70	89	4	33	28
Other non-metallic minerals	49	54	−7	3	11
Meat, fish, dairy	34	35	23	25	2
Chemical products	51	33	−4	−38	−35
Manufactured goods	17	20	578	710	19
Diamonds	23	19	32	10	−17
Crude and refined petroleum	23	3	10	−83	−85
Total	2,235	2,266	32	34	1
Italy					
Non-monetary gold & coin [1]	1,357	1,222	22	10	−10
Coal	214	171	4	−17	−20
Natural clothing materials	110	125	−12	0	14
Base metals	56	69	4	28	23
Ferro-alloys, associated ores	42	39	−7	−15	−8
Other non-metallic minerals	29	37	8	37	27
Wood, pulp, paper	27	25	463	419	−8
Meat, fish, dairy	17	22	48	83	24
Manufactured goods	9	15	109	228	57
Fruit, vegetables, grain	9	15	68	159	54
Miscellaneous farm products	4	12	127	574	197
Crude and refined petroleum	3	10	2	247	240
Iron ore and powder	9	10	−5	13	19
Total	1,889	1,772	17	10	−6
USA					
Platinum group metals	742	729	44	42	−2
Ferro-alloys, associated ores	196	178	31	19	−9
Base metals [2]	125	98	−1	−22	−21
Manufactured goods	132	95	64	19	−28
Diamonds [2]	360	87	−3	−77	−76
Wood, pulp, paper	65	72	76	94	10

Table 11 (cont.)

Country and commodity group	1986	1987	% change on 1983–5		% change 1987 on 1986
			1986	1987	
Chemical products	46	54	19	41	18
Other non-metallic minerals	40	41	−17	−15	2
Crude and refined petroleum	47	27	72	−2	−43
Unspecified[2]	32	26	−21	−36	−18
Natural clothing materials[2]	27	8	−26	−77	−69
Miscellaneous farm products[2]	11	5	−36	−72	−56
Iron and steel	184	5	4	−97	−97
Meat, fish, dairy[2]	40	2	−5	−94	−94
Fruit, vegetables, grain	72	0	−10	−100	−100
Uranium, radio-active material	270	0	67	−100	−100
Coal	52	0	54	−100	−100
Non-monetary gold and coin	79	0	−78	−100	−100
Total	2,519	1,428	8	−39	−43
West Germany					
Fruit, vegetables, grain	125	156	38	72	25
Platinum group metals	50	147	79	422	192
Base metals	160	136	−16	−29	−15
Ferro-alloys, associated ores	105	127	9	31	20
Non-monetary gold and coin	212	122	279	118	−42
Coal	172	94	55	−16	−46
Natural clothing materials	67	80	−8	−8	18
Manufactured goods	49	67	195	302	36
Other non-metallic minerals	66	57	78	56	−13
Miscellaneous farm products	43	52	−10	7	20
Iron and steel	44	45	45	49	3
Chemical products	30	27	22	12	−8
Uranium, radio-active material	12	25	−74	−45	109
Wood, pulp, paper	16	24	188	327	48
Iron ore and powder	27	14	−49	−73	−47
Crude and refined petroleum	11	9	67	33	−20
Diamonds	11	8	34	−2	−27
Silver, precious metal ores	2	7	−59	18	188
Total	1,203	1,195	30	29	−1
UK					
Ferro-alloys, associated ores	198	225	−10	2	14
Fruit, vegetables, grain	204	202	−1	−2	−1
Manufactured goods	129	145	−6	6	13
Silver, precious metal ores	126	100	−42	−54	−20

Table 11 (cont.)

Country and commodity group	1986	1987	% change on 1983–5 1986	% change on 1983–5 1987	% change 1987 on 1986
Natural clothing materials	80	92	−21	−9	16
Wood, pulp, paper	53	63	−10	8	20
Base metals	40	49	57	92	23
Platinum group metals	38	46	381	479	20
Iron ore and powder	27	33	79	122	24
Iron and steel	38	32	66	42	−15
Diamonds	222	23	83	−81	−90
Chemical products	20	23	22	39	13
Other non-metallic minerals	19	16	28	5	−18
Miscellaneous farm products	9	15	8	82	69
Coal	8	3	−31	−75	−63
Total	1,210	1,069	2	−10	−12
France					
Uranium, radio-active material	80	159	−34	31	99
Fruit, vegetables, grain	70	115	47	144	65
Ferro-alloys, associated ores	57	74	−5	23	30
Natural clothing materials	48	55	−28	−17	16
Coal	95	50	−57	−78	−48
Platinum group metals	21	27	91	144	27
Base metals	24	25	−28	−24	5
Non-monetary gold and coin	22	23	44	54	7
Wood, pulp, paper	15	21	226	349	38
Meat, fish, dairy	13	20	37	103	49
Other non-metallic minerals	16	18	−12	−3	11
Manufactured goods	11	18	88	208	64
Iron ore and powder	0	0	−100	−99	100
Total	472	606	−24	−3	28
Taiwan					
Coal	77	76	68	67	0
Iron and steel	55	124	67	277	126
Fruit, vegetables, grain	47	59	209	285	25
Base metals	30	64	−34	41	114
Wood, pulp, paper	26	34	51	97	30
Chemical products	19	18	49	40	−6
Manufactured goods	6	12	504	1,036	88
Ferro-alloys, associated ores	14	17	85	131	25
Natural clothing materials	13	19	42	101	42
Total	287	423	54	126	47

Table 11 (cont.)

Country and commodity group	1986	1987	% change on 1983–5 1986	% change on 1983–5 1987	% change 1987 on 1986
Belgium/Luxembourg					
Diamonds	91	111	91	135	23
Coal	97	89	−3	−11	−8
Base metals	72	54	−20	−40	−24
Fruit, vegetables, grain	29	39	41	88	33
Other non-metallic minerals	22	28	141	209	29
Ferro-alloys, associated ores	7	14	−18	56	91
Manufactured goods	10	14	102	170	34
Natural clothing materials	10	11	−18	−12	8
Chemical products	10	9	20	8	−10
Total	349	369	15	22	6
South Korea					
Coal	204	168	80	48	−18
Mineral products	NA	NA			
Fruit, vegetables, grain	NA	NA			
Total	NA	NA			
Hong Kong					
Iron and steel	129	109	155	116	−15
Coal	94	74	28	1	−21
Diamonds[2]	36	35	58	55	−2
Manufactured goods	13	12	65	63	−1
Fruit, vegetables, grain	18	22	−4	14	19
Wood, pulp, paper	18	19	30	41	8
Meat, fish, dairy[2]	12	11	41	37	−3
Natural clothing materials[2]	10	15	55	149	61
Chemical products	9	13	13	59	40
Base metals[2]	7	4	−25	−55	−40
Miscellaneous farm products[2]	2	3	−81	−77	24
Total	346	318	50	38	−8
Spain					
Coal	146	132	104	84	−10
Ferro-alloys, associated ores	35	43	47	82	23
Crude and refined petroleum	14	24	98	244	74
Natural clothing materials	19	21	−21	−13	10
Meat, fish, dairy	14	20	210	337	41
Fruit, vegetables, grain	17	12	60	15	−28
Iron and steel	12	12	39	38	0
Other non-metallic minerals	10	11	34	51	13
Total	269	277	69	74	3

Table 11 (cont.)

Country and commodity group	1986	1987	% change on 1983–5 1986	% change on 1983–5 1987	% change 1987 on 1986
Switzerland					
Diamonds	3	131	−66	1,324	4,066
Platinum group metals	13	46	−54	68	263
Fruit, vegetables, grain	27	32	12	32	18
Coal	14	18	254	359	30
Total	56	227	−13	251	302
Israel					
Coal	95	71	32	−1	−25
Iron and steel	55	52	42	35	−5
Fruit, vegetables, grain	15	20	31	75	34
Manufactured goods	9	20	−7	103	119
Unspecified[2]	4	25	−79	43	592
Total	178	190	19	27	7
Turkey					
Iron and steel	81	87	94	108	7
Base metals	16	38			130
Coal	22	35	188	359	59
Iron ore and powder	33	21	101	26	−37
Ferro-alloys, associated ores	8	15	51	188	91
Chemical products	19	14	185	116	−24
Other non-metallic minerals	18	6	258	21	−66
Total	197	215	133	155	9
Netherlands					
Coal	62	59	101	92	−5
Fruit, vegetables, grain	23	27	−8	8	18
Miscellaneous farm products	27	26	52	48	−3
Chemical products	20	24	−1	22	23
Manufactured goods	15	15	93	87	−3
Other non-metallic minerals	9	13	6	56	47
Natural clothing materials	2	3	−73	−58	54
Total	157	167	34	43	6
Austria					
Base metals	29	27	6	2	−4
Fruit, vegetables, grain	24	26	46	64	12
Coal	3	12			244
Chemical products	10	11	31	45	10
Iron ore and powder	10	7	252	155	−27
Non-monetary gold and coin	1	6	−86	−45	297
Total	77	90	20	39	16

Table 11 (cont.)

Country and commodity group	1986	1987	% change on 1983–5		% change 1987 on 1986
			1986	1987	
Australia					
Manufactured goods	20	21	−22	−16	7
Platinum group metals	9	13	414	680	52
Meat, fish, dairy	20	13	−1	−32	−32
Wood, pulp, paper	9	9	−3	−3	−1
Chemical products	9	9	−20	−23	−4
Ferro-alloys, associated ores	10	9	23	7	−13
Other non-metallic minerals	5	4	−55	−64	−19
Total	83	80	−7	−10	−4
Canada					
Manufactured goods	113	21	725	55	−81
Fruit, vegetables, grain	25	1	−8	−96	−96
Uranium, radio-active material	32	6	−8	−82	−80
Ferro-alloys, associated ores	15	19	1	23	21
Natural clothing materials	10	8	33	−3	−27
Iron and steel	10	0	86	−95	−98
Total	206	55	98	−47	−73
Portugal					
Coal	15	25	545	1,020	74
Iron and steel	16	12	16	−7	−20
Natural clothing materials	7	11	−30	3	48
Total	37	48	44	86	29
Brazil					
Chemical products	29	34	168	221	20
Singapore					
Iron and steel	21	30			45
Fruit, vegetables, grain	15	20			29
Wood, pulp, paper	8	11			35
Total	44	61			38
Sri Lanka					
Iron and steel	31	NA	236		
Greece					
Iron and steel	30	26	141	102	−16
Coal	5	13	−54	8	132
Total	36	38	47	57	6

Table 11 (cont.)

Country and commodity group	1986	1987	% change on 1983–5 1986	% change on 1983–5 1987	% change 1987 on 1986
Réunion					
Meat, fish, dairy[2]	11	12	34	49	11
Venezuela					
Fruit, vegetables, grain	3	NA	−74		
Base metals[2]	0	NA	−100		
Wood, pulp, paper	12	NA	60		
Total	16	NA	−30		
Argentina					
Iron and steel	17	NA	187		
Norway					
Ferro-alloys, associated ores	22	8	28	−54	−64
Sweden					
Ferro-alloys, associated ores	9	11	−38	−22	26
Fruit, vegetables, grain	0	1	−99	−95	804
Total	9	12	−67	−56	33
Thailand					
Wood, pulp, paper	12	NA	468		
Other non-metallic minerals	0	NA	−91		
Total	13	NA	87		
Denmark					
Coal	93	0	−28	−100	−100

Notes: Includes all countries with imports above US$10m in any one year 1983–7. 'Unspecified' includes SITC 911 (post) and 931 (special transactions), residuals under SITC 9, and differences between the country total and the sum of its listed commodities. [1] A roughly equivalent amount is estimated to enter via Switzerland. [2] Figures available for SACU only.

Sources: UN Statistical Office; OECD; national trade reports.

Table 12. Exports to South Africa by country (US$ million)

Trading partner	1986	1987	% change on 1983–5		% change 1987 on 1986	Rank	
			1986	1987		1983–5	1987
West Germany	1,940	2,546	−3	28	31	1	1
Japan	1,357	1,868	−12	22	38	4	2
UK	1,250	1,565	−19	2	25	3	3
USA	1,173	1,295	−38	−31	10	2	4
France	404	468	−13	1	16	5	5
Italy	352	457	−20	3	30	6	6
Taiwan	218	423	4	102	94	10	7
Netherlands	254	289	6	21	14	7	8
Belgium/Luxemb'g	210	284	−4	30	35	9	9
Switzerland	242	276	9	24	14	8	10
East Asia (other)[1]	47	126	0	172	171	26	11
Hong Kong	74	125	−25	25	67	16	12
SE Asia (other)[1]	90	121	26	68	34	21	13
Sweden	112	108	−24	−26	−3	11	14
Spain	85	99	−15	−2	16	15	15
Canada	137	87	2	−35	−36	12	16
Israel[2]	65	82	−23	−2	27	17	17
Austria	76	79	8	13	4	22	18
South Korea	59	79	3	36	33	24	19
Brazil[2]	NA	NA				14	20
Ireland	41	61	−7	61	50	28	21
Singapore	35	61	−27	26	72	25	22
Australia	53	57	−36	−31	7	18	23
Argentina[2]	49	NA	−61			13	24
Chile[2]	NA	NA				29	25
Venezuela[2]	NA	NA				27	26
Portugal	16	18	−42	−33	15	30	27
Denmark	46	14	−24	−76	−69	23	28
New Zealand[2]	11	11	−33	−32	1	32	29
Sri Lanka[2]	11	NA	−37			31	30
Ivory Coast[2]	NA	NA				34	31
Norway	46	7	−39	−91	−85	19	32
Neth. Antilles[2]	NA	NA				33	33
Peru[2]	NA	NA				36	34
Paraguay[2]	1	NA	−75			35	35
Finland	3	0	−97	−100	−100	20	36
Total	8,454	10,602	−18	3	25		

Notes: [1] Re-exports via Hong Kong and Singapore respectively. [2] Figures available for SACU only.

Sources: UN Statistical Office; OECD; national trade reports.

Table 13. Exports to South Africa by country (SDR million)

Trading partner	1986	1987	% change on 1983–5 1986	% change on 1983–5 1987	% change 1987 on 1986	Rank 1983–5	Rank 1987
West Germany	1,654	1,969	−14	2	19	1	1
Japan	1,157	1,445	−22	−2	25	4	2
UK	1,065	1,211	−28	−18	14	3	3
USA	1,000	1,002	−45	−45	0	2	4
France	345	362	−23	−19	5	5	5
Italy	300	353	−29	−17	18	6	6
Taiwan	186	327	−8	62	76	10	7
Netherlands	217	224	−6	−3	3	7	8
Belgium/Luxemb'g	179	219	−15	4	23	9	9
Switzerland	206	213	−4	−1	3	8	10
East Asia (other)[1]	40	98	−11	118	146	26	11
Hong Kong	63	96	−34	1	52	16	12
SE Asia (other)[1]	77	93	11	35	22	21	13
Sweden	95	84	−33	−41	−12	11	14
Spain	73	76	−25	−22	5	15	15
Canada	116	67	−10	−48	−42	12	16
Israel[2]	55	63	−32	−22	15	17	17
Austria	65	61	−4	−10	−6	22	18
South Korea	50	61	−9	9	20	24	19
Brazil[2]	NA	NA				14	20
Ireland	35	47	−5	29	36	28	21
Singapore	30	47	−35	2	56	25	22
Australia	45	44	−43	−45	−3	18	23
Argentina[2]	41	NA	−65			13	24
Chile[2]	NA	NA				29	25
Venezuela[2]	NA	NA				27	26
Portugal	13	14	−48	−46	4	30	27
Denmark	39	11	−33	−81	−72	23	28
New Zealand[2]	9	8	−40	−45	−8	32	29
Sri Lanka[2]	9	NA	−44			31	30
Ivory Coast[2]	NA	NA				34	31
Norway	39	5	−46	−92	−86	19	32
Neth. Antilles[2]	NA	NA				33	33
Peru[2]	NA	NA				36	35
Paraguay[2]	1	NA	−78			35	35
Finland	2	0	−97	−100	−100	20	36
Total	7,206	8,202	−27	−17	14		

Notes: [1] Re-exports via Hong Kong and Singapore respectively. [2] Figures available for SACU only.

Sources: UN Statistical Office; OECD; national trade reports.

Table 14. Exports to South Africa by commodity group, 1987 (US$ million)

Value	% of total	Commodity group and item
2,439	20	Vehicles and transport equipment of which:
		1,330 Vehicle parts and accessories
		244 Passenger cars
		223 Internal combustion engines
		194 Construction and mining machinery
		167 Goods vehicles
		133 Aircraft
		83 Tractors, farm machinery
1,880	15	Coal, gas, petroleum
1,667	14	Electrical and electronic goods of which:
		408 Electronic parts and components
		293 Computers
		168 Computer parts
		161 Consumer electronics
		117 Electronic measuring equipment
		92 Telephone equipment
		59 Medical electronics
		57 Electricity transmission equipment
1,498	12	Chemicals of which:
		361 Resins, plastics
		353 Organic chemicals
		181 Medicines, pharmaceuticals
		134 Inorganic chemicals
		86 Soap, cosmetics, perfumes
		23 Synthetic rubber
1,476	12	Machinery and tools of which:
		174 Pumps, compressors
		169 Hand and interchangeable tools
		157 Textile and leather machinery
		143 Steam engines and boilers
		140 Electric motors and generators
		122 Heating and cooling equipment
		97 Mechanical handling equipment
		71 Machine tools
		47 Printing machinery
		35 Metal-working machinery
		22 Pulp and paper machinery
976	8	Other manufactured goods of which:
		170 Scientific and control instruments
		102 Photographic equipment
		77 Books and printed matter
		67 Optical goods, watches
		44 Glass and glassware

Table 14 (cont.)

Value	% of total	Commodity group and item
874	7	Agricultural products of which:
		185 Paper and paperboard
		139 Meat and fish
		75 Alcoholic beverages
		68 Cereals
		59 Vegetable oils and animal fats
		54 Coffee, tea, beverages
		40 Rubber
		32 Fruit and vegetables
		21 Tobacco and cigarettes
566	5	Clothing and textiles of which:[1]
		284 Fabrics
		106 Clothing, footwear
		104 Synthetic fibres and yarns
294	2	Iron and steel of which:
		118 Tubes, pipes
		67 Bars, rods, shapes, plates, sheets
283	2	Other minerals of which:
		89 Non-ferrous metals
		33 Clay construction materials
		32 Fertilizer
		30 Diamonds, precious stones
		23 Sulphur
158	1	Unspecified
12,110		Sub-total
12,340[2]		Total

Notes: Includes all countries (except BLS) with exports above US$10m in any one year 1983–7. All commodity items above US$10m in 1987 are listed. 'Unspecified' includes SITC 9 and the differences between the country total and the sum of its listed commodities. Commodity group totals for South Africa only, but for some individual commodities a small quantity of direct exports to BLS is included. [1] Approximately US$50m excluded from the sub-totals for lack of details. [2] Reported partner-country trade plus estimated oil exports less estimated exports to BLS.

Sources: UN Statistical Office; OECD; national trade reports; Shipping Research Bureau.

Table 15. Exports to South Africa by commodity group: 1987 compared with 1983–5 average and 1986 (US$ million)

Commodity group	1986	1987	% change on 1983–5 1986	% change on 1983–5 1987	% change 1987 on 1986
Agricultural products	803	874	−35	−29	9
Coal, gas, petroleum	1,500	1,880	−55	−43	25
Iron and steel	230	294	−6	20	28
Other minerals	276	283	−12	−10	3
Chemicals	1,339	1,498	15	28	12
Clothing and textiles	435	566	−26	−3	30
Machinery and tools	1,130	1,476	−31	−10	31
Vehicles and transport equipment	1,767	2,439	−15	17	38
Electrical and electronic goods	1,461	1,667	−9	4	14
Other manufactured goods	767	976	−16	7	27
Unspecified	112	158	25	77	42
Sub-total	9,819	12,110	−26	−8	23
Total South Africa[1]	9,940	12,340	−26	−8	24
– coverage (%)	99	98			
– excluding oil	8,440	10,460	−16	4	24

Notes: Includes all countries with exports above US$10m in any one year 1983–7. 'Unspecified' includes SITC 911 (post) and 931 (special transactions), residuals under SITC 9 and differences between the country total and the sum of its listed commodities. For several countries, only SACU data are available. The aggregates given here are thus slightly overstated. [1] Reported partner-country trade plus estimated oil exports.

Sources: UN Statistical Office; OECD; national trade reports.

Table 16. Exports to South Africa by commodity group and country (US$ million)

Commodity group and country	1986	1987	% change on 1983–5 1986	1987	% change 1987 on 1986
Agricultural products					
UK	124	170	−7	28	38
USA[1]	143	154	−64	−61	8
West Germany	65	83	31	69	28
SE Asia (other)	65	73			12
France	29	50	8	86	73
Argentina[1]	45	NA	−62		
Netherlands	30	41	−10	24	37
Ireland	7	30	82	642	307
Chile[1]	NA	NA			
Italy	20	25	27	55	22
Canada[1]	30	24	12	−13	−22
Brazil[1]	NA	NA			
Japan	27	24	−20	−30	−13
Austria	11	18	4	68	63
Belgium/Luxemb'g	11	16	14	66	45
Australia	26	15	−34	−62	−43
Spain	10	11	1	16	15
Singapore	8	11			31
Ivory Coast[1]	NA	NA			
Israel[1]	3	9	−67	−2	200
Sri Lanka[1]	8	NA	−44		
Sweden	14	7	−21	−58	−46
Portugal	6	7	−59	−50	23
New Zealand[1]	7	7	−27	−31	−6
Denmark	8	2	−46	−88	−78
Paraguay[1]	1	NA	−75		
Peru[1]	NA	NA			
Finland	0	0	−100	−100	−164
Sub-total	700	778	−38	−31	11
Total	645	706	−45	−40	9
Minerals					
Coal, gas and petroleum products					
West Germany	17	21	−11	9	22
USA[1]	31	13	−15	−64	−57
UK	11	11	13	11	−2
Japan	7	7	−20	−29	−10
Neth. Antilles[1]	NA	NA			
Venezuela[1]	NA	NA			
Sub-total	66	51	−32	−47	−22
Total reported	82	61	−25	−45	−26
Total petroleum[2]	1,500	1,880			

Table 16 (cont.)

Commodity group and country	1986	1987	% change on 1983–5 1986	1987	% change 1987 on 1986
Iron and steel					
Japan	59	91	−22	22	55
West Germany	54	77	2	46	42
UK	33	50	15	74	51
France	36	22	18	−28	−39
Italy	7	12	6	77	67
USA[1]	5	8	−63	−35	74
Sub-total	193	259	−6	26	34
Total	236	300	−6	19	27
Other minerals					
West Germany	44	60	7	46	37
UK	42	41	23	20	−3
Belgium/Luxemb'g	12	29	103	390	141
USA[1]	20	28	−20	14	43
Canada[1]	49	25	−12	−55	−49
Italy	14	21	−44	−16	49
France	10	16	12	83	64
Japan	8	13	−23	24	60
Israel[1]	11	13	−6	15	23
Netherlands	10	10	−2	−6	−4
Norway	34	0	−41	−100	−100
Sub-total	254	257	−11	−10	1
Total	281	287	−12	−10	2
Chemicals					
West Germany	303	345	35	54	14
UK	292	327	8	20	12
USA[1]	225	234	−5	−1	4
Netherlands	101	107	28	36	6
Switzerland	70	88	21	52	26
France	71	82	26	44	15
Japan	72	78	27	37	8
Belgium/Luxemb'g	47	59	−3	23	26
Italy	26	37	2	44	40
Israel[1]	18	23	6	34	26
Spain	18	22	30	60	22
Singapore	13	18			41
Taiwan	7	15	48	221	117
Brazil[1]	NA	NA			
Sweden	10	13	12	49	33
Ireland	13	12	−7	−12	−5
Denmark	13	10	32	6	−19
Canada[1]	4	7	−48	−18	58
Sub-total	1,302	1,475	14	29	13
Total	1,310	1,481	12	27	13

Table 16 (cont.)

Commodity group and country	1986	1987	% change on 1983–5 1986	1987	% change 1987 on 1986
Manufactured goods					
Clothing, textiles and related goods					
Taiwan	80	140	−4	68	75
Japan	55	55	−40	−40	0
West Germany	38	55	−37	−9	45
South Korea[1]	NA	NA			
Italy	45	48	−14	−7	8
UK	28	37	−37	−17	32
Hong Kong[1]	18	33	−33	25	87
USA[1]	28	24	−48	−55	−13
East Asia (other)[1]	17	NA	−16		
Belgium/Luxemb'g	8	15	−35	26	95
Spain	6	14	−60	−12	116
Netherlands	7	11	−40	−7	55
France	9	10	−36	−30	9
Austria	7	9	−31	−7	35
Brazil[1]	NA	NA			
Sub-total	345	450	−34	−14	31
Total	349	475	−32	−7	36
Machinery and tools					
West Germany	345	449	−19	5	30
UK	172	242	−30	−2	40
Japan	138	162	−28	−15	18
Italy	85	139	−36	6	64
USA[1]	112	135	−51	−41	20
France	72	87	−28	−13	20
Switzerland	55	74	−25	0	34
Taiwan	17	40	−22	84	135
Sweden	33	35	−38	−35	5
Belgium/Luxemb'g	16	27	−36	11	72
Netherlands	19	23	−29	−13	22
Austria	21	18	24	7	−14
Spain	8	12	−51	−31	41
Israel[1]	6	9	−45	−23	40
Canada[1]	4	4	−50	−51	−1
Brazil[1]	NA	NA			
Denmark	9	2	−34	−88	−81
Finland	0	0	−99	−100	−100
Sub-total	1,114	1,459	−31	−10	31
Total	1,137	1,487	−31	−10	31

Table 16 (cont.)

Commodity group and country	1986	1987	% change on 1983–5 1986	1987	% change 1987 on 1986
Vehicles and transport equipment					
Japan	621	984	3	64	59
West Germany	651	857	− 3	27	32
USA[1]	168	228	− 46	− 27	36
UK	128	161	− 50	− 37	26
Italy	35	58	− 33	11	66
France	38	43	− 45	− 36	15
Taiwan	16	31	− 7	80	94
Belgium/Luxemb'g	8	19	− 34	63	149
Netherlands	12	14	13	27	12
Austria	10	7	− 11	− 40	− 32
Spain	19	6	87	− 39	− 67
Australia	6	6	− 50	− 54	− 9
Sweden	6	4	− 60	− 71	− 28
Canada[1]	28	3	182	− 65	− 88
Switzerland	2	1	− 73	− 83	− 36
Brazil[1]	NA	NA			
Sub-total	1,748	2,424	− 16	17	39
Total	1,776	2,453	− 15	17	38
Electrical and electronic products					
West Germany	305	367	3	24	20
Japan	238	292	− 22	− 5	22
USA[1]	256	252	− 19	− 20	− 2
UK	224	236	− 16	− 11	5
Taiwan	45	100	82	306	123
France	84	95	− 9	3	13
Italy	79	84	15	23	7
Netherlands	50	57	8	23	14
Switzerland	57	55	46	41	− 3
Hong Kong[1]	15	29	− 28	37	91
Belgium/Luxemb'g	22	22	− 14	− 11	3
Singapore	9	17			83
Spain	11	16	− 23	6	38
Sweden	17	11	− 20	− 48	− 35
Ireland	15	10	59	9	− 32
Israel[1]	10	8	− 35	− 47	− 18
Canada[1]	6	7	− 49	− 42	14
Sub-total	1,443	1,658	− 8	5	15
Total	1,475	1,680	− 9	4	14

Table 16 (contd.)

Commodity group and country	1986	1987	% change on 1983–5 1986	1987	% change 1987 on 1986
Other manufactured goods					
UK	145	194	− 10	20	34
West Germany	136	171	0	27	26
USA[1]	105	114	− 28	− 22	9
Japan	82	106	− 26	− 4	29
Taiwan	38	70	− 20	46	84
Italy	39	58	− 29	5	49
France	38	56	− 17	22	47
Hong Kong[1]	38	56	− 19	18	46
Switzerland	34	35	37	39	1
Belgium/Luxemb'g	20	22	− 8	1	10
Netherlands	17	19	5	17	12
Israel[1]	13	15	− 11	3	16
Spain	10	13	− 26	− 5	28
Austria	8	9	− 18	3	26
Sweden	6	6	− 27	− 20	10
Ireland	3	3	− 63	− 58	12
Sub-total	732	949	− 16	9	30
Total	762	971	− 16	7	27
Unspecified					
USA[1]	39	59	16	76	52
Belgium/Luxemb'g	47	52	26	41	12
Taiwan	9	14			55
West Germany	12	14			
UK	1	2	− 31	14	65
(UK unidentified/ arms[3])	(25)	(31)	(− 49)	(− 37)	(24)
Sub-total	108	141	28	67	31
Total	111	158	26	78	42

Notes: Includes all countries with exports above US$10m in any one year 1983–7. 'Unspecified' includes SITC 911 (post) and 931 (special transactions), residuals under SITC 9 and differences between the country total and the sum of its listed commodities. [1] Figures available for SACU only. [2] Estimated total exports of petroleum products. [3] Excluded: forms a large residual under SITC 9 1983–6 alongside arms exports at *c.* US$1m. In 1987 arms increase to US$31m and the residual disappears, indicating the probable nature of the trade. No other country reports arms exports above US$1m except Italy (US$3m in 1987).

Sources: UN Statistical Office; OECD; national trade reports.

Table 17. Exports to South Africa by country and commodity group (US$ million)

Country and commodity group	1986	1987	% change on 1983–5 1986	1987	% change 1987 on 1986
West Germany					
Vehicles and transport equipment	651	857	−3	27	32
Machinery and tools	345	449	−19	5	30
Electrical and electronic goods	305	367	3	24	20
Chemicals	303	345	35	54	14
Other manufactured goods	136	171	0	27	26
Agricultural products	65	83	31	69	28
Iron and steel	54	77	2	46	42
Other minerals	44	60	7	46	37
Clothing, textiles	38	55	−37	−9	45
Coal, gas, petroleum	17	21	−11	9	22
Unspecified	12	14	2	17	15
Sub-total	1,970	2,499	−1	26	27
Japan					
Vehicles and transport equipment	621	985	3	64	58
Electrical and electronic goods	238	292	−23	−6	22
Machinery and tools	138	162	−28	−15	18
Other manufactured goods	83	107	−26	−4	29
Iron and steel	59	91	−22	21	55
Chemicals	72	78	27	37	8
Clothing, textiles	56	56	−40	−40	0
Agricultural products	27	24	−20	−30	−13
Other minerals	9	14	−21	24	58
Coal, gas, petroleum	7	7	−20	−28	−10
Sub-total	1,310	1,814	−12	22	38
UK					
Chemicals	292	327	8	20	12
Machinery and tools	172	242	−30	−2	40
Electrical and electronic goods	224	236	−16	−11	5
Other manufactured goods	145	194	−10	20	34
Agricultural products	124	170	−7	28	38
Vehicles and transport equipment	128	161	−50	−37	26
Iron and steel	33	50	15	74	51
Other minerals	42	41	23	20	−3
Clothing, textiles	28	37	−37	−17	32
Coal, gas, petroleum	11	11	13	11	−2
Unspecified	1	2	−31	14	65
Unidentified/arms [1]	25	31	−49	−37	24
Sub-total	1,225	1,501	−19	0	23

Table 17 (cont.)

Country and commodity group	1986	1987	% change on 1983–5 1986	% change on 1983–5 1987	% change 1987 on 1986
USA[2]					
Electrical and electronic goods	256	252	−19	−20	−2
Chemicals	225	234	−5	−1	4
Vehicles and transport equipment	168	228	−46	−27	36
Agricultural products	143	154	−64	−61	8
Machinery and tools	112	135	−51	−41	20
Other manufactured goods	105	114	−28	−22	9
Unspecified	39	59	16	76	52
Other minerals	20	28	−20	14	43
Clothing, textiles	28	24	−48	−55	−13
Coal, gas, petroleum	31	13	−15	−64	−57
Iron and steel	5	8	−63	−35	74
Sub-total	1,132	1,251	−37	−30	11
France					
Electrical and electronic goods	84	95	−9	3	13
Machinery and tools	72	87	−28	−13	20
Chemicals	71	82	26	44	15
Other manufactured goods	38	56	−17	22	47
Agricultural products	29	50	8	86	73
Vehicles and transport equipment	38	43	−45	−36	15
Iron and steel	36	22	18	−28	−39
Other minerals	10	16	12	83	64
Clothing, textiles	9	10	−36	−30	9
Sub-total	387	461	−13	4	19
Italy					
Machinery and tools	85	139	−36	6	64
Electrical and electronic goods	79	84	15	23	7
Other manufactured goods	39	58	−29	5	49
Vehicles and transport equipment	35	58	−33	11	66
Clothing, textiles	45	48	−14	−7	8
Chemicals	26	37	2	44	40
Agricultural products	20	25	27	55	22
Other minerals	14	21	−44	−16	49
Iron and steel	7	12	6	77	67
Sub-total	349	482	−19	11	38

Table 17 (cont.)

Country and commodity group	1986	1987	% change on 1983–5		% change 1987 on 1986
			1986	1987	
Taiwan					
Clothing, textiles	80	140	− 4	68	75
Electrical and electronic goods	45	100	82	306	123
Other manufactured goods	38	70	− 20	46	84
Machinery and tools	17	40	− 22	84	135
Vehicles and transport equipment	16	31	− 7	80	94
Chemicals	7	15	48	221	117
Unspecified [3]	9	14			55
Sub-total	212	410	6	105	94
Netherlands					
Chemicals	101	107	28	36	6
Electrical and electronic goods	50	57	8	23	14
Agricultural products	30	41	− 10	24	37
Machinery and tools	19	23	− 29	− 13	22
Other manufactured goods	17	19	5	17	12
Vehicles and transport equipment	12	14	13	27	12
Clothing, textiles	7	11	− 40	− 7	55
Other minerals	10	10	− 2	− 6	− 4
Sub-total	246	282	5	20	15
Belgium/Luxembourg					
Chemicals	47	59	− 3	23	26
Unspecified	47	52	26	41	12
Other minerals	12	29	103	390	141
Machinery and tools	16	27	− 36	11	72
Other manufactured goods	20	22	− 8	1	10
Electrical and electronic goods	22	22	− 14	− 11	3
Vehicles and transport equipment	8	19	− 34	63	149
Agricultural products	11	16	14	66	45
Clothing, textiles	8	15	− 35	26	95
Sub-total	189	261	14	609	553
Switzerland					
Chemicals	28	5	− 52	− 92	− 82
Machinery and tools	26	7	− 57	− 88	− 73
Electrical and electronic goods	20	10	− 60	− 79	− 49
Other manufactured goods	34	2	− 43	− 97	− 94
Vehicles and transport equipment	35	1	− 52	− 98	− 96
Sub-total	144	26	− 53	− 91	− 82

Table 17 (cont.)

Country and commodity group	1986	1987	% change on 1983-5 1986	1987	% change 1987 on 1986
East Asia (other)[2]					
Clothing, textiles	19	NA	−4		
Other manufactured goods	12	NA	−17		
Sub-total	31	NA	−9		
Hong Kong[2]					
Other manufactured goods	38	56	−19	18	46
Clothing, textiles	18	33	−33	25	87
Electrical and electronic goods	15	29	−28	37	91
Sub-total	71	118	−25	24	66
SE Asia (other)					
Agricultural products	66	73			12
Sweden					
Machinery and tools	33	35	−38	−35	5
Chemicals	10	13	12	49	33
Electrical and electronic goods	17	11	−20	−48	−35
Agricultural products	14	7	−21	−58	−46
Other manufactured goods	6	6	−27	−20	10
Vehicles and transport equipment	6	4	−60	−71	−28
Sub-total	85	77	−31	−38	−10
Spain					
Chemicals	18	22	30	60	22
Electrical and electronic goods	11	16	−23	6	38
Clothing, textiles	6	14	−60	−12	116
Other manufactured goods	10	13	−26	−5	28
Machinery and tools	8	12	−51	−31	41
Agricultural products	10	11	1	16	15
Vehicles and transport equipment	19	6	87	−39	−67
Sub-total	83	94	−13	−1	13
Canada[2]					
Other minerals	49	25	−12	−55	−49
Agricultural products	30	24	12	−13	−22
Electrical and electronic goods	6	7	−49	−42	14
Chemicals	4	7	−48	−18	58
Machinery and tools	4	4	−50	−51	−1
Vehicles and transport equipment	28	3	182	−65	−88
Sub-total	122	70	1	−42	−43

Table 17 (cont.)

Country and commodity group	1986	1987	% change on 1983–5 1986	% change on 1983–5 1987	% change 1987 on 1986
Israel [2]					
Chemicals	18	23	6	34	26
Other manufactured goods	13	15	−11	3	16
Other minerals	11	13	−6	15	23
Agricultural products	3	9	−67	−2	200
Machinery and tools	6	9	−45	−23	40
Electrical and electronic goods	10	8	−35	−47	−18
Sub-total	61	77	−23	−3	26
Austria					
Agricultural products	11	18	4	68	63
Machinery and tools	21	18	24	7	−14
Other manufactured goods	8	9	−18	3	26
Clothing, textiles	7	9	−31	−7	35
Vehicles and transport equipment	10	7	−11	−40	−32
Sub-total	57	62	−3	6	9
South Korea					
Clothing, textiles	NA	NA			
Brazil [2]					
Vehicles and transport equipment	NA	NA			
Machinery and tools	NA	NA			
Clothing, textiles	NA	NA			
Chemicals	NA	NA			
Agricultural products	NA	NA			
Sub-total	NA	NA			
Ireland					
Agricultural products	7	30	82	642	307
Chemicals	13	12	−7	−12	−5
Electrical and electronic goods	15	10	59	9	−32
Other manufactured goods	3	3	−63	−58	12
Sub-total	38	56	9	61	48
Singapore					
Chemicals	13	18			41
Electrical and electronic goods	9	17			83
Agricultural products	8	11			31
Sub-total	30	45			51

Table 17 (cont.)

Country and commodity group	1986	1987	% change on 1983–5		% change 1987 on 1986
			1986	1987	
Australia					
Agricultural products	26	15	−34	−62	−43
Vehicles and transport equipment	6	6	−50	−54	−9
Sub-total	32	21	−38	−60	−36
Argentina[2]					
Agricultural products	45	NA	−62		
Chile					
Agricultural products	NA	NA			
Venezuela[2]					
Coal, gas, petroleum	NA	NA			
Portugal					
Agricultural products	6	7	−59	−50	23
Denmark					
Chemicals	13	10	32	6	−19
Machinery and tools	9	2	−34	−88	−81
Agricultural products	8	2	−46	−88	−78
Sub-total	30	14	−23	−65	−55
New Zealand[2]					
Agricultural products	7	7	−27	−31	−6
Sri Lanka[2]					
Agricultural products	8	NA	−44		
Ivory Coast[2]					
Agricultural products	NA	NA			
Norway					
Other minerals	34	0	−41	−100	−100
Neth. Antilles[2]					
Coal, gas, petroleum	NA	NA			

Table 17 (cont.)

Country and commodity group	1986	1987	% change on 1983–5 1986	% change on 1983–5 1987	% change 1987 on 1986
Peru[2]					
Agricultural products	NA	NA			
Paraguay[2]					
Agricultural products	1	NA	−75		
Finland					
Machinery and tools	0	0	−99	−100	−100
Agricultural products	0	0	−100	−100	−100
Sub-total	0	0	−99	−100	−100

Notes: Includes all countries with exports above US$10m in any one year 1983–7. 'Unspecified' includes SITC 911 (post) and 931 (special transactions), residuals under SITC 9 and differences between the country total and the sum of its listed commodities. [1] A large residual remains under SITC 9 for 1983–6 alongside arms exports (SITC 951) at *c.* US$1m. In 1987 arms increase to US$31m, and the residual disappears, indicating the probable nature of the trade. No other country reports arms exports above US$1m except Italy (US$3m in 1987). [2] Figures available for SACU only. [3] The 1986–7 figures include the residual values not allocated by commodity.

Sources: UN Statistical Office; OECD; national trade reports.

Table 18. Countries ranked by percentage change in trade with South Africa: first six months of 1988 compared with first six months of 1987 (US$ million)

Country	Total trade		
	1987	1988	Rise/fall (%)
Taiwan	431	904	110
Switzerland	198	392	98
West Germany	1,658	2,480	50
Turkey	104	154	47
Spain	182	265	46
France	476	660	39
UK	1,221	1,679	38
Hong Kong	238	320	35
Netherlands	213	287	35
Belgium/Luxemb'g	309	412	33
Austria	82	107	31
Canada	90	112	24
USA	1,225	1,511	23
Ireland	33	40	20
Portugal	43	51	20
Japan	1,925	2,172	13
Israel	147	144	−2
Australia	104	89	−14
Sweden	85	4	−96

Country	Imports from South Africa		
	1987	1988	Rise/fall (%)
Switzerland	71	238	223
Taiwan	244	618	153
West Germany	549	909	66
UK	528	746	41
Turkey	103	145	40
France	266	364	37
Canada	44	60	37
Netherlands	86	117	37
Spain	141	192	36
Belgium/Luxemb'g	185	241	30
Austria	50	64	28
Hong Kong	141	172	22
Ireland	5	6	19
USA	638	730	15
Portugal	36	39	9
Japan	1,136	1,034	−9
Israel	118	95	−19
Australia	54	33	−38
Sweden	16	0	−100

Table 18. (cont.)

Country	Exports to South Africa		
	1987	1988	Rise/fall (%)
Turkey	1	9	655
Spain	41	74	78
Portugal	7	12	76
Israel	29	49	69
Taiwan	187	286	53
Hong Kong	97	148	53
Japan	789	1,138	44
West Germany	1,110	1,571	42
France	211	296	40
Belgium/Luxemb'g	124	171	37
Austria	32	43	35
UK	693	933	35
Netherlands	128	170	33
USA	587	781	33
Switzerland	127	154	21
Ireland	28	34	21
Canada	46	52	12
Australia	50	56	12
Sweden	69	4	−95

Notes: Based on Table 19. Countries with total trade of less than US$25m in each half year omitted.

Table 19. Trade with South Africa: first six months of 1988 compared with first six months of 1987 (US$ million)

Country	Total trade			Imports from South Africa			Exports to South Africa		
	1987	1988	Rise/fall (%)	1987	1988	Rise/fall (%)	1987	1988	Rise/fall (%)
West Germany	1,658	2,480	50	549	909	66	1,110	1,571	42
Japan	1,925	2,172	13	1,136	1,034	-9	789	1,138	44
UK	1,221	1,679	38	528	746	41	693	933	35
USA	1,225	1,511	23	638	730	15	587	781	33
Taiwan	431	904	110	244	618	153	187	286	53
France	476	660	39	266	364	37	211	296	40
Belgium/Luxemb'g	309	412	33	185	241	30	124	171	37
Switzerland	198	392	98	71	238	233	127	154	21
Hong Kong	238	320	35	141	172	22	97	148	53
Netherlands	213	287	35	86	117	37	128	170	33
Spain	182	265	46	141	192	36	41	74	78
Turkey	104	154	47	103	145	40	1	9	665
Israel	147	144	-2	118	95	-19	29	49	69
Canada	90	112	24	44	60	37	46	52	12
Austria	82	107	31	50	64	28	32	43	35
Australia	104	89	-14	54	33	-38	50	56	12
Portugal	43	51	20	36	39	9	7	12	76
Ireland	33	40	20	5	6	19	28	34	21
Norway	9	10	19	5	10	109	4	1	-78
New Zealand	9	10	10	5	3	-28	4	7	52
Denmark	9	8	-12	2	2	-6	7	6	-14
Sweden	85	4	-96	16	0	-100	69	4	-95
Iceland	0	1	54	0	1	69	0	0	-50
Finland	0	0	0	0	0	-100	0	0	100
Total	8,792	11,812	34	4,421	5,818	32	4,371	5,993	37

Notes: Data for OECD countries plus South Africa's three largest non-OECD partners. OECD data from OECD Monthly Statistics of Foreign Trade, January 1989. Data for Israel, Hong Kong and Taiwan drawn from national statistics. Hong Kong exports include re-exports (in contrast to previous tables). No 1988 data for Greece or Italy. Rates of exchange: OECD and Israel data in US$; HK$ fixed at US$1 = HK$7.8; Taiwan mid-period rates – 1987 US$1 = NT$32, 1988 US$1 = NT$28.7.

Table 20. Trade with South Africa: first six months of 1988 compared with first six months of 1987 (SDR million)

Country	Total trade			Imports from South Africa			Exports to South Africa		
	1987	1988	Rise/fall (%)	1987	1988	Rise/fall (%)	1987	1988	Rise/fall (%)
West Germany	1,297	1,812	40	429	664	55	868	1,148	32
Japan	1,503	1,588	6	887	756	-15	616	832	35
UK	995	1,227	28	413	545	32	543	682	26
USA	959	1,104	15	499	534	7	459	571	24
Taiwan	337	661	96	191	452	136	146	209	43
France	373	482	29	208	266	28	165	216	31
Belgium/Luxemb'g	242	301	24	145	176	22	97	125	28
Switzerland	155	287	85	56	174	213	99	113	14
Hong Kong	186	234	26	110	126	14	76	108	42
Netherlands	167	209	26	67	86	28	100	124	24
Spain	143	194	36	110	140	27	32	54	67
Turkey	82	112	37	81	106	31	1	7	618
Israel	115	105	-9	92	69	-25	23	36	58
Canada	70	82	16	34	44	28	36	38	5
Austria	64	78	22	39	47	20	25	32	27
Australia	82	65	-20	42	24	-43	40	41	4
Portugal	33	37	12	28	28	1	5	9	65
Ireland	26	29	12	4	4	10	22	25	13
Norway	7	8	11	4	7	94	3	1	-80
New Zealand	7	7	3	4	3	-32	3	5	42
Denmark	7	6	-18	2	3	-12	6	4	-20
Sweden	66	3	-96	13	0	-100	54	3	-95
Iceland	0	0	43	0	0	58	0	0	-54
Finland	0	0	-7	0	0	-100	0	0	84
Total	6,878	8,633	26	3,458	4,253	23	3,420	4,381	28

Notes: Data for OECD countries plus South Africa's three largest non-OECD trading partners. OECD data from OECD Monthly Statistics of Foreign Trade, January 1989. Data for Israel, Hong Kong and Taiwan drawn from national statistics. Hong Kong exports include re-exports. No 1988 data for Greece or Italy. SDRs per US$: 1987 Q1 = 0.79313, Q2 = 0.77271; 1988 Q1 = 0.77098, Q2 = 0.73096. Rates of exchange: OECD and Israel data in US$; HK$ fixed at US$1 = HK$7.8; Taiwan median rates – 1987 US$1 = NT$32, 1988 US$1 = NT$28.7.

Table 21. Trade with South Africa: first nine months of 1988 compared with first nine months of 1987 (US$ million)

Country	Total trade			Imports from South Africa			Exports to South Africa		
	1987	1988	Rise/fall (%)	1987	1988	Rise/fall (%)	1987	1988	Rise/fall (%)
West Germany	2,589	3,739	44	839	1,269	51	1,750	2,470	41
Japan	3,018	3,153	4	1,730	1,515	-12	1,288	1,638	27
UK	1,914	2,538	33	821	1,105	35	1,093	1,433	31
Taiwan	676	1,255	86	360	791	120	317	464	47
Switzerland	366	628	72	171	395	132	196	233	19
Hong Kong	405	549	36	233	302	29	172	248	44
Netherlands	339	409	20	137	158	15	202	250	24
Spain	298	387	30	229	282	23	68	105	53
Israel	229	212	-7	174	136	-22	55	76	38
Canada	143	194	36	77	107	39	66	87	33
Austria	130	161	24	76	92	21	54	69	28
Ireland	49	76	54	7	11	66	42	65	53
Norway	12	17	37	6	16	168	6	1	-84
New Zealand	15	17	10	8	6	-31	7	11	55
Denmark	14	15	4	3	5	55	11	10	-10
Finland	0	0	40	0	0	-50	0	0	100

Notes: Data for OECD countries that have reported for the first nine months plus South Africa's largest non-OECD partners. OECD data from OECD *Monthly Statistics of Foreign Trade,* January 1989. Data for Israel, Hong Kong and Taiwan drawn from national statistics. Hong Kong exports include re-exports (in contrast to previous tables). Rates of exchange: OECD and Israel data in US$; HK$ fixed at US$1 = HK$7.8; Taiwan median rates – 1987 US$1 = NT$31.5, 1988 US$1 = NT$28.7.

Table 22. Japan, West Germany and gold, 1987 and 1988

Japanese and West German trade with South Africa (US$ million)			
	Jan.–Oct. 1987	Jan.–Oct. 1988	Rise/fall (%)
Japan			
Total imports	2,019	1,611	−20
Gold	340	57	−83
PGMs	450	289	−36
Diamonds	7	2	−69
Imports excluding gold, PGMs, diamonds	1,221	1,263	3
Total exports	1,462	1,777	22
Total trade excluding gold, PGMs, diamonds	2,684	3,040	13
West Germany			
Total imports	1,044	1,430	37
Gold	87	303	248
PGMs	124	147	18
Diamonds	6	7	10
Imports excluding gold, PGMs, diamonds	826	973	18
Total exports	1,987	2,764	39
Total trade excluding gold, PGMs, diamonds	2,812	3,736	33

Notes: In 1988 West Germany replaced Japan as South Africa's largest trading partner. Analysis of the trade data shows that West German and Japanese commodity trade both increased in 1988, but West German trade increased much faster. Japanese imports fell only because it imported South African gold and platinum through third parties; excluding gold, platinum and diamonds, Japanese imports from South Africa rose slightly in 1988 (measured in both US$s and SDRs). Statistics for West Germany are available only for the first ten months of 1988, so Japan and West Germany have been compared for that period. PGMs = platinum group metals.

Rates of exchange:	Average of first three quarters (per US$)		Full year (per US$)	
	1987	1988	1987	1988
Japan	147.6	129.1	145	128
West Germany	1.828	1.75	—	—
SDRs	—	—	0.773	0.746

Appendices

Table 22. (cont.)

	Japan's full-year trade with South Africa					
	US$ (million)		Rise/fall (%)	SDR (million)		Rise/fall (%)
	1987	1988		1987	1988	
Total imports	2,265	1,934	−15	1,750	1,442	−18
Gold	221	35	−84	171	26	−85
PGMs	554	329	−41	429	245	−43
Diamonds	12	4	−69	10	3	−70
Imports excluding gold, PGMs, diamonds	1,476	1,566	6	1,141	1,168	2
Total exports	1,856	2,049	10	1,435	1,528	7
Total trade	4,121	3,982	−3	3,185	2,971	−7
Total trade excluding gold, PGMs, diamonds	3,333	3,614	8	2,576	2,696	5

	Japanese gold and platinum purchases (tonnes)		
	1987	1988	Difference
Gold			
Total imports	229.2	292.4	63.2
From South Africa[1]	15.5	4.5	−11.0
From UK, Switzerland[2]	121.1	148.0	26.9
From USSR, Australia and Canada[1]	56.8	107.9	51.1
Platinum			
Total imports	52.2	67.6	15.4
From South Africa[1]	27.1	16.6	−10.5
From UK[2]	7.5	15.2	7.7
From USA, West Germany[2]	4.2	7.9	3.7
From USSR[1]	11.6	13.7	2.1

Notes: This table shows that Japan has decreased its gold and platinum imports from South Africa but has increased by a larger amount its gold and platinum imports from countries that themselves import from South Africa. [1] Producer. [2] Imports from South Africa.

NOTES AND REFERENCES

PART I   SANCTIONS ARE ESSENTIAL FOR NEGOTIATIONS

1 *Introduction*

1 *Mission to South Africa: The Findings of the Commonwealth Eminent Persons Group on Southern Africa* (Penguin Books, Harmondsworth, 1986), p. 132 (hereafter *EPG*).
2 ibid., p. 122.
3 ibid., p. 140.
4 *Optima*, December 1988.

2 *How Sanctions Work*

1 Note that Britain dissented from most references to sanctions in the Okanagan Statement.
2 See contribution by Lodge in *South Africa: The Sanctions Report – Documents* (James Currey, London, 1989) (hereafter *SRD*).

3 *Partial Sanctions: a Partial Success*

1 *Economic Report*, Trust Bank, October 1988.
2 Article by John Battersby reprinted in the *International Herald Tribune*, 15 November 1988.
3 *Guardian*, London, 13 August 1988.
4 Speaking in Washington, DC, and quoted in the USIA 'Africa Wireless File', No. 487 13/1/89.
5 *Financial Mail*, Johannesburg, 26 September 1988.
6 *The Times*, London, 17 August 1988.
7 *EPG*, p. 127.
8 Ken Flower, *Serving Secretly* (John Murray, London, 1987), p. 227.

9 *Financial Mail*, 28 November 1986.
10 *Financial Mail*, 29 November 1985.
11 *Weekly Mail*, Johannesburg, 29 January 1988.
12 *Finance Week*, Johannesburg, 5–11 May 1988.
13 *Financial Mail*, 13 May 1988.
14 *Star*, Johannesburg, 20 July 1988.
15 *Finance Week*, 18 August 1988.
16 *Finance Week*, 22 September 1988.
17 *Star*, 12 December 1988.
18 *EPG*, p. 135.
19 Widely published as an advertisement – for example, in the *Independent*, London, 14 July 1987.
20 'South African Alert', *Business International*, London, March 1988.
21 BBC monitoring report (Johannesburg), 20 August 1988.
22 *Independent*, 9 February 1989.
23 'British Policy Towards South Africa', Foreign and Commonwealth Office, 1988.
24 'Report to the Congress Pursuant to Section 501 of the Comprehensive Anti-Apartheid Act of 1986 for the Year Ending October 2, 1988'.
25 Speaking at a Polish Government dinner, Warsaw, 3 November 1988.
26 See CIIR in *SRD*.
27 'The Art of Counter-Revolutionary Warfare', published by the State Security Council and quoted in the *Weekly Mail*, 26 May 1988.
28 *Star*, 19 July 1987.
29 Quoted in Van Heerden in *SRD*.
30 *EPG*, p. 140.

4 *Why is South Africa the Exception?*

1 Speaking at a seminar, 'How to Counter South African Destabilization', Athens, Greece, 20–23 October 1988.
2 *Los Angeles Times*, 26 July 1987.
3 'Mishap or Crisis? The Apartheid Economy's Recent Record in Historical Perspective', paper presented by Terence Moll at the Institute of Commonwealth Studies, London, 4 March 1988.
4 *Star*, 14 February 1989.
5 See Marcus in *SRD*.
6 Lynda Chalker, British Deputy Foreign Secretary, speaking at the British Council of Churches Conference 'Britain and Southern Africa', London, 28 February 1989.
7 Francis Wilson and Mamphela Ramphele, *Uprooting Poverty*, the Report for the Second Carnegie Inquiry into Poverty and Development in Southern Africa (David Philip, Claremont, South Africa, 1989), p. 350.

8 ibid., p. 230.
9 Lynda Chalker, speaking at the British Council of Churches Conference 'Britain and Southern Africa'.
10 *Children on the Front Line – 1989 Update* (Unicef, New York, 1989), pp. 11, 38.
11 See David Martin and Phyllis Johnson, *South Africa: The Destabilization Report* (title under review: James Currey, London, 1989).
12 See Jourdan in *SRD*.
13 In 1986.
14 *New York Times*, 5 July 1988.
15 See Hanlon in *SRD*.

PART II   CURRENT SANCTIONS: IMPACT AND SHORTCOMINGS

5 *The Sanctions Juggernaut*

1 See Ferguson and Sluiter in *SRD*.

6 *Sales to South Africa*

1 See Crown in *SRD*.
2 A researcher at the Stockholm International Peace Research Institute estimates South African sales at under US$150 million per year: Signe Landgren, *Embargo Disimplemented: South Africa's Military Industry* (Oxford University Press, Oxford, 1989), p. 177.
3 See Woldendorp in *SRD*.

7 *Purchases from South Africa*

1 *Financial Mail*, 11 March 1988.
2 Zimbabwe, which does export steel through Mozambican ports, reports no sales of this size to Singapore. The Expert Study Group made several requests to the Government of Singapore to clarify the position. So far no reply has been received.
3 *Mail on Sunday*, London, 28 February 1988.
4 *Contraband*, New Zealand Customs Department, Wellington, January–February 1989.

8 *Other Government Measures*

1 See Keith Ovenden and Tony Cole, *Apartheid and International Finance: A Program for Change* (Penguin Books, Ringwood, Victoria, Australia, 1990).
2 See Bailey in *SRD*.

3 See Lewis in *SRD*.
4 Oliver Tambo, Canon Collins Lecture, London, 28 May 1987.

9 *Disinvestment*

1 See Ovenden and Cole, *Apartheid and International Finance*, for a detailed discussion of disinvestment.
2 A survey by the Investor Responsibility Research Centre of 377 firms found that only 86 had cut all ties with South Africa, while 153 retained non-equity links, and 138 had direct investments or employees in South Africa.
3 *Africa News*, Durham, North Carolina, USA, 20 February 1989.
4 Under this system money to pay for withdrawals comes from outside South Africa. See Ovenden and Cole, *Apartheid and International Finance*, for more details of the Financial Rand mechanism.

10 *People's Sanctions*

1 Export consultant John Bell, quoted in the *Financial Mail*, 18 March 1988.

PART III   FRUSTRATING SANCTIONS
11 *Changing Patterns of Trade*

1 See Appendix 7 for detailed trade tables.
2 See Appendix 7, Table 22.
3 *South African Coal Streams via the Netherlands*, Working Group Kairos, Utrecht, Netherlands, 1989.
4 See Robbins in *SRD*.
5 Answer to a question in the Swiss Conseil National, 88.1044, of 7 October 1988.
6 *Financial Times*, London, 4 November 1986.

12 *Encouraging South African Trade*

1 See also Ovenden and Cole, *Apartheid and International Finance*.
2 *Finance Week*, 9 March 1989.
3 *Financial Mail*, 11 November 1988.
4 *Finance Week*, 25 August 1988.
5 See, for example, *Financial Mail*, 6 May 1988.

13 *Blocking and Bypassing Sanctions*

1 See Goodison in *SRD*.
2 In 1987 EC fruit, vegetable and grain imports from South Africa were

more than US$265 million higher than the 1983–5 average (see Appendix 7, Table 10). By contrast, official EC figures show that 1985 imports of South African steel covered by sanctions were only US$140 million.

3 *Daily Telegraph*, London, 16 February 1989.
4 See Ferguson and Sluiter in *SRD*.
5 'Minorco and Consolidated Gold Fields plc: A Report on the Merger Situation', the Monopolies and Mergers Commission, London, Cm 587.
6 *Guardian*, London, 3 December 1988.

14 *The Role of South African-owned Companies*

1 See Lewis in *SRD*.
2 See Ovenden and Cole, *Apartheid and International Finance*.
3 Allied Technologies Ltd, Annual Report 1986.
4 *Israeli Foreign Affairs*, January 1989.
5 *Star*, 24 August 1988.

PART IV VULNERABILITY AND SANCTIONS POTENTIAL

15 *Trade Vulnerability*

1 This is discussed in detail by Robbins in *SRD*.
2 See Robbins in *SRD* and Joseph Hanlon and Roger Omond, *The Sanctions Handbook* (Penguin Books, Harmondsworth, 1987), p. 250.
3 See Jourdan in *SRD*.
4 See World Gold Commission in *SRD*.

16 *Technology and Skills*

1 South Africa is changing over to a system of measuring local content by value instead of weight.
2 Board of Trade and Industry Report No. 2627, Interim Report, 'Investigation into the Industry Manufacturing Passenger Cars and Light Commercial Vehicles', Pretoria, 3 March 1988.
3 See Woldendorp in *SRD*.
4 *Financial Mail*, 12 June 1987.
5 See Swainson in *SRD*.
6 *Financial Mail*, 15 July 1988.
7 *Financial Mail*, 4 August 1988.
8 See Swainson in *SRD*.
9 *Financial Mail*, 24 October 1986.

17 How Much Pressure is Needed?

1 For more detail see Ovenden and Cole, *Apartheid and International Finance*.
2 *Wall Street Journal*, New York, 25 March 1987.
3 An estimated US$3 billion has been converted into medium-term debt 'outside the net'.
4 Christopher Wilson, 'South Africa's Debt Overhang', *Optima*, June 1987.
5 Quoted in 'The Case for a Gold Sanction', World Gold Commission, London 1989.
6 GDP in the 1980s has risen by 1 per cent per year on average, while population growth is approximately 3 per cent per year.
7 *Financial Mail*, 28 November 1986.
8 *Economic Report*, Trust Bank, October 1988.
9 *Business Day*, Johannesburg, 22 May 1986.
10 See Ovenden and Cole, *Apartheid and International Finance*.
11 *Financial Times*, 23 November 1988.
12 See Stoneman in *SRD*.
13 ibid.
14 This was explicitly proposed by Nedbank chairman Owen Horwood, *Financial Times*, 22 November 1988.

PART V POSSIBLE FURTHER ACTION

18 A Strategy for Action

1 See Robbins in *SRD*.

19 Targeting Pretoria's Trade

1 GATT, in turn, follows the International Standard Industrial Classification (UN Statistical Papers, Series M, No. 4). GATT defines three 'broad product groups', one of which is 'agriculture'. See the GATT *International Trade* annual volumes for definitions and detailed discussion of trade in the various product groups.
2 This definition excludes cotton and wool yarn and thread, leather, paper and sawn wood, and vegetable tanning products. We would include all of these in 'agricultural' products and have used this broader definition in our statistics. These additional 'agricultural' products would in any case be included in our proposed ban on manufactured goods; if both agricultural products and manufactured goods were banned, their categorization would not be an urgent question.
3 See Robbins in *SRD*.
4 See Robbins and Jourdan in *SRD*.

5 *Finance Week*, 18 August 1988.
6 Memorandum to the House of Commons Foreign Affairs Committee dated 22 October 1985.

20 *Arms and Oil*

1 Our views on violations of the arms embargo are based largely on reports of the World Campaign Against Military and Nuclear Collaboration with South Africa, the International Seminar on the Arms Embargo held in London in May 1986 and the '421 Committee' established by the United Nations Security Council under Resolution 421 in 1977.
2 See Signe Langdren, *Embargo Disimplemented*, p. 207.
3 *US Department of Commerce News*, Washington, DC, 3 March 1982.
4 See, for example, Ernie Regehr, *Arms Canada* (James Lorimer, Toronto, 1987).
5 House of Commons Trade and Industry Committee, Second Report of the 1988–9 session, 'Trade with Eastern Europe'.
6 Lord Glenarthur, speaking for the Government in the House of Lords, 8 March 1988.

21 *Cars and Computers*

1 Board of Trade and Industry Report No. 2627, Interim Report, 'Investigation into the Industry Manufacturing Passenger Cars and Light Commercial Vehicles', Pretoria, 3 March 1988.
2 *Finance Week*, 26 May 1988.
3 'South Africa Status Report on Implementation of the Comprehensive Anti-Apartheid Act', General Accounting Office, Washington, DC, October 1987.
4 See Chataway in *SRD*.

22 *Enforcement*

1 'South Africa Status Report on Implementation of the Comprehensive Anti-Apartheid Act'.
2 See Rich in *SRD*.
3 See 'Implementation of the Comprehensive Anti-Apartheid Act of 1986', Lawyers Committee for Civil Rights Under Law, 1400 Eye St, Washington, DC, 20005.

23 *Influencing Market Forces*

1 See Ferguson and Sluiter in *SRD*.

PART VI   SUMMARY AND CONCLUSIONS

25 Sanctions are a Life-and-death Issue

1 *Independent*, 4 August 1988.
2 *EPG*, p. 141.

INDEX